Updated 2022

The Ancient Egyptian Universal Writing Modes

Moustafa Gadalla

**Ancient Egyptian Universal
Writing Modes
by Moustafa Gadalla**

All rights reserved. No part of this book may be reproduced or transmitted in any form or by any means, electronic or mechanical, including photocopying, recorded or by any information storage and retrieval system without written permission from the author, except for the inclusion of brief quotations in a review.

Copyright © 2017 , 2018, 2020 and 2022 by Moustafa Gadalla, All rights reserved.

CONTENTS

About the Author ... xiii

Preface ... xv

Standards and Terminology ... xxi

The 28 ABGD Letters & Pronunciations ... xxv

Map of Ancient Egypt ... xxix

Map of Egypt and Surrounding Countries ... xxxi

PART I : DENIAL, DISTORTION AND DIVERSION

Chapter 1 : The Archetypal Primacy of ... 3
The Egyptian Alphabet

1.1 The Divine "Inventor" of The Egyptian ... 3
Alphabetical Letters
1.2 Remote Age of Egyptian Alphabets ... 6
1.3 The Distinctive Pre-Hyksos Egyptian ... 8
Alphabetical Papyri

Chapter 2 : The Concealment of The Supreme Egyptian Alphabet 13

2.1. Smoke Screening Thousands of Egyptian Alphabetical Writings 13
2.2. Egyptian is Dead, Long Live "Arabic" 14
2.3. The Mighty Western-Fabricated Egyptian Alphabet and "Sequence" 15
2.4. The Double Talk and Double Take of Two [Egyptian Sourced] Alphabets 16

Chapter 3 : The Diversion of A Proto-Sinaitic "Phoenician Connection" 19

3.1. Mining History in Sinai 19
3.2. "Proto-Sinaitic" Graffiti — A Manufactured "Straw" 21
3.3. B'alat Who Saved The Day! 25
3.4. Understanding Names, Epithets and Titles of Egyptian Deities 26
3.5. Phoenicians' Homeland 28
3.6. "Phoenicia" : The Egyptian Satellite 30

PART II : FORMATION AND FORMS OF EGYPTIAN ALPHABETIC WRITINGS

Chapter 4 : Genesis of Egyptian Alphabetic Letters/Writings 37

4.1. The Unfounded Obsession That Letters Were Derived from Picture 37
4.2. Differences Between Ideograms, Signs and Alphabetical Writing 38
4.3. "Evolution" of Alphabet from "Signs" to "Real" Alphabets 40

Chapter 5 : The Egyptian Sound Organization of Letters 43

5.1 The Universal Three Primary/Quantal Egyptian Vowel 43
5.2 From Three to Five Vowels 46
5.3 The Seven Harmonic Tones/Vowels 47
5.4 The Infinite Vowels Derivatives 48
5.5 Consonants as Derivatives of Vowels 49
5.6 The 25 Articulated Alphabetical Consonants 50
5.7 Balanced Phonology Range 51
5.8 Special Phonetics of Each Letter 52
5.9 Sound Ligaturing of Letters in a Word 53

Chapter 6 : The Egyptian Alphabetic Writing Styles 55

6.1 The Devious Western Categorization of Egyptian Alphabetical Scripts 55
6.2 False Distinctions of Egyptian Cursive Writing 59
6.3 The True Two Primary Egyptian Alphabetic Scripts [Uncials and Cursive] 63
6.4 Forms and Functions of Calligraphy 67

Chapter 7 : The Profession of Egyptian Scribes 69

7.1 The Writing Civilization 69
7.2 The Profession of Scribes 71
7.3 Writing Surfaces & Instruments 72
7.4 Mobile Scribes 76

Chapter 8 : Multiple Writing Forms of a Single Document 81

8.1 Commonality Of Multiple Writing Forms 81
8.2 Egyptian Magical Divination Forms 82
8.3 Egyptian Stela 83

Chapter 9 : Multiple Writing Forms of The Rosetta Stone 85

9.1. Place of its Original Location 85
9.2. Dating Falsehoods 86
9.3. Shameless Change of the Word "Priestly" to "Greek"! 88
9.4. Scandalous Cartouches "Decipherment" 89
9.5. The Egyptian Three Function and Forms of The Decree 92
9.6. Shamelessly Substituting 'god/goddess' For Ptolemaic 'King/Queen' 96
9.7. Self-Serving Conjectural "Decipherment" 97

PART III : HOW THE ONE WORLD LANGUAGE BECAME THE MANY

Chapter 10 : The Beacon of The Ancient World 101

10.1. Egyptian Settlements Throughout The World 101

10.2. Ancient Egypt and The Seven Seas 106
10.3. Ancient Egypt: The World Economic Engine 107
10.4. The Dominant Egyptian Language 109
10.5. The Egyptian Mother Language of All Language Families 113

Chapter 11 : Common Characteristics of Ancient Egyptian Alphabetic Writing System 115

Chapter 12 : Letterforms Divergence of World Alphabets From Its Egyptian Origin 123

12.1. The Apparent Variations of Letter-forms in World Alphabets from Its Egyptian Origin 123
12.2. Overview of Archetypal 28 Egyptian Letter-forms and Divergence Into Other Regions 125

Chapter 13 : Sound Divergence of World 165
Alphabets From Its Egyptian Origin

13.1. The Systematic Sound Variations [Sound 165
shifts]
13.2. Causes and Effects of Sound Divergence 167
From Its Egyptian Origin into Other World
Alphabets

Chapter 14 : Cavalier Designations of 171
New Languages

14.1. Rewarding A New Language For Each 171
Historical "Winner"
14.2. Fabricating "New" Languages From 173
Egyptian Scripts

PART IV : THE PRIMARY LINGUISTIC
CHARACTERISTICS OF THE EGYPTIAN
LANGUAGE

Chapter 15 : The Primary Linguistic 177
Characteristics of The Egyptian
Language

15.1. The Four Distinctive Pillars of a Language 177
15.2. The Egyptian Prototypal Interconnected 178
Lexicon, Grammar and Syntax

PART V : OUT OF EGYPT—DIFFUSION
PATTERNS TO ASIA AND AFRICA

Chapter 16 : Hebrew and Moses of 191
Egypt

16.1. Moses and Writing 191
16.2. Moses and Maah 193
16.3. The Two Writing Forms [Old & New!] 194
16.4. Sameness of Egyptian Prototypal 198
Interconnected Lexicon, Grammar and Syntax

Chapter 17 : The Ancient Egyptian Hegemony of Asiatic Neighbors 201

17.1. The Egyptian Settlement at Moab 201
17.2. False Designations of Various Alphabets in 203
North Arabia [Nabatean, Aramaic and Ugariti]
17.3. False Designations of South Arabian 210
Alphabets
17.4. "Arabic" : The Stolen Egyptian Language 218
17.5. Distinction Without A Difference [Same 221
Writing System & Linguistics]

Chapter 18 : The African Connections 227

18.1. The Traditional "Immigrants" Ge-ez 227
Language [Dead or Alive?!].
18.2. Amharic — A Reshuffled Ge-ez 231
18.3. The Direct Egyptian-Ethiopic Connections 236
18.4. Eastern African languages 241

Chapter 19 : From Egypt To India and 243
Beyond

19.1. From Egypt Via Yemen To The Indian Sub- 243
Continent
19.2. The Two Primary Inscription Styles in The 244
Indian Sub-Continent
19.3. The Apparent Large Number of Indian 247
Letters
19.4. Punjab — Both Styles Together 249
19.5. India & Far East 250

Chapter 20 : From Egypt to The Black 253
Sea Basin [Georgia and Armenia]

20.1 Affinities of Languages From Central Asia 253
To The Black Sea
20.2 Ancient Egyptian Settlements in The Black 254
Sea Basin
20.3 Pre-Existence of "Armenian/Georgian" 256
Alphabets in Ancient Egypt
20.4 Vocalic Limitation of Armenian/Georgian 257
Tongue vis-à-vis Its Number of Alphabet
20.5 Sameness of Ancient Egyptian Alphabetical 258
Writing System in Later "Georgian & Armenian Languages"
20.6 Linguistic Characteristics with Their Ancient 259
Egyptian Roots

PART VI : OUT OF EGYPT—DIFFUSION PATTERNS TO EUROPE

Chapter 21 : Greek : A Shameless 263
Linguistic Heist

21.1 The Egyptian Settlers and Kings of Greece 263
21.2 Greeks As Employed Security Guards in 266
Egypt
21.3 Greek Mercenaries and the Abu Simbel 267
Inscriptions
21.4 Pre-Existence of The Proclaimed "Greek" 269
Alphabetical Letter-forms in Ancient Egypt
21.5 Robbing and Postdating Egyptian Scripts To 274
Rename Them as "Greek"
21.6 Vocalic Limitation Effects of Greek Tongue 283
on the 28 Prototypal Alphabetical Letters
21.7 Sameness of Ancient Egyptian Alphabetical 286
Writing System in Later "Greek Language"
21.8 Sameness of Egyptian Prototypal 295
Interconnected Lexicon, Grammar and Syntax

Chapter 22 : The European Languages 299
22.1. Etruscan: The Foremost Ancient Italian 299
Language
22.2. The Rise and Abrupt Fall of the Romans' 302
Latin!
22.3. Broken Empire—Eastern Orthodox 304
22.4. Wild Goose Chase of A "Latin" In Hispania 305
22.5. The Egyptian Alphabets of Hispania 306
22.6. The Egyptian-Iberian Linguistic Oneness 310
22.7. Warmongers and The "Romance" Languages! 313

PART VII : THE ANCIENT FUTURE OF THE
UNIVERSAL LANGUAGE

Chapter 23 : Egyptian Alphabetical 317
Vocalic Language [Past, Present &
Future]

23.1. The Unchanging Egyptians 317
23.2. The Enduring Egyptian Alphabetical Vocalic 318
Language
23.3. Vocabularies Now and Then 320
23.4 Arabic Corruption of Original Egyptian 321
Letter-forms and Reshuffled Letters Order/
Sequence
23.5 Sameness of Alphabetical Writing System 323
23.6 Reinstatement of Original Letter-forms and 325
Its ABGD Sequence

Chapter 24 : Renaissance & Seeking the 327
Universal Language The Ancient Future

24.1 English Language Flawed Dominance 327
24.2 The Renaissance Search For A Universal 330
Language

Glossary 333

Selected Bibliography 339

Sources and Notes 347

1
ABOUT THE AUTHOR

Moustafa Gadalla is an Egyptian-American independent Egyptologist who was born in Cairo, Egypt in 1944. He holds a Bachelor of Science degree in civil engineering from Cairo University.

From his early childhood, Gadalla pursued his Ancient Egyptian roots with passion, through continuous study and research. Since 1990, he has dedicated and concentrated all his time to researching and writing.

Gadalla is the author of twenty-two published internationally acclaimed books about the various aspects of the Ancient Egyptian history and civilization and its influences worldwide. In addition he operates a multimedia resource center for accurate, educative studies of Ancient Egypt, presented in an engaging, practical, and interesting manner that appeals to the general public.

He was the Founder of Tehuti Research Foundation which was later incorporated into the multi-lingual Egyptian Wisdom Center (https://www.egyptianwisdomcenter.org) in more than ten languages. He is also the Founder and Head of the online Egyptian Mystical University (https://www.EgyptianMysticalUniversity.org). Another ongoing activity has been his creation and production of performing arts projects such as the Isis Rises Operetta (https://www.isisrisesoperetta.com); to be followed soon by Horus The Initiate Operetta; as well other productions.

2

PREFACE

This book will show that the Egyptian Alphabetical language is the MOTHER and origin of all languages; and how it was diffused to become other 'languages' throughout the world.

It is the aim of this book to provide such an exposition: one which, while based on sound scholarship, will present the issues in language comprehensible to non-specialist readers. Technical terms have been kept to a minimum. These are explained, as non-technically as possible, in the glossary.

The book is divided into seven parts with a total of 24 chapters, as follows:

Part I. Denial, Distortion and Diversion has 3 chapters—Chapters 1 to 3:

> **Chapter 1: The Archetypal Primacy of The Egyptian Alphabet** will show the role and remote history of alphabetical letter-forms writing in Ancient Egypt prior to any other place on Earth.

Chapter 2: The Concealment of The Supreme Egyptian Alphabet will show the incredible Western academia scheme to conceal the Ancient Egyptian alphabetical letter-forms from its prominent position in the history of writing.

Chapter 3: The Diversion of A Proto-Sinaitic "Phoenician Connection" will uncover all the facts about having "Phoenicians" as the inventor of alphabets on Egyptian soil!

Part II. Formation and Forms of Egyptian Alphabetic Writings has 6 chapters—Chapters 4 to 9:

Chapter 4: Genesis of Egyptian Alphabetic Letters/ Writing will refute the unfounded obsession that alphabetical letter-forms were derived from pictures; and will explore the differences between ideograms, signs and alphabetical writing.

Chapter 5: The Egyptian Sound Organization of Letters will cover the primary three vowels as the originators of all vowel sounds and associated consonants.

Chapter 6: The Egyptian Alphabetic Writing Styles will sort out the present common confusion of Ancient Egyptian styles of writing and set the two primary styles as uncials and cursive.

Chapter 7: The Profession of Egyptian Scribes will cover the range of Egyptian writings; the profession of scribes; writing surfaces and instruments; and the documentation of official missions by Egyptian scribes.

Chapter 8: Multiple Writing Forms of a Single Document will cover the commonality of having several styles of the same language on a single document; and will give examples of multiple writing forms on Egyptian magical divination papyri as well as on Egyptian stelae.

Chapter 9: Multiple Writing Forms of The Rosetta Stone will expose the total misrepresentation of the three Egyptian writing forms on the Rosetta Stone as (incorrectly) being Egyptian and "Greek"!

Part III. How The One World Language Became The Many has five chapters—Chapters 10 to 14:

Chapter 10: The Beacon of the Ancient World will cover Egyptian settlements throughout the world; Ancient Egypt and The Seven Seas; Ancient Egypt as the world economic engine; the dominant Egyptian language; and the Egyptian Mother language of all language families.

Chapter 11: Common Characteristics of Ancient Egyptian Alphabetic Writing System will detail such characteristics.

Chapter 12: Letter-forms Divergence of World Alphabets From Its Egyptian Origin will cover the apparent variations of alphabetical letter-forms in world alphabets from its Egyptian origin as well as providing an overview of the archetypal 28 Egyptian alphabetical letter-forms and their divergence into other regions of the world.

Chapter 13: Sound Divergence of World Alphabets

From Its Egyptian Origin will cover the systematic sound variations as well as causes and effects of sound divergence from its Egyptian origin into other world alphabets.

Chapter 14: Cavalier Designations of New Languages will cover how a new language has been awarded as a symbol of identity for winners of wars and new religions; as well as how "new" languages were fabricated from Egyptian scripts.

Part IV. The Primary Linguistic Characteristics of The Egyptian Language has one chapter—Chapter 15:

Chapter 15: The Primary Linguistic Characteristics of The Egyptian Language will cover the four pillars of a language; as well as reviewing the Egyptian prototypal interconnected lexicon, grammar, and syntax.

Part V. Out of Egypt—Diffusion Patterns To Asia and Africa has 5 chapters—Chapters 16 to 20:

Chapter 16: Hebrew and Moses of Egypt will show the Egyptian origin of Hebrew and the absence of any linguistic distinction between Hebrew and the Ancient Egyptian language.

Chapter 17: The Ancient Egyptian Hegemony of Asiatic Neighbors will discuss the found scripts in North and South Arabia, and will clear up all apparent differences between them and the Ancient Egyptian writing system.

Chapter 18: The African Connections will discuss

the history and details of the Ethiopic language(s) and will clear up all apparent differences between them and the Ancient Egyptian writing system.

Chapter 19: From Egypt To India and Beyond will cover the two primary inscription styles in the Indian Sub-Continent; and will clear up all apparent differences between them and the Ancient Egyptian writing system.

Chapter 20: From Egypt to The Black Sea Basin [Georgia & Armenia] will cover affinities of languages from Central Asia To the Black Sea Basin; Ancient Egyptian settlements in the Black Sea Basin; the pre-existence of "Armenian/Georgian" alphabets in Ancient Egypt; and the sameness of the Ancient Egyptian alphabetical writing system to later "Georgian & Armenian languages".

Part VI. Out of Egypt—Diffusion Patterns To Europe has two chapters—Chapters 21 & 22:

Chapter 21: Greek: A Shameless Linguistic Heist will cover the role of Greeks in Ancient Egypt as hired security guards; the pre-existence of the proclaimed "Greek" alphabetical letter-forms in the Ancient Egyptian system; robbing and postdating Egyptian scripts to rename them as "Greek"; and the absence of any linguistic distinction between Greek and the Ancient Egyptian language.

Chapter 22: The European Languages will cover Etruscan, Latin and Hispanic languages and the absence of any linguistic distinction between them and the Ancient Egyptian language.

Part VII. The Ancient Future of The Universal Language has two chapters—Chapters 23 & 24:

Chapter 23: Egyptian Alphabetical Vocalic Language [Past, Present & Future] will cover the state of the vocalic and written language in Egypt and the minor changes that occurred over thousands of years.

Chapter 24: Renaissance and Seeking the Universal Language—The Ancient Future will cover an overview of the English language's inconsistent phonetic writing system; the Renaissance search for a Universal Language; and how such a language, by all accounts, is the [Ancient] Egyptian Language.

Moustafa Gadalla

3

STANDARDS AND TERMINOLOGY

1. The Ancient Egyptian word neter and its feminine form, netert, have been wrongly, and possibly intentionally, translated as 'god' and 'goddes's by almost all academicians. Neteru (plural of neter/netert) are the divine principles and functions of the One Supreme God.

2. You may find variations in writing the same Ancient Egyptian term, such as Amen/Amon/Amun or Pir/Per. This is because the vowels you see in translated Egyptian texts are only approximations of sounds which are used by Western Egyptologists to help them pronounce the Ancient Egyptian terms/words.

3. We will be using the most commonly recognized words for the English-speaking people that identify a neter/netert [god, goddess], a pharaoh, or a city; followed by other 'variations' of such a word/term.

It should be noted that the real names of the deities (gods, goddesses) were kept secret so as to guard the cosmic power of the deity. The Neteru were referred to by epithets that describe particular qualities, attributes and/or aspect(s) of their roles. Such applies to all common terms such as Isis, Osiris, Amun, Re, Horus, etc.

4. When using the Latin calendar, we will use the following terms:

> **BCE** – Before Common Era. Also noted in other references as BC.
>
> **CE** – Common Era. Also noted in other references as AD.

5. The term Baladi will be used throughout this book to denote the present silent majority of Egyptians that adhere to the Ancient Egyptian traditions, with a thin exterior layer of Islam.[See *Ancient Egyptian Culture Revealed* by Moustafa Gadalla, for detailed information.]

6. There were/are no Ancient Egyptian writings/texts that were categorized by the Egyptians themselves as "religious", "funerary", "sacred", etc. Western academia gave the Ancient Egyptian texts arbitrary names, such as the "Book of This" and the "Book of That", "divisions", "utterances", "spells", etc. Western academia even decided that a certain "Book" had a "Theban version" or "this or that time period version". After believing their own inventive creation, academia then accused the Ancient Egyptians of making mistakes and missing portions of their own writings (?!!).

For ease of reference, we will mention the common but arbitrary Western academic categorization of Ancient

Egyptian texts, even though the Ancient Egyptians themselves never did.

4

THE 28 ABGD LETTERS & PRONUNCIATIONS

– Actual Egyptian 28 ABGD letters are indicated in Capitals—non-capitals letters are inserted to help English speaking people pronounce the Egyptian words.

– When 2 letters are underlined together (in the "Roman" script) they represent one sound. For example T̲h̲ sounds like 'Th' in the English word 'Three'. Another example is D̲h̲ sounds like the Th' in the English word 'There'.

– An underlined letter followed by a dot indicates an Egyptian letter close to the English sound of such a letter.

– Three Egyptian letters [A,W&Y] are "weak consonants" i.e. each can be pronounced as a consonant or a vowel sound, depending on the word and its context.

Letter Sound	Numerical Value	Letter sound in English words
1. ALeF	1	Adam (as a cons.), fat (as a vowel sound)
2. BeYT	2	Boy
3. GyM	3	Girl
4. DaL	4	Delta
5. Heh	5	He
6. Waw	6	We (as a cons. sound), FOOD (as a vowel sound)
7. Zayn	7	Zero
8. H.et	8	strongly aspirant H made in the throat which is defined as a ' fricative faucal,' that is a strongly marked continuous guttural sound produced at the back of the palate. The sound does not exist in English, French, or Italian, but comes near to the ch in the German lachen, or the Scotch loch (Spanish x and j.)
9. T.a	9	emphatic T (close to the sound of double 't' at the end of the English word 'butt')
10. Yad	10	Yes (as a cons. sound), Feet (as a vowel sound), a semi-consonantal glide, like the y in "yellow"
11. Kaf	20	Milk
12. Lam	30	Lane
13. Meem	40	Milk
14. Noon	50	No
15. Seen	60	Safe

16. **A.yn**	70	does not occur in English, but represents a deeper guttural consonant, perhaps a voiced glottal stop
17. **F**	80	**F**ood
18. **S.ad**	90	emphatic S (close to the sound of letter 's' in the the English word 'sun' or in the name 'Sandra')
19. **Qaf**	100	It is defined as a 'hard. explosive ultra guttural,' and may be described as a guttural having an affinity with k, but formed further back, between the posterior soft portion of the palate and the back of the tongue. Sounds like a backward k; rather like q in queen
20. **R**	200	**R**ise
21. **Sheen**	300	**Sh**ow
22. **T**	400	**T**able
23. **Th**	500	**Th**ree
24. **Kh**	600	Gutteral Aspirate—like ch in Schotch loch—perhaps like ch in German ich
25. **Dhal**	700	O**Th**er
26. **D.ad**	800	emphatic D
27. **Z.**	900	emphatic Z
28. **Ghyn**	1000	A voiced velar fricative /ɣ/ or a voiced uvular fricative

5

MAP OF ANCIENT EGYPT

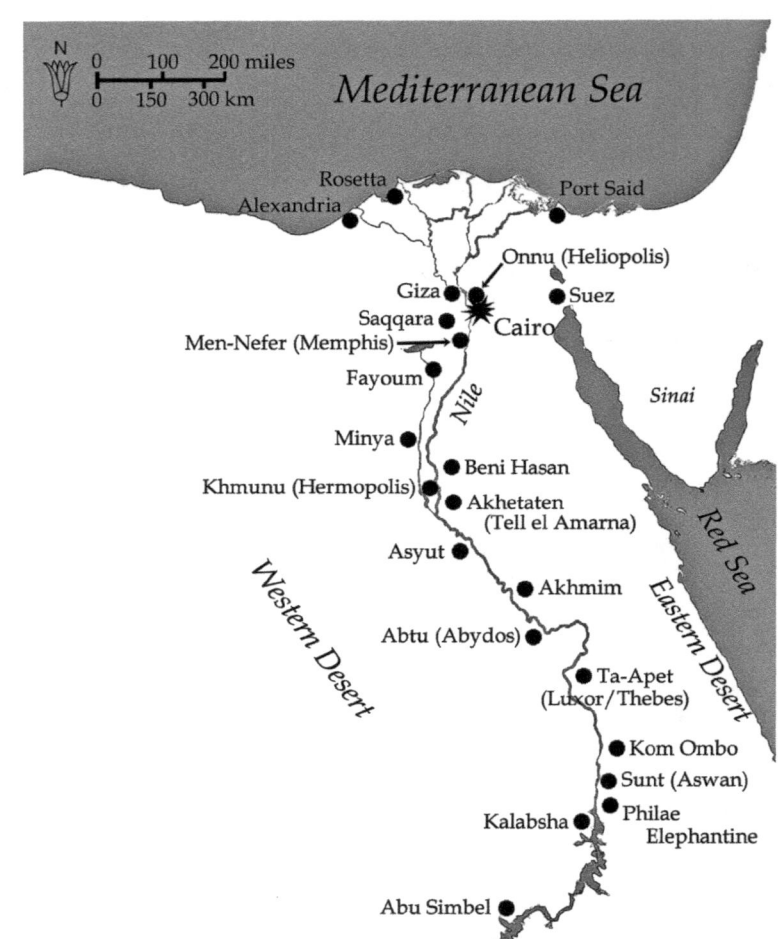

6

MAP OF EGYPT AND SURROUNDING COUNTRIES

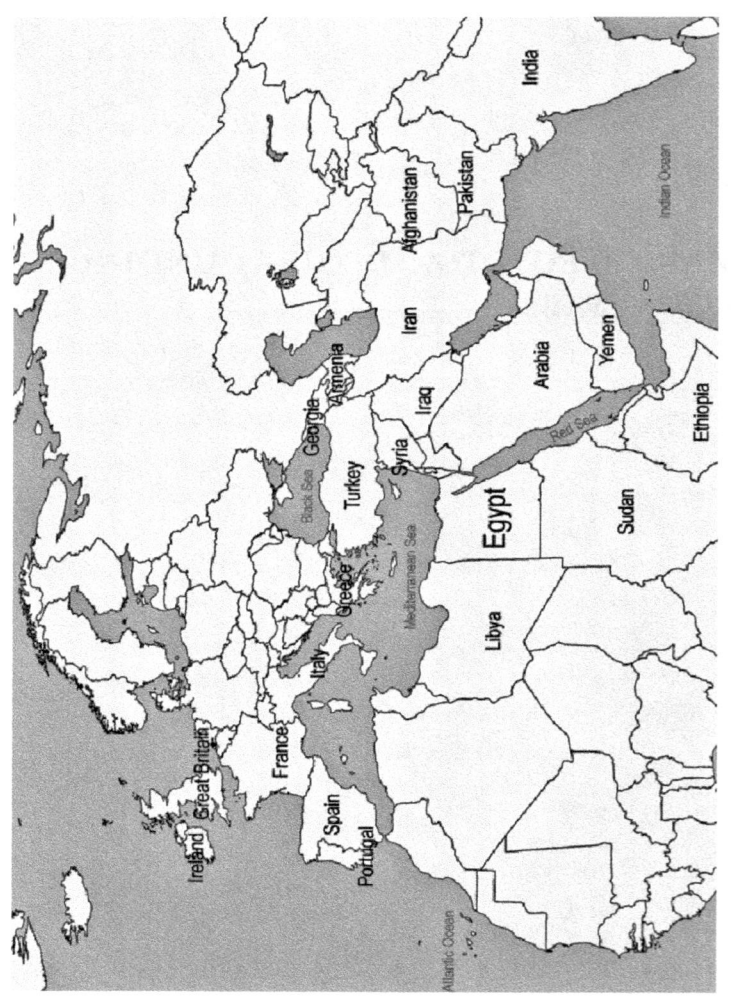

PART I : DENIAL, DISTORTION AND DIVERSION

Chapter 1 : The Archetypal Primacy of The Egyptian Alphabet

1.1 THE DIVINE "INVENTOR" OF THE EGYPTIAN ALPHABETICAL LETTERS

In Genesis II:1, we are informed:

> *"And the whole earth was of one language and of one speech".*

The more one studies the various languages (and dialects) in the world, the more it becomes clearer and clearer that there was originally one language that split into various tongues. The Bible and ancient writers affirm such an original language. Because of false pride and the prejudices of Western academia and religious (Judaism, Christianity, and Islam) zealots, the origin of this universal mother language has been ignored. Evidence confirms that Ancient Egypt is the single source of universal language.

On this subject matter, Plato admits the role of Egypt in his *Collected Dialogues* [*Philebus* 18-b,c,d]:

> *"SOCRATES: The unlimited variety of sound was once discerned by some god, or perhaps some godlike man;*

you know the story that there was some such <u>god in Egypt called Theuth</u>...

It was because he realized that none of us could ever get to know one of the collection all by itself, in isolation from all the rest, that he <u>conceived of 'letter'</u> as a kind of bond of unity, uniting as it were all these sounds into one, and so he gave utterance to the expression '<u>art of letters,' implying that there was one art that dealt with the sounds.</u>"

The reference to "Theuth" above [in Plato's *Collected Dialougues*] is the same "Theuth" mentioned in the Phaedrus, where we are explicitly told that he was an Ancient Egyptian neter (god), **"the one whose sacred bird is called the Ibis"**, so as to exclude all doubt about his identity. It is obvious that his account is based on a genuine Egyptian tradition, because the ibis-headed Theuth [Thoth] is an Egyptian neter (god).

Theuth [Thoth] is portrayed as an ibis-headed figure, writing on a tablet.

It must be noted that the Ancient Egyptians NEVER gave credit to a mortal human for any "invention" and always gave the credit to the Divine's attributes/qualities/energies being represented by the Neteru (gods, goddesses) as the only source of knowledge.

It is very clear that Plato (in *Philebus* [18-b, c, d]) did not refer to pictorial forms of expression (hieroglyphs), but rather to expression by individual and diverse letters, each with its own particular sound value.

Theuth [Thoth] represents the Divine Messenger who articulates and writes the spoken/written language, knowledge, etc.

Several of Theuth [Thoth]'s attributes were confirmed by Diodorus of Sicily:

> "*It was by Thoth, according to Ancient Egyptians, <u>that the common language of mankind was first further articulated</u>, and that many objects which were still nameless received an appellation, <u>that the alphabet were defined</u>, and that ordinances regarding the honors and offerings due to the neteru* (gods, goddesses)*were duly established; he was the first also to observe the orderly arrangement of the stars and the harmony of the musical sounds and their nature.*"
> [Book I, Section 16-1]

The Ancient Egyptian alphabet consists of 28 letters. Plutarch referred to the number of articulated letters in the Ancient Egyptian alphabet in *Moralia, Vol. V*, [56A]:

> "*Five makes a square of itself, as many as the letters of the Egyptian alphabet.*"

The three primary/quantal vowels A, Y and W were not

counted in the number of the 25 consonants/letters because they were/are not produced by the human articulating organs.

Such practice was universal at that time. Moreover, it continues to be endorsed by modern-day linguists.

More about the three primary/quantal vowels A, Y and W in a later chapter of this book.

[For a complete list of the ABGD letters and their corresponding numbers and sound values, look at the beginning of this book: The 28 ABGD Letters and Pronunciation.]

1.2 REMOTE AGE OF EGYPTIAN ALPHABETS

Most modern Western scholars affirm, explicitly and implicitly, that the Ancient Egyptian alphabet (and language) is the oldest source in the world. In his book *The Literature of the Ancient Egyptians* [page xxxiv-v], the German Egyptologist Adolf Erman admits:

> *"The Egyptians alone were destined to adopt a remarkable method, following which they attained to the highest form of writing, the alphabet..."*

The British Egyptologist, W.M. Flinders Petrie, in his book *The Formation of the Alphabets* [page 3], concluded:

> <u>*"From the beginning of the prehistoric ages, a cursive system consisting of linear signs, full of variety and distinction was certainly used in Egypt."*</u>

The most eminent authority on languages, Isaac Taylor, in his book *History of the Alphabets,* Volume 1, page 62:

> "The immensely early date at which symbols of an alphabetic nature are found on the Egyptian monuments is a fact of great interest and importance. It is of great interest, inasmuch as it constitutes the starting point in the history of the Alphabet, establishing the literal truth of the assertion that <u>the letters of the alphabet are older than the pyramids—older probably than any other existing monument of human civilization.</u>"

Isaac Taylor, in his book *History of the Alphabets* Volume I, pg. 64, wrote about the Egyptian King Sent:

> "King Sent, in whose reign the alphabetic characters were already in use, may be taken to have lived <u>between 4000 and 4700 BCE</u>. Startling as the result of such calculations may appear, it must be affirmed to be probable that the <u>beginnings of the graphic art in the valley of the Nile must be relegated to a date of seven or eight thousand years from the present time.</u>"

It is very clear that the Ancient Egyptian alphabetical language was the FIRST in the world thousands of years prior the much-to-do-about nothing "Sinai scripts" [see a later chapter about this topic].

In his book *The Formation of the Alphabet*, W.M. Flinders Petrie has collected and tabulated alphabetical letter-forms that extended from the early prehistoric age of Egypt to the Greek and Roman eras. Petrie also compiled (from several independent scholars) similar-looking alphabetical letter-forms from 25 locations in Asia Minor, Greece, Italy, Spain, and other locations throughout Europe. All are much younger than the Ancient Egyptian alphabetical letter-forms.

Petrie's tabulation of these alphabetical letter-forms shows that:

> 1. All alphabetical letter-forms were present in Ancient Egypt since early pre-dynastic eras (over 7,000 years ago), prior to any place else in the world.
>
> 2. All the Egyptian alphabetical letter-forms are clearly distinguishable in the oldest recovered so-called Egyptian "hieratic writing" more than 5,000 years ago.
>
> 3. The same exact Ancient Egyptian alphabetical letter-forms were later adopted and spread to other people throughout the world.

1.3 THE DISTINCTIVE PRE-HYKSOS EGYPTIAN ALPHABETICAL PAPYRI

The eminent German Egyptologist Adolf Erman wrote, in his book *Life in Ancient Egypt*, page 339:

> **"Even under the Old Kingdom [2575-2040 BCE]*a special cursive hand had already been invented for daily use, the so-called hieratic."***

Isaac Taylor, in his book *The History of the Alphabet*, Vol.1, pages 94 and 95, referred to three important Ancient Egyptian manuscripts from the Old and Middle Kingdom eras [2575-1783] prior to the Hyksos period [c.1600

BCE], which had very clear and distinctive alphabetical cursive scripts. The three papyri agree essentially with each other as to the general style of the writing and the forms of the individual alphabetical characters in neat cursive.

These early alphabetical writings [Hieratic] clearly show a true cursive character: black, rounded, and bold.

The three Ancient Egyptian manuscripts referred to by

Isaac Taylor are:

> 1. An Egyptian manuscript in the possession of Prof. Lepsius in which mention is made of the builder of the Great Pyramid of Giza, Khufu [Cheops], and other kings of the earlier dynasties of Memphis [2649 -2465 BCE].

> 2. The most perfect specimen of the alphabetical neat cursive writing of the early period is the celebrated papyrus which was acquired at Thebes by M. Prisse d'Avennes, given by him to the Bibliotheque Nationale at Paris. This manuscript is usually called the "Papyrus Prisse." It was published in facsimile by M. Prisse in 1847, and consists of eighteen pages of a magnificent alphabetical cursive writing, unequaled in size and beauty, the characters being unusually large, full, and firm. A statement at the end of the papyrus shows that it is only a copy of the original work, which purports to have been composed by Prince Ptah-Hotep, who lived during the reign of Assa, a king of the fifth dynasty [2465-2323 BCE].

> 3. In the Museum at Berlin, there are some fragments

of a Hieratic papyrus during the times of the Egyptian kings Amenemhat and Usurtasen, who belonged to the twelfth dynasty [1991-1783] which preceded the invasion of the Hyksos.

Here is the Facsimile of papyrus Prisse, where letter-forms look exactly like letter-forms throughout the recognized Ancient Egyptian history and beyond.

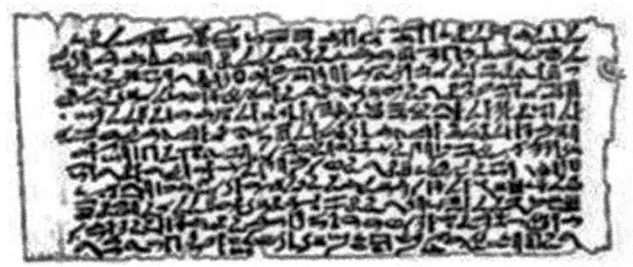

Here is an enlarged portion of this very Ancient Egyptian papyrus showing distinctive alphabetical letter-forms which every other country will adopt, as the evidence will show throughout this book.

Other early alphabetical writings are numerous. Here are a few examples:

1. Clear alphabets from the Old Kingdom era [2575-2040 BCE] from a letter from a widow, written on linen, Egyptian Museum, Cairo, JE25975.

2. This is the third of a cycle of five hymns to Senwosret III, which was found in the town of el-Lahun. The hymn to Senwosret III shows the strophic arrangement, and was written in mid 12th Dynasty [1991-1783 BCE].

3. The writing shown here is a memorandum from the Overseer of the temple to the Lector priest at Nubkaura Temple at el-Lahun (during the time of Senwosret II, 1897–1878 BCE), notifying him that Sirius would rise on the 16th day of the 4th month, so as to take note of its exact location and time to enter it into the temple records.

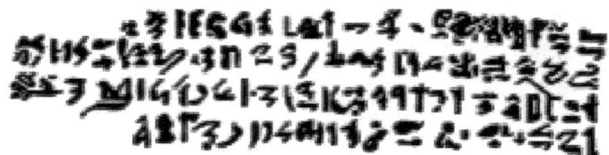

4. Several other similar samples on various topics and purposes can be found in R.B. Parkinson's book [see Selected Bibliography.]

5. Other Ancient Egyptian papyri with neat alphabetical writings on all kinds of subjects from this very early era are referred to throughout various publications by Moustafa Gadalla and are in most Egyptological references.

Chapter 2 : The Concealment of The Supreme Egyptian Alphabet

2.1 SMOKE SCREENING THOUSANDS OF EGYPTIAN ALPHABETICAL WRITINGS

The BIGGEST smoke screen in history is concealing the (Ancient) Egyptian alphabetical writing system. They made everyone think of the Egyptian language as a collection of "primitive pictures" called hieroglyphics. They concealed the Egyptian alphabetical system as the MOTHER of ALL languages in the world.

Here is how Alan Gardiner, in his book *Egyptian Grammar,* tries to "rationalize" how they concealed the Egyptian alphabetical system:

> *"Egyptologists have experienced the practical need of adopting some common standard to which different hieratic hands could be reduced, and instead of selecting one simple style of hieratic for the purpose, have preferred to transcribe all hieratic hands into hieroglyphic".*

Gardiner's "explanation/justification" for burying alphabetical [hieratic] writings assures us that there were <u>various forms of writings for various purposes</u>. The very same Western academies NEVER used the same "lame excuse" with Greek, Roman, or any other language in the world!

This lame excuse was ONLY used in Egyptian writings to deceive and conceal the Ancient Egyptian's alphabetical writing language.

There is NOT A SINGLE reference—prior to this 19th-20th century "Western Egyptologists" conspiracy—that stated a relationship between hieroglyphics (pictorial signs) and Hieratic/demotic alphabetical letterforms. On the contrary, EVERY single reference stated EXPLICITLY how unrelated they are.

2.2 EGYPTIAN IS DEAD, LONG LIVE "ARABIC"

After concealing the (Ancient) Egyptian alphabetical writing system that makes everyone thinks of the Egyptian language as a collection of "primitive pictures" called hieroglyphics, their second blow was declaring that the Ancient Egyptian language is DEAD and that it was replaced—out of thin air—by the "Arabic" language!

To say that Egyptians speak "Arabic" is totally false and illogical. It is the other way around: the "Arabs" long ago "adopted" and continue to speak EGYPTIAN.

The British Egyptologist Alan Gardiner in his book, *Egyptian Grammar*, page 3, writes:

"<u>The entire vocalic system of Old Egyptian may indeed</u>

> *be proved to have reached a stage resembling that of Hebrew or modern Arabic"*

Egyptian is the mother of all Semitic languages, as proven and concluded by ALL academicians.

More detailed information will be shown throughout the book, in later chapters.

2.3 THE MIGHTY WESTERN-FABRICATED EGYPTIAN ALPHABET AND "SEQUENCE"

Western Egyptologists—contrary to ALL historical evidence—invented an arbitrary group of symbols as being an Egyptian alphabet. Western Egyptologists declared, without a single supporting piece of evidence, that their created Egyptian alphabetical symbols were "degraded forms" of some hieroglyphic symbols. They then declared that they "settled" on an arbitrary selection of 24 letters to be the Egyptian Alphabet!!!

To further conceal the TRUTH, they arbitrarily arranged their 24 letters based on "frequency of use in texts". They have never applied the same "methodology" to "Greek", "Latin" or any other language!

Some contrary evidence was mistakenly left among these conspirators. A well-known reference, *Atlas of Ancient Egypt*, admits that Egyptians had an orderly sequence of alphabetical letters. Buried on page 198 of this reference, we read:

> *"The Egyptians had an <u>alphabetical order into which lists were sometimes arranged.</u>"*

The fact of the matter is that the order of the Ancient Egyptian alphabet was the ABGD sequence. Hebrews have always followed this sequence and the Arabs only in the 10th Century changed the ABGD sequence by a childish reshuffling of the ABGD sequence. More details will be found in later chapters of this book.

The arbitrary sequence of fabricated 24 letter signs was an intentional act so nobody would notice the obvious: that Ancient Egyptian letter-forms are the archetypes of letter-forms for all other languages!

2.4 THE DOUBLE TALK AND DOUBLE TAKE OF TWO [EGYPTIAN SOURCED] ALPHABETS

Western academia claims—with no basis in fact whatsoever—that an Egyptian alphabet was developed by the Ancient Egyptians, from their hieroglyphics. Western academia arbitrarily gave such alphabetical writings the names "hieratic" and "demotic".

Yet, the very same Western academics decided to give credit for the invention of the alphabet to someone else; and for that they chose the "Phoenicians"! Without any evidence, logic, or rationale, Western academia declared that it was some "Phoenician labors" working the Egyptian mines in Sinai who invented the *REAL alphabet* that forms the basis of Semitic alphabets—and, later, Greek and other European alphabets!!

Such a loud group of Western academics gave some imaginary "Phoenicians" (known in the ancient world as "seafarers") a "land assignment" far away from their homeland of present-day Lebanon and DEEP into the hostile wilderness of the Egyptian land of Sinai, so as to perform "mining work" for the Egyptians!

Not only did Western academia use an Egyptian location for such an invention; but furthermore, they claimed that the Egyptian hieroglyphs were used to produce these "Phoenician" alphabetical letter-forms! In this, as in every other regard, the mighty Western academia is consistent in denying the Egyptians ("Anyone but Egyptians")!

Unfortunately, we have to spend time and space to refute the negative – i.e., the unaccounted Phoenician claims by Western academia.

Several knowledgeable and honest academicians were drowned by a loud and hateful group. The following quotation from Isaac Taylor's book *The History of the Alphabets*, Vol. I [pg. 83], separates the facts from fiction:

> " — *[Ancient writers such as] Eusebius has preserved a passage from the alleged writings of the so-called Tyrian historian Sanchuniathon, from which we gather that the <u>Phoenicians did not claim to be themselves the inventors of the art of writing, but admitted that it was obtained by them from Egypt. Plato, Diodorus Siculus, Plutarch, Aulus Gellius, and Tacitus, all repeat the same statement</u>, thereby proving <u>how widely current throughout the ancient world was the opinion that the ultimate origin of letters must be sought in Egypt</u>. It may suffice to quote the words of Tacitus, who says, "Primi per figures animalium Aegyptii sensus mentis effingebant; (ea antiquissima monimenta memoriae humanae inpressa saxis cernuntur) et litterarum semet inventores perhibent. Inde Phoenicas, quia mari prae-*

pollebant, intulisse Graeciae, glorimque adeptos, tan-quam reperirint quae acceperant." Tacitus, Ann., xi. 14."

We will next give an overview of the history of mining activities in the Egyptian Sinai Peninsula so as to provide a complete context of the subject matter.

Chapter 3 : The Diversion of A Proto-Sinaitic "Phoenician Connection"

3.1 MINING HISTORY IN SINAI

In keeping with the orderly manner of the Ancient Egyptian civilization, they maintained written records showing the nature of their expeditions and the arrangements of their mining activities. The surviving Ancient Egyptian records show a tremendous organization of mining activities more than 5,000 years ago, in numerous sites throughout Egypt and beyond.

At the mines of Wadi Maghara, in Sinai, there still stand the stone huts of the workmen as well as a small fort, built to protect the Egyptians stationed there from the attacks of the Sinai Bedouins. There was a water well not far from these mines, and sizable cisterns in the fortress to hold water. The mines of Wadi Maghara were actively worked all throughout the dynastic era [3050– 343 BCE]. Inscriptions during the reign of the Great Pyramid of Giza (Khufu [Cheops]) are found engraved in the mines of Wadi Mahgara in Sinai.

The turquoise mines at Serabit el Khadem in the Sinai Peninsula show a typical Ancient Egyptian mining quarry consisting of a network of caverns and horizontal and vertical passages carefully cut with proper corners—as were the quarries of the Ancient Egyptians in all eras.

The very religious Egyptians have always built temples/shrines, along with commemorative stelae, near/at each mining site.

The Ancient Egyptian mining site at Serabit el Khadem in Sinai is a typical mining site, with its small temple of Hathor (called *"the Lady of the Turquoise"*) which stood on a high rocky terrace that dominated the valley since the 4th Dynasty [2575–2465 BCE] or possibly much earlier. This temple was enlarged afterwards by various kings of the New Kingdom, especially by Tut Homosis III. In front of the temple for at least a half mile is a kind of avenue that was arranged through numerous massive stelae, covered on four sides with inscriptions commemorating mining expeditions. Inscribed stelae describing the work at each mining site are also found at other mines throughout Egypt.

Ancient Egyptian records also show the various division and specialties of manpower at the mining sites. Egyptian mining activities were very organized, with people traveling back and forth to check the site work to ensure properly efficient operations and to provide a frequent rotation of the workforce at the mining sites, as well as providing amenities to these fortified sites.

In all the countless numbers of documents and inscriptions, is there a single reference to the employment of foreigners in the Ancient Egyptian mine sites; which were always fortified and guarded against the nomads of the Sinai Peninsula?

[For more detailed information, see *Ancient Egyptian Culture Revealed*, *Egyptian Romany of Hispania* and *Egyptian Pyramids Revisited* or its older edition, *Pyramid Handbook*, all by Moustafa Gadalla.]

3.2 "PROTO-SINAITIC" GRAFFITI—A MANUFACTURED "STRAW"

Western academia has decided that the letter-forms of the alphabet were developed from pictures. They have also pre-determined what they described as a "missing link between pictures and letter-forms". They gave their "missing link" terms such as "pre-alphabet signs". It was the 30 characters of the so-called "Proto-Sinaitic finding" that served their intended purpose!

Such a "finding" was not even a case of "grasping a straw". In reality, it was a manufactured "straw" so that they can grasp onto it!

So let us look at the elements of their proclaimed "finding":

> 1. As a part of Sir Wm. Flinders Petrie's work to collect alphabetical letters/signs from different regions of the ancient world, he made a reference that in the winter of 1904-1905, he found what appeared to him to be 30 crude signs/inscriptions at Serabit elKhadim (where the site contained turquoise mines which were mined from expeditions over thousands of years, as mentioned above in this chapter) that

became known as "Proto-Sinaitic". The 30 characters/inscriptions were scattered at various locations in the area among hundreds of well-executed inscriptions. They are nothing more than some graffiti that were made in restricted areas such as the main temple at this mining site. It should be noted that Ancient Egyptian temples were restricted and not accessible to the public—a fact known to all Western academicians.

2. Petrie, who is an accomplished British Egyptologist, himself never claimed his collection of 30 characters to be of any special significance. He was 'used' by other academicians to make a big deal about 30 graffiti that he collected in his worldwide task in preparation for his book, *Formation of Alphabets*.

Here are some significant to be made:

1. The "collection" is basically a collection of some distinct hieroglyphics, some symbolic signs, and some that appear as alphabetical character forms. Because it is basically a random "collection", no one can make any sense of it.

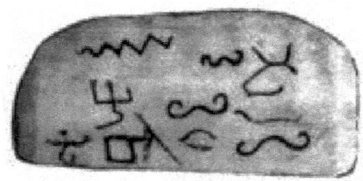

G.R. Driver, among practically all other scholars in this field, clearly admitted so in his book, *Semitic Writing: From Pictograph to Alphabet*, page 141:

> *"Sinaitic signs can hardly be used for purposes of interpretation"*

Neither Petrie nor any other Western academician was able to identify the 30 characters, except for one Alan Gardiner, who claimed that he was able to identify a single word from 4 characters. [More about such a claim later in this chapter.]

These signs are random, and to call them a "collection" gives a wrong sense of coherence/relationship to each other or to anything whatsoever!

2. <u>The "discoverer" himself, the accomplished British Egyptologist and linguist Petrie, never advocated that letter-form shapes were derived from pictures.</u> The British Egyptologist Petrie, in his book *The Formation of the Alphabets*, page 6, states:

> *"The question as to whether the* [alphabetical letter-forms]*signs were derived from the more pictorial hieroglyphs, or were an independent system, has been so little observed by writers on the subject, that <u>the matter has been decided more than once without any consideration of the various details involved.</u>"*

To insist that signs/letters/characters are derived from Egyptian hieroglyphics is without any basis and is contrary to the facts recorded by ALL writers of antiquities.

3. Regarding the subject of dating such crude signs, Western academia made up dates to concur with

their "Phoenicians" diversion tactics. They shamelessly dated them to circa 1700-1400 BCE!

4. Despite their acknowledgment that they can't make any sense out of such random "collection" of signs, Western academia insisted that said "signs" were alphabetical signs and the ancestor of the Phoenician alphabet from which nearly all modern alphabets descend.

5. Western academicians are basically all in agreement about the **graphic similarities of such a "collection" of random signs with the Egyptian "hieratic" script**. In the 1950s and 60s it was common to show the derivation of the Canaanite alphabet from the Egyptian script 'hieratic', using William Albright's interpretations of Proto-Sinaitics as the key. It was generally accepted that the language of the **inscriptions was Semitic and that the script had an Egyptian "hieratic" prototype.**

6. Godfrey Driver, in his book *Semitic Writing: from Pictograph to Alphabet,* provided the case to prove that the alphabetic characters of such a "collection" were well established from much earlier times in the Sinai.

7. It is a total fabrication to assume that Phoenicians worked the mines in the Egyptian Sinai. Then, add another assumption to the first baseless assumption: that those miners (who were not a literate people), after working the mines all day, were able to "invent" the consonantal alphabet during their "after hours spare time"!

Godfrey Driver continues, in his book *Semitic Writing: From Pictograph to Alphabet*, page 140:

> *"Further, the writing, however crude, could not have been the work of indigenous Semitic nomads eking out a bare existence in the Sinaitic Peninsula from time immemorial; and neither miners nor their foremen are likely inventors of an alphabet. These monuments were the work of the Egyptians."*

3.3 B'ALAT WHO SAVED THE DAY!

A decade after Petrie's original discoveries, and after the "discoverer" Petrie (being himself an accomplished British Egyptologist with extensive research in the history and formation of alphabets as well as all academic linguistic specialists) could make no sense of the 30 random "collections" of undeciphered characters, it has been claimed that Alan Gardiner was able to figure out a **SINGLE** "word" in all the referenced Petrie "discovered" ProtoSinaitic characters!

Conveniently, this very single word was b`lt, (B`alat). B'alat is an Egyptian epithet that means "Lady", describing the Ancient Egyptian netert [goddess] Hathor. Notwithstanding that she was an Egyptian deity and that the Ancient Egyptians used such an "epithet", it was claimed that since the same "epithet" was used by the "Phoenicians" elsewhere, that this single word provides the "evidence" that the inscriptions were made by "Phoenicians" working in Sinai!!! An incredible act of desperation!

It was admitted that Alan Gardiner could not establish,

with clear authority, the phonetic value or even the stable visual form of the rest of the signs in the Sinaitic "collection".

He singularly claimed that he found five Egyptian hieroglyphic pictures conveying the epithet "Balat". He theorized that the first letter of each Egyptian hieroglyphic will spell out the epithet "Balat"! There is not a SINGLE historical or practical piece of evidence to support his theory. Furthermore, it is common knowledge that Hathor is not a "name", but an epithet that means "House [Hat] of Horus [Hor]."

It is also common knowledge among all Egyptologists—including Gardiner himself—that the Ancient Egyptians used several epithets and titles to refer to any of the Egyptian deities.

3.4 UNDERSTANDING NAMES, EPITHETS AND TITLES OF EGYPTIAN DEITIES

The role of the name in Ancient and Baladi Egypt was not, as per our modern-day thinking, a mere label. Egyptian creation texts repeatedly stress the belief of creation by the Word. We find that in the Book of the Divine Cow (found in the shrines of Tut-Ankh-Amen), Re creates the heavens and its hosts merely by pronouncing some words whose sound alone evokes the names of things—and these things then appear at his bidding. As its name is pronounced, so the thing comes into being. For the name is, in reality; the thing itself.

The real names of the deities (gods, goddesses) were kept secret. The real name was/is imbued with magical powers and properties. To know and pronounce the real name of a neter/netert (god/goddess) is to exercise power over it.

In keeping with this belief, the names of deities often relate to their roles. They were referred to by epithets that describe particular qualities, attributes and/or aspect(s) of their roles. Because of their multiple and overlapping roles, deities can have many epithets.

Here are a few examples of Egyptian epithets of Neteru (gods, goddesses) that were cavalierly called "names" by academicians:

    1. Amen/Amun means "hidden one".

    2. The netert (goddess)

1. Sekhmet is actually two words, Sekh and -Mut—meaning *Elder Mother* or *Den Mother*, with all the qualities of a *Den Mother*.

    3. The neter [god] Ausar [commonly recognized as 'Osiris'] actually consists of two words—*Aus* and *Ra*. The word **Aus** means ***the power of***, or the root of. As such, Ausar [Aus-Ra] means *the power of Ra*, meaning the re-birth of Ra the creation in the abyss of a pre-creation state.

In most (or practically all) references about Ancient Egypt, writers dealt with Egyptian epithets with total disregard for the intent and nature of the Egyptian language. Epithets and the like must be understood in the context of the Egyptian language.

The Ancient Egyptians also used generic words that were

also confused by foreign academicians as "names", while in reality they are simple words with religious connotations. 'Baal' simply means 'lord' or 'ruler', and so we hear of the Baal or the Baalat (Lady) of such-and-such a city. Similarly, a deity will be called Melek, meaning King. So, too, Adon, which means Lord or Master. Melqart meant King of the City. Other "names" meaning 'favored by the gods' or 'granted by the gods' were translated into Latin as Fortunatus, Felix, Donatus, Concessus, and so on.

To the contemptuous Western academia mindset, whenever the "name" of a deity appears either in or outside Egypt, they declare such a "name" of non-Egyptian origin!! The truth is that Egypt influenced the world in every regard because it was the most populated and richest country in the ancient world for several millennia. The ancient writers of antiquities acknowledged such a fact, but Western academia cannot stand it! [More information about names, epithets, and titles can be found in other publications by Moustafa Gadalla such as *Egyptian Cosmology* and *Egyptian Divinities*.]

Next, we will give an overview of the identity of the people known as "Phoenicians" and their real and "presumed" homeland.

3.5 PHOENICIANS' HOMELAND

The Phoenicians are arbitrarily credited with introducing many aspects of a truly complete civilization into different parts of the world. Yet, the Phoenicians never had a history of such "talents" in their presumed home country.

Phoenicians actually means **people of reddish/tanned**

skins—the typical look of a sunburned sailor. They were sailors, and should not be associated with a specific region of the world. Not withstanding this fact about the meaning of "Phoenicians" for the people at that time in history, we are going to presume that Western academia is "correct", and will investigate the presumed land of "Phoenicia".

Present-day Lebanon is assumed to be the location of "Phoenicia". The mountains of modern-day Lebanon extend some 110 miles [175 km] from north to south, with many of its western foothills reaching the Mediterranean. The Lebanon range presents a monolithic facade to the Mediterranean coast, with no natural passes (other than difficult gorges) to the interior. Travel inland went over—not through. A day's journey in either direction consisted of a long, laborious ascent followed by a lengthy but somewhat less arduous descent. Such land topography makes it inaccessible to travel from the Mediterranean shore towards the east. As a consequence, the destiny of the inhabitants of Phoenicia was linked with the sea because of how cramped they may have felt on land, with its formidable mountain barriers and impenetrable, torrential rivers. The sea, with its wide expanse, was their only way of making a living.

As in Greece, a country devoid of great plains and traversed by steep mountain chains and deep gorges of torrential streams, the natural resources of Phoenicia were limited.

Phoenicia's main natural resource was lumber. Byblos became the center of a lumber trade where vast quantities of cedar and pine trees were felled in the adjacent

Lebanon hills, rolled or carted down to Byblos, and from there, towed on rafts to Egypt. The destiny of the Phoenicians was thus tied to the Egyptian demand for lumber.

3.6 "PHOENICIA": THE EGYPTIAN SATELLITE

The tenure of Byblos in a sort of alliance was necessary because Egypt, which was one of the largest timber-consuming countries of antiquity, lacked timber that was essential for her buildings, her boats, her furniture and fuel, and especially, her funerary equipment. Alabaster vases bearing the names of most of the Egyptian kings of the 3rd–6th Dynasties (2649–2152 BCE)—especially those of Pepi I and Pepi II of the 6th Dynasty—were found in large quantities at Byblos during excavations, by chance discovery. A large number of these vases are at the National Museum in Beirut and a smaller number may be seen at the Louvre Museum and the Archaeological Museum of the American University of Beirut. Furthermore, the Palermo Stone states that 40 vessels loaded with fir trees arrived in Egypt during the reign of Snefru (2575-2551 BCE), or as early as 2800 BCE, during the reign of Khasekhem, the last king of the 2nd Dynasty.

The need for timber supplies explains, at least in part, the importance of the permanent settlement—a kind of protectorate—which the Egyptians had at Byblos in the middle of the Phoenician coast from the earliest days of the Old Kingdom (c. 2575 BCE). The kings of Byblos were invested with such Egyptian titles as "prince", "count", or "sheikh of sheikhs". Their precise political standing in relation to Egypt is unknown, but they were probably vassal kings or high commissioners controlling a local population subject to Egypt.

Byblos was dependent on the Egyptian economy. During the anarchy that prevailed in Egypt under the 7th–10th Dynasties (2150–2040 BCE), contact with Byblos seems to have been disrupted, and Byblos lay in ruins at the time.

During the Middle Kingdom, whose central period was that of the 12th Dynasty (1991–1783 BCE), Egypt revitalized its relations with the Phoenician coast and principally with Byblos. The relationship with Egypt was especially close. Royal tombs built into the cliffs on the shore of Byblos have been found with their treasures intact, and objects from rifled tombs have found their way to museums in Paris and Beirut.

Among the intact tombs are those of Abi-shemu (Abi-ismyfather) and his son Ypshemu-abi (my-father's-name-is-good), contemporaries of Pharaohs Amenemhet III and IV (1844–1787 BCE). An obsidian ointment jar bearing the cartouche of Amenemhet III was found in Abishemu's tomb and a gift box of incense from Amenemhet IV in the tomb of his son; while golden pectorals, other pieces of jewelry, and ornamented jars were sent to unnamed kings.

During the early New Kingdom era (c. 1575 BCE), Phoenicia enjoyed a period of prosperity under the Pharaohs, who succeeded Tuthomosis III. Amenhotep II, and Tuthomosis IV, during the early part of the reign of Amenhotep III (c. 1400 BCE).

Egypt fulfilled its alliance obligations by providing all means to protect its allies in Asia. The letters of Tell el Amarna convey the stress and strain of the times and the anxiety of the various correspondents. When the Hittites invaded the Egyptian allies in Asia, Seti I (1333–1304 BCE) took the field against the Hittites and was able to recover Phoenicia and Palestine. His successor, Ramses II (1304–1237 BCE), carried on a long struggle with the Hittites as well, which ended in a treaty whereby Egypt retained Phoenicia and Palestine and Hatti maintained its sovereignty over the Amorites of the hinterland and Naharin. Shafatbaal and Ahiram were contemporary kings of Byblos, and welcomed the return of the Egyptians to their country. Ahiram, a contemporary of Ramses II, was buried in a stone sarcophagus carved with motifs strongly reminiscent of Egyptian art.

The livelihood of the Phoenicians was totally dependent on Ancient Egypt, and Egyptian goods are prominently found in Phoenician tombs. It should not be a surprise to find that the Phoenicians were Egyptianized in all aspects of their existence. Their temples, tombs, artifacts, religion, language, system of government, etc., were all Ancient Egyptian.

The Egyptian temple at Byblos, evidently the seat of the Egyptian governor where the kings of Egypt had offerings made in their name, is a significant indication of this special relationship. According to the finds yielded by excavations in the Egyptian temple at Byblos, the duration of that temple and of the occupation to which it bears witness extended from the Old Kingdom (2575–2150 BCE) throughout the Middle and New Kingdoms (2040–1070 BCE). Many Egyptian scarabs of the Middle Kingdom [i.e. the period of the 12th Dynasty and the period immediately following] have been found among the deposits in the temple. A remarkable royal monument has also been recovered—a great bas-relief depicting the Prince of Byblos, before the legend of a Pharaoh of the period following the 12th Dynasty, with all these names and particulars in Egyptian hieroglyphics. In art, sculpture, and architecture, the Phoenicians copied the Egyptian style. However, their execution is far inferior to that of Egypt.

With such a total and complete dependence on Egypt in all aspects of its existence, how can anyone expect the Phoenicians not to speak and write the Egyptian language? Egyptian inscriptions are found everywhere and in all periods throughout Phoenicia.

[More about the Phoenicians and their activities can be found in the book *Egyptian Romany: The Essence of Hispania* by Moustafa Gadalla.]

PART II : FORMATION AND FORMS OF EGYPTIAN ALPHABETIC WRITINGS

Chapter 4 : Genesis of Egyptian Alphabetic Letters/Writings

4.1 THE UNFOUNDED OBSESSION THAT LETTERS WERE DERIVED FROM PICTURE

All early Greek and Roman writers affirmed that there were basically two forms of Ancient Egyptian writings: an imagery form of expression [the pictorial hieroglyphics] and alphabetical form of writing. The pictorial forms are a series of images conveying conceptual meanings and not individual sound values. [More about this form in the book *The Egyptian Hieroglyph Metaphysical Language* by Moustafa Gadalla.]

Despite all contrary evidence, a loud group of Western academics has dominated the subject of the 'genesis of alphabets' in Egypt and elsewhere. With no basis whatsoever, they declared that the graphic form of letters was originally derived from Egyptian hieroglyphs, and that they were given the sound value of the first consonant of the Semitic translation of the hieroglyph.

It must be emphasized that not a single classical writer—including Clement of Alexandria (in *Stromata Book V* [chapter IV]) – ever indicated that the Egyptian alphabetical form of writing was a "cursive" or "degenerated" form of Ancient Egyptian pictorial hieroglyphics. Yet, shamelessly, some "scholars" invoked the writing of Clement of Alexandria to insist that out of hieroglyphs sprang a more cursive writing known to us as *hieratic*, and out of *hieratic* there again emerged a very rapid script sometimes called *enchorial* or *demotic*.

Many rational scholars, however, recognized that the pictorial writings are a series of images conveying conceptual meanings and not individual sound values, such as the British Egyptologist W.M. Flinders Petrie, who wrote in his book, *The Formation of the Alphabets* [pg. 6],

> *"The question as to whether the [alphabetical] signs were derived from the more pictorial hieroglyphs, or were an independent system, has been so little observed by writers on the subject, that the matter has been decided more than once without any consideration of the various details involved."*

4.2 DIFFERENCES BETWEEN IDEOGRAMS, SIGNS AND ALPHABETICAL WRITING

– Ideograms are what the Egyptian hieroglyphics represent.

Each pictorial symbol is worth a thousand words, representing that function or principle on all levels simultaneously; from the simplest, most obvious physical manifestation of that function to the most abstract and metaphysical. This symbolic language represents a wealth of physical, physiological, psychological and spiritual data in the presented symbols.

The metaphorical and symbolic concept of the hieroglyphs was unanimously acknowledged by all early writers on the subject such as Plutarch, Diodorus, Clement, etc.

The best description came from Plotinus, who wrote in *The Enneads* [Vol. V-6]:

> *"The wise men of Egypt, either by scientific or innate knowledge, and <u>when they wished to signify something wisely, did not use the forms of letters which follow the order of words and propositions and imitate sounds and the enunciations of philosophical statements, but by drawing images and inscribing in their temples one particular image of each particular thing</u>, they manifested the non-discursiveness of the intelligible world, that is, that <u>every image is a kind of knowledge and wisdom and is a subject of statements</u>, all together in one, and not discourse or deliberation. But [only] afterwards [others] discovered, starting from it in its concentrated unity, a representation in something else, already unfolded and speaking it discursively and giving the reasons why things are like this, so that, because what has come into existence is so beautifully disposed, if anyone knows how to admire it he expresses his admiration of how this wisdom, which does not itself possess the reasons why substance is as it is, gives them to the things which are made according to it."*

Clement of Alexandria, in *Stromata, Book V*, chapter IV, never associated alphabetical writing system with that of hieroglyphics and/or that hieratic was a "cursive" or "degenerated" form of hieroglyphics. He clearly did not make the hieroglyphic as the origin/basis of other forms/styles when he stated *"and finally, and last of all, the Hieroglyphic."*

> *"Now those instructed among the Egyptians learned first of all <u>that style of the Egyptian letters</u> which is called Epistolographic* [cursive i.e. 'composed as a series of letters']; <u>*and second, the Hieratic style, which the Priestly scribes perform*</u>; *and finally, and last of all, the Hieroglyphic..."*

[For more details read *The Egyptian Hieroglyphic Metaphysical Language* by Moustafa Gadalla.]

– **Signs** are indicative symbols, just like our modern traffic signs. Such signs represent things such as the seven astronomical planets, astronomical constellations, particular stars, zodiac constellations, metals, the four elements, %, #, @, etc. Signs can also be for trade and/or a profession's uses.

– **Alphabetical Writing** signifies a unity of form and sound; i.e. one sound value for each letter-form.

4.3 "EVOLUTION" OF ALPHABET FROM "SIGNS" TO "REAL" ALPHABETS

The difference between an alphabetical letter-form and a "sign" was clearly delineated above: a letter has its own particular sound, while a sign like a 'traffic sign' has no sound value.

In the field of alphabet studies, Petrie collected a large number of elements/letter-forms that clearly do not look like pictures. He then arranged them in groups of look-alikes and called them "alphabetical signs"! He considered such "alphabetical signs" to be the "forerunners" of alphabetical letter-forms! Because the number of letter-forms that Petrie collected exceeded the number contained in the recognized 'Semitic' alphabet, he then *theorized* that what he'd collected were the "forerunners" of "alphabetical letter-forms".

Petrie was incorrect in not calling them alphabetical letter-forms because they were and continued to look the same in various languages. The 'apparent' large number can easily be reduced to the archetypal 28 Ancient Egyptian letters once certain unique writing techniques are explained. Variations in letter-forms are easily explained in the context of the Ancient Egyptian alphabetical language as well as of the later Semitic Languages Group:

1. Each Ancient Egyptian letter (as well as later in Arabic/Persian) have 4 forms:

> a. detached
> b. initial
> c. medial
> d. terminal

2. Dots are found in some letters to represent the last six letters in the Egyptian alphabet that has a sonic-twin letter in the top 22 letters. These last six letter-forms have the same letter-form of each's primary letter plus an added dot or a bar to distinguish each from its prime sonic-twin. Western academics have always confused such distinctions of these last six letters of the 28-letter alphabet.

3. Alphabetical letter-forms were also used for other purposes such as musical texts, numbers, etc. In such uses, letter-forms are used by adding a bar above/below a letter or letter-form turned around in different directions. More details will be shown in a later chapter in this book about the Egyptian 'tonal' writing system.

Such variations confused unknowledgeable Western academics, and therefore they came up with the term "sign" and described it [wrongly] as being an intermediate step in the "evolution" of letters from pictures to "final/refined letter-forms"!

Chapter 5 : The Egyptian Sound Organization of Letters

5.1 THE UNIVERSAL THREE PRIMARY/QUANTAL EGYPTIAN VOWEL

In order to utter a consonant, we must close (or almost close) the month in a particular manner, and in order to produce the vowel, we must open the mouth more or less widely, in a particular manner. The vowels, as such, are similar to the sounds of free/uninterrupted musical instrument sounds.

As acknowledged by all involved, Ancient Egyptian has had three primary vowels thousands of years before the "Phoenicians":

- High being the letter/vowel 'A'—as in mad
- Low being the letter/vowel 'Y/I'—as in me
- Medium being the letter/vowel 'W/O/U'—as in moo

The sounds of these three vowels indicate the central and two extreme positions, in the first mode, of the first kind of action of the parts of the mouth upon the voice, and were all needed to provide the sounds of the letters of the alphabet.

These three sounds, considered in relation to the human organs of speech, correspond respectively to the greatest diminution of the aperture of the throat by means of the tongue to nearly the greatest diminution of the external orifice of the mouth by means of the lips, and to nearly the greatest opening of the mouth and throat.

It is from these three primary/basic sounds/pitches/tones that ALL sounds are created.

These three primary quantal vowels are unique in several ways:

> 1. First, they are present in the sound patterns of the vast majority of human languages.

> 2. Second, these vowels represent extreme positions of the tongue, with tight constrictions in each of three widely separate regions of the vocal tract: palatal, velar, and pharyngeal.

> 3. Third, Apes, most fossil hominids, and newborn infants cannot make these three "extreme" vowels because they do not have a two-tube resonating system. That might not be extraordinary in itself, but [Y/ I, A, W/O/U] are special or quantal in nature. They can be produced only if the vocal tract is tightly constricted in such a way as to form two tubes.

>> – For [Y/I], the oral cavity is tightly constricted and the pharyngeal cavity is expanded.

>> – For [A], the opposite holds: The oral cavity is fully expanded and the pharyngeal tube is tightly constricted.

– For [W/O/U], the oral cavity is slightly more expanded than the pharyngeal cavity, with a tight constriction between the two tubes.

For all three vowels, there are sharp changes in vocal tract size near the midpoint of the vocal tract. It is this midpoint discontinuity in the two-tube vocal tract of humans that permits quantal vowel sounds to be produced.

Any speaker can be relatively imprecise in positioning the tongue and jaw for these three vowels. That is: sloppy articulation still produces reasonably good acoustic approximations of these three vowels.

Other vowel sounds demand more careful articulation.

The resistance of [i, a, u] to precise articulation (they can be spoken sloppily, yet be understood) means that they are stable speech signals.

Quantal vowel sounds are satisfactory for communication in many ways:

1. First, they are acoustically powerful and can carry hundreds of yards in the open air.

2. Second, since only a quasi-human vocal tract can produce them, hearing them would indicate a human signal rather than that of prey or predator.

3. Third, rapid, efficient speech production involves the swift articulation of streams of syllables. Since each syllable generally contains a vocalic (vowel-like) nucleus, [i, u, a] could serve as the basis for an efficient, syllable-based speech production code.

Because [i, u, a] are quantal in nature, most members of a human group could produce these sounds sufficiently accurately to be recognized, despite sloppy articulation. And because it is known that many consonant sounds are identified by the accompanying vowel, the differences in identical vowels caused by differences in vocal tract length could be calibrated. That is, both sex and age of the speaker could be identified so that the consonant sounds could be more easily identified.

Efficient verbal communication also demands that speech sounds be distinctive and not easily confused with one another. The quantal vowels fulfill this requirement because their resonance frequency patterns are quite different and not easily confused, even under adverse conditions.

It must be emphasized that ONLY the way these three sounds are delivered in the Egyptian [later Arabic] tongue constitute the only true precise quantal sounds.

The above discussion establishes the primary role of these particular "vowels" regarding other vowels, consonants, etc, as will be explained throughout this chapter.

5.2 FROM THREE TO FIVE VOWELS

As stated above, these three primary vowels [A,Y/I & W/O/U] indicate the central and two extreme positions in the first mode of the first kind of action of the parts of the mouth upon the voice. But between these extreme positions lies an infinite number of others, and the subtlety of our organs is such that we are able to glide, by almost imperceptible degrees, from one position to another, and each position will of course correspond to a different modification of the voice.

The vowels are formed by the voice and are modified but not interrupted by the various positions of the tongue and lips. Their differences depend on the proportions between the aperture of the lips and the internal cavity of the mouth, which is altered by different elevations of the tongue.

The five sounds, in the order i, e, a, o, u, constitute what are commonly called the five vowels, to which number the vowel sounds are usually supposed to be restricted. The additional two vowels are derived from the three primary vowels as follows:

- Intermediate to 'i' and 'a' is represented by 'ay' in may.

- Intermediate to 'a' and 'u', is 'o', as represented by 'ow' in mow.

5.3 THE SEVEN HARMONIC TONES/VOWELS

To follow from the same basis above, the seven sounds are derived from the above 5 vowels as follows:

- between 'a' and 'o', we have the 6th derived vowel, as represented by 'aw' in maw; and,

- between 'o' and 'u', is the 7th derived vowel, which corresponds to 'y' in myrrh.

If we pronounce the seven vowels in this order, we see clearly that they follow one another in a natural manner.

Vowels, in sequence and in set configurations, were commonly used in spells, utilizing their cosmic powers.

Mystics of many persuasions found special significance in the seven vowels, relating them to the major heavenly bodies: the sun, the moon, and the five known planets. [For more detailed information about the harmony and sounds of the seven planets/spheres and its applications in [Ancient] Egyptian traditions read, *The Enduring Ancient Egyptian Musical System* by Moustafa Gadalla.]

5.4 THE INFINITE VOWELS DERIVATIVES

To follow from the same basis above, more and more intermediate vowels are derived from the seven vowels above. In other words, there are an infinite number of vowels, all derived from the particular Egyptian three-quantal vowels. The recognition of the significance of vowels and other sound-producing elements were all accredited to the Ancient Egyptians, as admitted by Plato, per his Collected Dialogues [*Philebus* 18-b, c, d]:

> **SOCRATES:** *The unlimited variety of sound was once discerned by some god, or perhaps some godlike man; you know the story that there was some such person in Egypt called Theuth. He it was who originally <u>discerned the existence, in that unlimited variety, of the vowels—not 'vowel' in the singular but 'vowels' in the plural</u>—and then of other things which, though they could not be called articulate sounds, yet were noises of a kind. There were a number of them too, not just one, and as a third class he discriminated what we now call the mutes. Having done that, <u>he divided up</u> the noiseless ones or mutes <u>until he got each one by itself, and</u>*

<u>did the same thing with the vowels</u> and the intermediate sounds; ..."

The reference to "Theuth" above is the same "Theuth" mentioned in the Phaedrus, where we are explicitly told that he was an Ancient Egyptian neter (god), **"the one whose sacred bird is called the Ibis",** so as to exclude all doubt about his identity. It is obvious that his account is based on a genuine Egyptian tradition because the ibis-headed Theuth [Thoth] is an Egyptian neter (god).

All these shades/intermediate vowel sounds are recognized in writing by phonetic/vocalic markings and most of them are known/learned "from mothers"—such as in other languages like English, where phonetics are used in dictionaries to set the proper sounding pronunciation of letters, syllables, and words.

The type of a vowel is determined entirely by its position inside a word.

5.5 CONSONANTS AS DERIVATIVES OF VOWELS

Phonology and its related subjects show that vowels are the origin sounds, and that consonants are derived from them.

The vocal tract in the production of a vowel can be regarded as a tube open at the lip end and closed at the glottal end.

We next have to consider that modification which the action of the consonant produces in the vowel. Now, in order to utter a consonant, we must close, or almost close, the month in a particular manner; and in order to produce the vowel, we must open the mouth more or less widely, in a particular manner. There may, therefore, be affirmed to be as many species of each consonant as there are different vowels to which it may be applied.

5.6 THE 25 ARTICULATED ALPHABETICAL CONSONANTS

As mentioned above, vowels are primary sounds and "consonants" are merely stopping of the flow of the vowel in a certain way, in our human vocal system.

Thoth represents the Divine Messenger who articulated and wrote the spoken words, knowledge, etc.

Several of Thoth's attributes were confirmed by Diodorus of Sicily in his *Book I*, Section 16-1:

> *"It was by Thoth, according to Ancient Egyptians, that <u>the common language of mankind was first further articulated</u>, and that many objects which were still nameless received an appellation, that <u>the alphabet were defined</u>, ..."*

The Ancient Egyptian alphabet consists of 28 letters. Plutarch referred to the Ancient Egyptian 25 articulated consonants in *Moralia, Vol. V*, [56A]:

> *"Five makes a square of itself, as many as the letters of the Egyptian alphabet."*

The three primary/quantary vowels A, Y and W were not counted in the number of the 25 consonants/letters because they were/are not produced by the articulating human organs. Such practice was universal at that time.

Moreover, it continues to be endorsed by modern-day linguists.

The letter-forms of the 28 [Ancient] Egyptian alphabet will be shown later in chapter 12 so as to compare them with other later languages of the world in Africa, Asia and Europe.

Our focus in this chapter continues to be about the subject of the sound values of the [Egyptian] alphabet.

5.7 BALANCED PHONOLOGY RANGE

The number of alphabetical sounds in the ideal language is best described by Richard A. Firmage in his book *The Alphabet ABECEDARIUM: Some Notes on Letters*, page 288:

> *"The theoretical ideal goal of an alphabet is to reproduce every shade of sound with the greatest possible exactitude."*

Since, as admitted by all, the vocalic properties of the Ancient Egyptian tongue is identical to later "Arabic", it is easy to recognize see that the [Ancient] Egyptian 28 letters concurs with the ideal goal as stated by Firmage [above].

See The 28 ABGD Letters and Pronunciations in the pre-text materials of this book.

For more detailed information about the distribution and location of as well as the sound production ways of the various sounds of the alphabet, read *The Alphabet of Nature* by Alexander John Ellis.

5.8 SPECIAL PHONETICS OF EACH LETTER

Upon careful observation, we find that the sound of a particular letter will change depending on the location of the letter in a word, as well as its relationship to letters preceding and following it. An example in English is found in the articulations of the words *pin, spin,* and *tip,* where there exists a slight variation in the pronunciation of the letter 'p' in each of these three words.

These highly idealized abstract patterns are called *phonemes*.

A *phoneme* may be operationally defined as representing the sound segment which, when changed by the substitution of another sound segment, changes the meaning and sound shape of a word.

A phoneme as the smallest acoustic value enables us to recognize and distinguish the sound shades of a letter/musical note.

There is generally a close correspondence between the letters and phonemes of a given language, but it is hardly exact in any language—except in the Egyptian system, where there are more phonemes than letters, which allows for the 4 sound variations of each letter by using more than one phoneme.

The various tonality of each letter was/is reflected in the Egyptian writing system, where each letter can have up to four forms:

> o **Detached** – the letter as it appears by itself, no letters joining to it either before or after.

o **Initial** – the letter as it appears when not preceded by a joining letter.

o **Medial** – the letter as it appears when there are joining letters both before and after the letter.

o **Terminal** – the letter as it appears when it is preceded, but not followed, by joining letters.

5.9 SOUND LIGATURING OF LETTERS IN A WORD

The phoneme phenomenon is realized and recognized in the Egyptian [and later Arabic] writing system, where not all letters of a word can be connected depending on the relationship between each two consecutive letters in any given word.

For an example, the word "to plant" in Egyptian is 'ZRA', where none of the three letters are connected to each other.

The word "to harvest/gather/add" is 'GMA' where all three letters of the word are connected.

Such a writing system with its [sound] connectivity rules was NEVER recognized by Western academia. This single issue has caused fatal mistakes in Western academia's works on languages—such as describing a connected group of letters as a "syllable" and thus calling something a "syllabic writing".

To add insult to injury, their ignorance of the principles of cursive writing was made worse when they consistently and arrogantly accused Egyptians of making mistakes in their writings?! The arrogance of ignorance!

Western academies, with their colonial attitudes, made up rules as they went along instead of admitting their own shortcomings. Western academia declared themselves more superior in the language of the Ancient Egyptians than the Egyptians themselves! An example of such irrational arrogance is made by Adolph Erman in his book *The Literature of the Ancient Egyptians*, page xliii:

> **"Besides the obstacles presented by this ambiguous system of writing, yet another, laughable may be, but for us only too serious, is to be found in the levity and ignorance of the scribes. That manuscripts swarm with mistakes is unfortunately no unusual thing elsewhere, but in hardly any other script are mistakes in writing so fatal as in hieroglyphic".**

[For more detailed information about syllables, their types, properties, structures and forms, their rhythmic flows within an utterance, etc., read *The Musical Aspects of the Ancient Egyptian Vocalic Language* by Moustafa Gadalla.]

Chapter 6 : The Egyptian Alphabetic Writing Styles

6.1 THE DEVIOUS WESTERN CATEGORIZATION OF EGYPTIAN ALPHABETICAL SCRIPTS

As stated earlier, despite all the facts, Western academia fabricated a story of how the 'Hieratic' script was degenerated from of the hieroglyphic pictorial symbols, and that the "demotic" script was further degeneration of the already-degenerated "Hieratic" script! They then invented the story that the Christians in Egypt adopted the "Greek" alphabet and added some additional letters from the most degenerated "demotic" version so that they could use it for their religious writings! No supporting facts whatsoever. The whole devious scheme is twofold:

1. To deny Egypt as the origin of the alphabet.

2. To place a European country as the source of *real* alphabets with "vowels".

Here are the artificial delineations of Western academia on the Ancient Egyptian alphabetical writing styles:

i. The Erroneously-called "Hieratic" Script is claimed, by Western academians, to be a unique form of cursive writing of the Egyptian Language. It is further claimed by Western academians that this "unique" style was used extensively by the priests for literary or religious texts as well as for business and personal documents.

This is absolutely false and misleading, for "hieratic" means *sacred/religious,* and it is an oxymoron to call a script "hieratic" which has no sacred/religious mundane purpose! Western academia has categorized Egyptian writings of the most mundane nature as being "hieratic"; such as those found on bits of pottery and stone called ostraka, as well as labels on vessels!!

Yet, there is nothing sacred/hieratic about labels on bottles!

Even chips of ostraka [shown below] have inscriptions that are erroneously called "hieratic" by western academies! Subject matters found on such ostraka are mundane [non-hieratic/sacred], such as:

- Work records, working memorandum, inspection reports.
- Lists of workmen, rations, and supplies.
- A record of a visitor to the construction site.
- The roster of a quarrying expedition.
- Daily records of work done.
- Notes of visits of inspection by scribes and superiors.
- Rosters of the skilled and unskilled workmen employed on a construction site.

. . .

ii. Enchorial/Demotic Script is claimed by Western academians to be a unique form of cursive writing of the Egyptian Language. It is further claimed by Western academies that this "unique" style was used for everyday affairs, for the Ancient Egyptians. It is claimed by Western academians that it was kind of a very cursive shorthand for rapid writing which was replete with ligatures, abbreviations and other orthographic peculiarities. As such, these academies claim that the demotic record is dominated by legal, administrative, and commercial material, literary compositions, scientific and even "religious texts" which were written in a more calligraphic hand.

If academies claim that this script was used for "religious texts" as well as business documents, how is it possible to call this rapid cursive form *"Demotic"* when it was used for *Hieratic/sacred* purposes in religious writing?!

. . .

iii. Coptic Script is claimed by Western academians to be a unique form of cursive writing of the Egyptian Language. It is further stated by Western academies by sheer repetition (and contrary to facts), that a "Coptic" form of writing was developed about 300 CE for the use of the Christian population in Egypt which consisted of the letters of the Greek alphabet with an additional six characters (derived from the Ancient Egyptian demotic script) to express sounds that were peculiar to the Egyptian language!Shown below is "Coptic script" from the Nag Hammadi Codices. It is written in uncials and has the same exact Ancient Egyptian letter-forms thousands of years before the Greek era.

The so-called "Coptic"/"Greek" script is in fact an Ancient Egyptian uncials form of writing. It was the Greeks who adopted them from the Egyptians, when they came to Egypt as mercenaries or to study, and not the reverse.

In the 17th century, Father Athanasius Kircher has acknowledged, in his extensive analytical works, that the "Greek" script is Ancient Egyptian in origin. And for that, he was badly ridiculed by his fellow Europeans.

6.2 FALSE DISTINCTIONS OF EGYPTIAN CURSIVE WRITING

The above Western arbitrary three scripts delineations (where it is claimed that the first two are of Egyptian origin while the third is of a "Greek" origin) are totally false distinctions. The first and second claimed "scripts" are a distinction without a difference of the Egyptian cursive style of writing. As for the uncial writing style, it is an Egyptian style that was adopted by the Greeks, as will be shown in several areas of this book.

Let us leave the uncials style [so-called Coptic/Greek] for later discussion and concentrate our efforts here on the cursive writings which were arbitrarily delineated by Western academics as "hieratic" and "demotic". The clear evidence is that what Western academies called "Hieratic Script" and "Demotic Script" have no SPECIAL real Hieratic purpose.

There were various styles of writing (formal, cursive, semi-formal, or semi-cursive). Some were extremely stylized/ornate/ornamented, while others were simple and plain. The purpose of each document determines the style of writing used. These ways of writing produced different forms of the letters at various times.

Here are the results of writing variations between the erroneously "hieratic", Demotic, and the so-called "abnormal Hieratic" by Western academians; as published in *A Palaeographical Study of Demotic Papyri* by Ola El-Aguizy. It should be noted that despite the misleading title of this reference, it actually lists and makes comparisons between the erroneously "hieratic", Demotic, and so-called "abnormal Hieratic" scripts throughout the book.

Ola El-Aguizy also writes in her book *A Palaeographical Study of "Demotic" Papyri* on page 18:

> *"It is generally difficult to base the dating on either of these forms, because, as just mentioned, they <u>were used</u>*

equally in all periods, with no apparent reason for the choice of either of them."

Ola El-Aguizy also writes in her book *A Palaeographical Study of "Demotic" Papyri* on page 18:

"The hieratic simplified forms illustrated in the following figure are quite similar to the demotic form of this group."

Again and again we see pathetic ways of finding differences where there are none. An example is the letter 'm', where Ola El-Aguizy writes in her book *A Palaeographical Study of "Demotic" Papyri*, on page 25:

"The demotic writing of the sign is the same as the simplified form used in hieratic; except that in demotic, the lower curve is usually more rounded than the hieratic one"

Really: *"the lower curve is more rounded".* How pathetic!

Quotations regarding other letters that Ola El-Aguizy writes about in *A Palaeographical Study of "Demotic" Papyri include,* on page 36:

"It seems that the abnormal hieratic and demotic writings of this sign are a result of the simplification of the hieratic sign in the Middle and New Kingdoms":

"This sign in its abnormal hieratic form is quite similar to the hieratic examples of the same period and later, in as much as it does not add any unnecessary line to the main elements of the sign."

– and on page 37 of her book: *"The demotic examples, on the other hand resemble the hieratic examples of the middle kingdom."*

– On page 38 of her book: *"The demotic variants of this sign [phonetic [q] are not very different from their hieratic equivalents."*

– On page 40 of her book: *"The resemblance of the abnormal hieratic letter 'g' with its hieratic equivalent is very obvious."*

– On page 41 of her book: *"The Abnormal Hieratic examples [for 'D'] are not very different from the Hieratic."*

– On page 137 of her book: *"The demotic form depicts a simplification of previous forms."*

– On page 141 of her book: *"The similarity of the abnormal hieratic forms with the hieratic ones needs no description."*

– On page 147 of her book: *"Like the previous sign, the early demotic forms of this sign are very much like the hieratic ones".*

– On page 168 of her book: *"The demotic forms of the sign are not very different from the preceding hieratic forms. Only the upper closed curve is opened on the left side"*

...

By their own words, western academies and their paid proxies admit to no [material] difference between their erroneously called "hieratic" and "demotic" as

well as any other inbetween; the so-called "abnormal hieratic".

6.3 THE TRUE TWO PRIMARY EGYPTIAN ALPHABETIC SCRIPTS [UNCIALS AND CURSIVE]

Clement of Alexandria, in *Stromata Book V*, Chapter IV, tells us clearly of the REAL two primary styles of alphabetic writings; as well as the unrelated pictorial Egyptian hieroglyphs:

> *"Now those instructed among the Egyptians learned first of all <u>that style of the Egyptian letters</u> which is called Epistolographic* [cursive i.e. 'composed as a series of letters']; <u>*and second, the Hieratic style, which the Priestly scribes perform;*</u> *and finally, and last of all, the Hieroglyphic, ..."*

The third item, being the Egyptian Hieroglyphics and its nature, meanings, etc., was discussed earlier.

Clement never stated that the Egyptian "hieratic" style was a "cursive" or "degenerated" form of hieroglyphics. Hieroglyphics was notably the very last form that he mentioned.

The last mode of script being hieroglyphics is NOT of letters and words, but Clement re-affirmed what ALL writers of antiquities had indicated: that Egyptian hieroglyphics are of three natures—imitative, figurative and allegorical.

So Clement of Alexandria specifies two primary alphabetic writing modes—one for domestic/common/public use and another that is performed exclusively by the Egyptian priests and used exclusively for religious writings.

Cursive Style	Priestly [Religious] Style
A fluid, rounded,	Square, unslanted, segmented
Ligatured	Uncials—letters written separately
Hand writing [Kufic]	Formal/Book
Easy to write	Easy to read
Domestic Affairs [secular/civil]	Theological Matters

In order to make it easier for readers who have been mislead by Western academics' false categorizations, we offer here the true delineations with cross reference to the incorrect Western academia-referenced Egyptian writing styles:

i. Neat cursive style [erroneously labeled by Western academia as "hieratic" style]

This was a more careful application used for legal, professional [scientific and medical], and governmental documents. These were carefully executed by specialized and highly qualified scribes according to standards set in each of such applications, which are identified as specific calligraphic forms [to be discussed later in this chapter].

As in all Egyptian cursive writing, it was ligatured/not ligatured according to a specific system, as discussed earlier. As such, it shows that some letters have different forms when used as the first letter in a word (initial) than when used elsewhere in the word (medial, final).

Shown above is a sample of the erroneously-labeled (by Western academia) "hieratic" style as it appears in the Ebers Papyrus, which looks exactly like the erroneously-labeled (by western academia) "Demotic script!

ii. Public cursive style [erroneously labeled by Western academics as "demotic" style]

Scripts that are not intended to be of public records but for business and everyday affairs were not confined to any set standard [calligraphic] form(s) and were not executed by official scribes.

Such category of scripts/documents/writings extended to private letters.

As in all Egyptian cursive writing, it was ligatured/not ligatured according to a specific system, as discussed earlier. As such, it shows that some letters have different forms when used as the first letter in a word (initial) than when used elsewhere in the word (medial, final)..

Since such scripts were done by non-professional scribes, there were differences – often minor but still evident – in script, vocabulary, morphology, and/or syntax; as one would expect the same with modern handwriting.

As was common with this type of uncontrolled writing category, there was frequent use of abbreviations, especially with words that are used frequently.

iii. Sacred/Hieratic style [erroneously labeled by Western academia as "Coptic" style]

In their sacred writings, the Ancient Egyptian priests [as confirmed in Clement's statement above] used Uncials—the unconnected non-cursive form of alphabetic letters. As stated in an earlier chapter, each alphabetic letter in the Ancient Egyptian language [which was copied in later "Arabic"] has four forms—the first of which is the uncial letter-form.

Despite all the academic noise/assertions, there is NOT a single Egyptian religious text written in what they erroneously labeled "Hieratic" script, which is a cursive and not uncials writing.

Western academia renamed the REAL uncial script that the Ancient Egyptians used for religious purposes as "Coptic", which they declared to be "an Egyptian adoption of Greek alphabet with some additional letters from demotic"! There is not a single historical record to confirm their fabricated assertions.

The so-called "Coptic" and Greek scripts are basically an ancient Egyptian form of writing which was later adopted by the Greeks!

More detailed information about this subject in later chapters.

6.4 FORMS AND FUNCTIONS OF CALLIGRAPHY

An important element in calligraphy is the connection between form and function. Scripts broadly speaking, are either:

> i. Easy to read—Book hands were used foremost for the copying of literature, and aimed for clarity, regularity, and (to some extent) impersonality. Usually the work of professional scribes, deliberate stylization can give these hands an element of imposing beauty.

> ii. Easy to write—Documentary styles cover a much wider range of purpose. They include chancery hands as well as the workaday writings of officials and private persons. For this type of script, the ability to write quickly is of great importance; and to achieve this, the pen should be lifted as rarely as possible from the writing material.

Apart from form and function, calligraphy is also closely connected with the materials and instruments used for writing, which will be discussed in the next chapter of this book.

The purpose of scripts determines the style of writing: "formal," "'cursive," "semi-formal" or "semi-cursive." The terms 'cursive' and 'formal' refer neither to the material used for writing nor to the content of inscriptions. Rather, they refer fundamentally to script types – that is, to the manner in which letters are written, and to the resultant forms.

A formal script tends to be square or segmented, and

apparently required a more frequent lifting of the writing instrument from the writing material.

Egyptian scribes had (and in many ways, still do) different calligraphic forms for corresponding uses—legal documents, governmental offices, petitions, business transactions, medical, mathematical, astronomical forms, etc. The very same forms are still employed nowadays in Egypt under names such as Kufic, Naskh [copying], ThuluthTaliq/Nastaliq-Riqa, Diwani, etc. Several of these forms in a particular field/function are hard to read, for untrained eyes.

The line of Egyptian cursive writing suggests an urgent progression of the characters from right to left. The nice balance between the vertical shafts above and the open curves below the middle register induces a sense of harmony. For writing, the Egyptian calligrapher employed a reed pen (qalam) with the working point cut on an angle. This feature produces a thick down stroke and a thin upstroke with an infinity of gradation in between. The line traced by a skilled calligrapher is a true marvel of fluidity and sensitive inflection, communicating the very action of the master's hand.

Chapter 7 : The Profession of Egyptian Scribes

7.1 THE WRITING CIVILIZATION

The Ancient Egyptians were very organized, and people often communicated with one another by letter, in their daily existence. All government business was put in writing. The well-known proposition that *"what cannot be put into documental form does not exist"* was in force in Egyptian affairs. The Egyptians kept economic and labor records on papyri and other writing surfaces.

An example of the orderly and organized Ancient Egyptian society can be recognized in a requisition displayed in the Egyptian Museum in Cairo, which shows a wife's request to get her travel expenses paid for so that she could visit her husband, who was on an official duty. This example shows the level of a highly organized, well-oiled government order.

Writing formed the basis of official organization. Nothing in the Egyptian government was done without documents. Lists and protocols were indispensable even in the simplest matters of business. The pictures in the old tombs testify to this fact, for whether the corn is measured out, or the cattle are led past, the scribes are always there to record.

In the mode of executing deeds, conveyances, and other civil contracts, the Egyptians were very detailed. Marriage contracts, wills, sales of property, etc. always began with the date of the transaction and the names of the president of the court and the clerk by whom they were written. The body of the contract then followed. The document was witnessed by as many as 16 witnesses.

Numerous documents have come down to us, showing how accounts were kept in various departments. These documents show exactly how much was received, from whom, when it came in, and the details of how it was used. This minute care is not only taken in the case of large amounts, but even the smallest quantities of corn or dates, are conscientiously entered.

The various documents were orderly, and were archived and stored for future reference. Each document would indicate where it would go; e.g. a scribe would note: "to be copied" or "to be kept in the archives of the governor". The documents were then given into the care of the chief librarian of the appropriate department, who then placed them in large vases and cataloged them carefully.

The legal and official documents may be classed according to their titles, such as the amt-per or deed recording the transfer of property from one person to another either prospectively or immediately, and either with or without benefit to the granter (or, as it is technically expressed, with or without consideration). A species of will and of marriage settlement would appear to have been commonly committed to writing, under this name.

Writing was not just limited to official and governmental business, but extended to all aspects of daily activities—letters, inventory records, receipts, travel accounts, construction plans, musical texts, medical texts and formulae—and on and on.

Such written records and documents were recovered thousands of years before Egypt's 'Dynastic history'. In such a very remote age, alphabetical writing defined the Egyptian civilization more than anything else.

7.2 THE PROFESSION OF SCRIBES

All official public and governmental business writings were exclusively conducted by certified scribes. All practical tasks of writing were delegated to bureaucratic clerks.

To superintend and to write deeds was much the same thing, according to Egyptian ideas, and a "scribe" was an official. Scribes were employed in all levels of public administration: civil, military and religious.

It must also be noted that their training and expertise was equivalent nowadays to bureaucrats in deed and document recording offices, requiring knowledge of the language's grammar and syntax [not just writing], legal laws and principles, various forms/styles of writings, and the applicable form for each task/subject for the subject matter that is being scribed, etc.

For other non-official purposes, writings were conducted

by common people for all private matters—whether for business or personal letters.

7.3 WRITING SURFACES & INSTRUMENTS

Apart from form and function, calligraphy is also closely connected with the materials and the instruments used for writing.

Egyptians were able to utilize writings in all aspects of their lives by inventing excellent writing materials and books.

The Ancient Egyptians manufactured books by gumming separate sheets of papyrus together; and there are magnificent manuscripts measuring 65 and 130 feet [20 and 40 m].

The Egyptians utilized pens and ink of indestructible permanence, which they ground on wooden palettes.

These writing surfaces and tools were plentiful, allowing the scribes to write manuscripts in clear, elegant, round, firm signs. Using a pen (instead of a pointed tool) results in more round-shaped letters.

The following is more detailed information about the

Ancient Egyptian writing surfaces and devices:

i. Writing Materials/Surfaces:

In addition to stone inscriptions for monumental use, there were many other sorts of writing surfaces such as papyrus, pottery, ostraca, wood, and parchment.

- **Papyrus**—Egyptians invented an excellent material on which to write—papyrus. This was a paper-like material that was used for books, letters, documents, and any other writing.

The papyrus plant is a kind of giant swamp grass that grows in river mud. It sometimes grows to a height of ten feet and its roots are often as thick as a man's arm.

Writing papyri could be made in any size or weight, and papyri have been found that are one hundred and forty feet long. Fortunately, it was more durable than much of our paper. The oldest known piece goes back several thousand years B.C.E.

Egyptian papyrus became the most generally used writing material of the ancient world. There are no papyri extant which are not Egyptian papyri.

- **Ostraca** are rough flakes or chunks of limestone not retouched, smoothed, or finished in any way. The complete examples range in size from 20 x 15 x 2.25 cm to 56 x 46 x 12 cm.

- **Parchment** was used for permanent documents and books, in Egypt. It was primary used as the enveloping cover of a book consisting of several pages of papyri—front, sides and back—or even its title tag.

- **Tablet and stylus**. The tablet was simply a section of **wood** with a raised rim, like a shallow pan, containing a coating of wax. The stylus was a pointed instrument of metal or ivory. The writer scratched his letters into the wax with the point of his stylus. To erase what had been written, he scraped the wax away or melted it slightly until the surface was again smooth. Such a tablet was handy and cheap. It was used in schoolrooms and for letters, notices, and memoranda.

As the stylus was pushed through the soft surface of the tablet, it tended to collect the wax on its point. The lines therefore were irregular and necessarily short, since the stylus had to be lifted often to remove the waste wax from the point.

ii. Writing Instruments:

When the Egyptians developed papyrus, they produced something which could be written upon with several writing devices, utilizing inks that will be discussed later in this book. The utilized writing devices have a great consideration/impact on the shapes of the written cursive writing. The forms of letters are determined largely by the tools with which they were made.

The manuscript quill and reed gave to letters their thick/thin character.

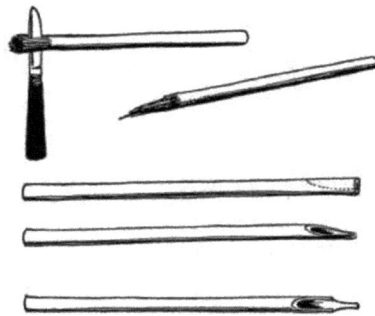

The neat Egyptian cursive writing looked as it did because it was written with a wide, flat reed pen.

Writing with a pen on papyrus instead of with a brush was bound to make a difference in the style of writing.

The main writing devices were:

– **Brush** was made out of the stem of a rush, with its end frayed. The line produced by this brush is fine or coarse according to the thickness of the rush, and is neat and evenly black or untidy and "dragged" according to the care with which the tip of the rush was prepared.

– **Reed Pen** with its working point cut on an angle produces compact and round forms with a thick down stroke and a thin upstroke with an infinity of gradation in between. The line traced by a skilled calligrapher is a true marvel of fluidity and sensitive inflection, communicating the very action of the master's hand.

Later, the reed was shaped and split at the point, very much like our present-day pen. Actually, such a pen, made from a reed or quill, is far superior to a steel pen for fine writing. It is softer and more pliable; and, even to this day, fine writing is almost always done with a reed or a quill pen, prepared almost exactly as the Egyptians used to do.

The earliest remaining Egyptian manuscripts, written on papyrus with a reed pen, are over 5,000 years old.

The Egyptian cursive style used for daily public purposes [not requiring official scribes] could be made rapidly, and were true "pen forms". This was the writing used in trade, commerce, and personal matters.

The character of the tools, as in all other cases that we have seen, gave a particular character to the letters.

Basically, black, red, and blue inks were used. The dilution and mixing of colors yielded several shades such as red (varying in shade from maroon to pink), brown, yellow, green, bluish green, blue (bright or pale), jet black, and chalky white.

Black ink and red ink were occasionally employed to mark out a special section, like the beginning of a text or a numerical total, or to indicate punctuation points in literary compositions as well as vocalic markings (diacritics).

For the outlines of drawings and the writing of inscriptions, the standard black and ocher red inks are used almost uniformly.

A scribe's palette of ivory had two holes: one for black ink, one for red, and a slot for holding brushes; as displayed in the British Museum [Eighteenth Dynasty. H. 30 cm. BM 5524.]

7.4 MOBILE SCRIBES

Here are a few representative examples of how Egyptian scribes have always accompanied business and military expeditions to record events:

i. Egyptian Scribes and Mining Expeditions

The surviving Ancient Egyptian records show a tremendous organization of mining activities more than 5,000 years ago, in numerous sites throughout Egypt and beyond.

The Ancient Egyptian records show the organizational

structure of mining operations. Ancient Egyptian surviving records show the names and titles of various officials who, during the Old and the Middle Kingdoms, directed the works at Hammamat and at Bechen mines in the Eastern Desert. They included engineers, miners, smiths, masons, architects, artists, security details, and ship captains who maintained the integrity of the parts of the ships that would be put back together when the expedition reaches navigable waters.

A document that dates to the reign of Ramses IV [1163–1156 BCE] provides the report of an expedition to the mountain of Bechen in the Eastern Desert, under the direction of the "superintendent of the works". Altogether, the expedition consisted of 8,368 people. These men included more than 50 civil officials and ecclesiastics as well as 200 officials from various departments. The fieldwork was carried out by miners, stonemasons, other related work forces who worked under three superintendents, and the "chief superintendent". The labor was carried out by 5,000 miners, smiths, masons, etc., and there were 2,000 various types of labor. There were at least 110 officers supervising 800 men of the barbarian mercenaries, for security detail. The security forces were needed for the protection of the mining sites and the transportation of people and material. The management of this large number of people is extraordinary—8,368 people is the size of a large community, even nowadays.

[Also see 'Mining History in Sinai' in Chapter 3 of this book.]

ii. Egyptian Scribes and Trade Expeditions in Africa

The town of Buhen, within a few miles of the Second Cataract, provides extensive Egyptian archaeological evidence since the early years of the Old Kingdom (2575-2150 BCE). The names of the following kings have been identified on clay sealings and ostraca: Khafra, Menkaura, Userkaf, Sahura, Neferirkara, Neuserra.

Professor Emery, the discoverer of most of its finds, found a countless numbers of Egyptian Papyri that indicated, to him, that a well-organized dispatch service was maintained with northern Egypt throughout the 4th and 5th Dynasties.

The Princes of Sunt (Aswan) stood high in the hierarchy of the Old Kingdom. One of his major responsibilities was organizing and equipping the caravans heading deep into Africa, and maintaining records of such activities. [Detailed information can be found in *Exiled Egyptians: the Heart of Africa* by this same author.]

iii. Sea Expedition to Lebanon and Cyprus

There were a host of scribes in each business expedition, such as the report of Wenamun on his trip to Phoenicia and Cyprus to negotiate and pay for the wood (and its transportation) for the Egyptian building of ships.

iv. Egyptian Scribes and the Foreign Security Guards

Egyptians are renowned worldwide as un-warlike people who can't (and don't) fight. It is therefore that the Ancient Egyptians hired foreign mercenaries to guard and fight on behalf of the Egyptians. The European presence in Egypt began when the Assyrians marched into Egypt and conquered the country as far as Luxor (Thebes) during the 7th century BCE. In 654 BCE, the Egyptian Psammatichus, from Sais, hired Greek (Ionian and Carian) mercenaries to drive the Assyrians out of Egypt. They were always accompanied by Egyptian governmental scribes who recorded all their activities.

Chapter 8 : Multiple Writing Forms of a Single Document

8.1 COMMONALITY OF MULTIPLE WRITING FORMS

It is very common nowadays, just like in Ancient Egypt, to have multiple writing forms of language in a single document, monument, etc.

There are various types of documents whose language varies with its intended subject matter, such as business, legal, contractual agreements, correspondence, etc. However, there are common general themes among them:

– At the top there is usually some form of a 'divine acknowledgement' such as *"In God we trust"*

– There is a logo, the symbol that represents the essence of the organization. The logo is a combination of a representative pictorial symbolic form together with a few supporting words and/or a motto.

– An exchange between two parties such as in a contract, for one party to do something and the receiving party to exchange such work for an agreed payment/consideration.

– Date, signatories, certification and entries into the records.

The very same arrangements are found in thousands of Ancient Egyptian documents and hundreds of stone stelae throughout the long history of Ancient Egypt.

Next, we will discuss in some detail the application of multiple writing forms in magical/divination purposes and stelae.

8.2 EGYPTIAN MAGICAL DIVINATION FORMS

The subject of magical divination in Ancient Egypt is beyond the scope of this book. We will just provide a background overview, followed by the application of various writing forms on magical divination items.

Egyptian magic dates from the time when the pre-dynastic and prehistoric dwellers in Egypt believed that the Earth, the underworld, the air, and the sky were peopled with countless beings, visible and invisible, which were held to be either friendly or unfriendly to man, according to whether or not the operations of nature, which they were supposed to direct, were favorable or unfavorable to him.

The object of Egyptian magic was to endow man with the means of compelling both friendly and hostile powers to do as he wished.

Among the Greeks and Romans, considerable respect was

entertained not only for the "wisdom" of the Egyptians, but also for the powers of working magic, which they mastered.

Egyptian magical texts are imbued with Egyptian divinities, and Egyptian allegorical references abound in their magical texts. They are consistent in all their aspects, forms, and details that go back to the earliest Egyptian religious/magic literature and are well documented in the "Pyramid Texts" of about 5,000 years ago.

As detailed in the book *Egyptian Alphabetical Letters of Creation Cycle* by Moustafa Gadalla, the twenty-eight Egyptian [and later, "Arabic"] letters are connected directly with the twenty-eight stations/mansions/phases of the moon. They were also connected with the heavenly bodies, the signs of the zodiac, and the Dekans. Alphabetical letters, to the early Egyptians, were the essence of things. Each letter had its own special powers. The powers of the letters are intimately associated with numbers; for each letter in the Egyptian [and later "Arabic"] alphabet has a numerical value.

In such divination items, Egyptians often used various forms of alphabets, numbers [reflecting their mystical significance], geometrical shapes, hieroglyphic symbols, signs for the four elements, metals, stars, astronomical, astrological, constellations, zodiac signs, etc.

8.3 EGYPTIAN STELA

Stelae are upright monolithic stone slabs. They are usually carved from granite, limestone, marble, sandstone, wood, pottery, faience, or other natural stone.

Stelae are bulletins of records of public or private affairs.

Such announcements in stone, in modern days or in Ancient Egypt, follow the same documentation arrangements as indicated above with various writing styles.

The Rosetta Stone, being a typical Ancient Egyptian stele, is divided into three sections which corresponds very much to the three categories of Clement's statement of hieroglyphs and two styles of alphabetical scripts—one cursive and the other uncials, for religious purposes.

A complete analysis of the Rosetta Stone will take place in the next chapter of this book.

Chapter 9 : Multiple Writing Forms of The Rosetta Stone

9.1 PLACE OF ITS ORIGINAL LOCATION

The Rosetta Stone is a black granite tablet which was discovered in 1799 in Rosetta during Napoleon's expedition in Egypt, and is now placed in the British Museum.

It measures about 3' 9" x 2' 4 1/2" x 11' on the inscribed side. The texts inscribed upon it consist of fourteen lines of Egyptian hieroglyphics, thirty-two lines of Egyptian alphabetical Cursive Style, and fifty-four lines of the Egyptian religious uncials style [arbitrarily designated as *'ancient Greek' by Western academia*].

The Stone was found built into a wall in an important Egyptian temple dedicated to Tum/Atum/Atam. As is the case for all Ancient Egyptian temples, it was built a long time ago and went through reconstruction every few centuries. The latest of such re-construction was during the time of the Egyptian Pharaoh Necho I [672-664 BCE] about 500 years earlier than the falsified "ascribed" date for the "Rosetta Stone" made by Western academia!!

Despite its being found built into the wall of a temple

dedicated to Tum/Atum in Rosetta, Western academics cavalierly decided that the Stone must have its origin in Memphis. Why, you ask? Western academia's incredible answer is that because the text pays homage to the deity Ptah (among other deities), that it must have its origin in Memphis, as Western academics have decided that Memphis is the only place that 'can' relate to Ptah! This is absolute nonsense: for Ptah was a 'universal' deity and not a local god in Egypt; being depicted in practically every and all Egyptian temples! Not to mention the fact that these very same Western academics agree that the Rosetta's temple, where the 'Stone' was found, is dedicated to the deity Tum/Atum!

One may ask: how can academia reconcile the fact of the location of this Stone in Rosetta; which is about 150 miles north of Memphis? The colonial-minded academics had no problem proclaiming that the Rosetta Stone "states that this exact Decree will be duplicated in every Egyptian temple of the first, second and third class". Yet, no a single copy [or a part thereof] of this Decree was ever found anyplace in Egypt!

Such a shameless act from those who will seek any/all means towards one end: that the uncial religious style of writing on the Rosetta Stone must be attributed to a *superior* European source—the Greeks!

9.2 DATING FALSEHOODS

Despite the absolute fact that there was neither a reference to a calendar year nor of the name of any pharaoh, Egyptian or otherwise, on the Rosetta Stone, it was mischievously dated by European Western academia to be

196 BCE. during the time of Ptolemy V Epiphanes (205-180 BCE)!!

The actual "dating" set on the Rosetta Stone follows the very same arrangements in ALL Ancient Egyptian documents/monuments throughout its recovered archaeological history, as follows:

1. A lunar reference to a day and a lunar month [no year is EVER mentioned]

For postings that relate to festivals, the day and month of the lunar month is stated, in addition to the [solar/Sothic] Ancient Egyptian calendar. Most Egyptian festivals were/are related to both solar and lunar timing, just like our modern day Easter' dating which, as a result, varies from one year to another.

In their usual European frenzy, academia was eager to "assign" the lunar month to a fictional "Macedonian [lunar] Calendar"! There is nothing to support a "Macedonian Calendar" anywhere, anytime. It is another pathetic attempt to drill the 'Greek' relevance into our heads.

2. The day, month and season of the solar/Sothic Egyptian calendar [no year is EVER mentioned]

Egyptian Public Notifications ["Decrees"]—especially those related to festival activities—specify both the date of the lunar month followed by the day of the solar month as it related to one of three [Egyptian] seasons. A year is NEVER mentioned.

3. The year of the sitting Pharaoh

The year of the reign of a sitting Pharaoh only refers to the title of such a pharaoh and NEVER his "name"—as is the case on the Rosetta Stone. Here, again, is another pathetic attempt by Western academia to insert the name of "Ptolemaic ruler" where the text clearly did NOT name such a person/king/ruler!!!

The decree, like all other Egyptian decrees, such as the undamaged Damanhur Stele, reads:

> *"year of the reign of HORUS-RA the CHILD, who hath risen as King upon the throne of his "father", the lord of the shrines of NEKHEBET and UATCHET, the mighty one of two-fold strength, the stabilizer of the Two Lands"*

No name is ever stated. A detailed explanation of lack of names will be shown later in this chapter.

9.3 SHAMELESS CHANGE OF THE WORD "PRIESTLY" TO "GREEK"!

This decree (like hundreds like it) is inscribed in three styles for its three registers.

Western academia translated the three styles into various forms:

Top register – Hieroglyphs

Middle register – Common [cursive] writing style

Bottom register – *"Writing of the Greeks"*

Calling the third style "Greek" is a lie, for according to

Budge himself in his book *Rosetta Stone*, Volume 1, page 167, Budge admits:

> *"but when the allusion is to Greek, the word used is called is a very old one, and is in the dual, "H.aui-nebui"; the germ H. a-nebu, i.e. "lords of the north," or "lords of the marshes [in the Delta]" occurs in the Pyramid Texts."*

Budge admits that the term used is found in the Pyramid Texts, three thousand years prior to the Greeks!!

Additionally the Egyptian word does NOT say anything about 'marshes' or 'north'. It only and simply means 'Priestly' and is translated as such hundreds of times from Egyptian documents of all eras by the very same Western academia, who wants to give a 'different' meaning just this single time!

The 'Priestly' Style is the uncials style, as discussed earlier in this book. It is this 'style' that was dubbed the Egyptian 'Coptic Style'. Such a writing style was found in Ancient Egyptian texts and documents a long time before the Greeks.

9.4 SCANDALOUS CARTOUCHES "DECIPHERMENT"

Egyptian documents never refer to the name of a pharaoh—including the Rosetta Stone—but to titles and epithets. The dishonest Western academics claimed that some inscribed cartouches in the hieroglyphic text of the Rosetta Stone contains names of "Ptolemaic Royalties"! This is even contrary to ALL scholars' views regarding the nature of the content within a cartouche. The following facts are acknowledged and agreed upon by ALL—with not a single exception!

The royal titulary or royal protocol of a pharaoh is the standard naming convention taken by the kings of Ancient Egypt. The full titulary, consisting of five designations, was very evident from the Middle Kingdom era until the end of the Greco-Roman era, as agreed by all Egyptologists.

Only two of such 'designations' were written in cartouches; namely the 'Throne Designation' and his 'Personal Designation.'

As an example, in the case of the famous Pharaoh who is recognized as Tuthomosis III', his:

'Throne Designation' was Menkheperre – meaning *'He of the Sedge and the Bee, Enduring of form is Re.'*

'Personal Designation' was Neferkheperu – meaning *'Son of Re, beautiful of forms.'*

As is very evident, these are not names, but they are titles and epithets for the pharaohs which were not particular to any singular pharaoh, but were shared by numerous other pharaohs. As mentioned above, this practice did not change during the Greco-Roman era, as affirmed by all Egyptologists.

However, a loud group of Western academics wanted to find 'Greek' evidence at any dishonest cost. Those scholars who were brave enough not to 'play along' were ridiculed by the dishonest 'scholars' who contradicted themselves by arbitrarily assigning alphabetical values for hieroglyphic symbols. An example of many is found in Budge's book *Rosetta Stone*, Volume I, page 35:

> "The <u>hieroglyphic text</u> had also been studied in 1802 and 1803 by M. le Compte de Pahlin. Count Pahlin <u>failed to discover the alphabetic character of the Egyptian hieroglyphics</u>, and thus it came to pass that he did not even succeed in suggesting that certain groups of picture characters represented the proper names in the Greek text."

And the lies did not even stop there. They claimed that they were able to "decipher" the names of 'Ptolemy' and 'Cleopatra'. They have ignored the fact that they have themselves established that all Ptolemaic kings and queens are called Ptolemy and Cleopatra! So which one of them is the inscribed name(s)?! As one researches deeper into academia's claim, one discovers that the dishonest 'scholars' admit that there was no mention of Cleopatra on the Rosetta Stone!! Budge, in his book *Rosetta Stone*, Volume I, page ix, says:

> "*It is a well-known fact that the name of <u>Cleopatra</u> in its hieroglyphic form played a prominent part in the Egyptian decipherment, but it is not so well known that it <u>does not appear on the Rosetta Stone</u>*"

Budge (also in his book *Cleopatra Needles*, page 233) mentions:

> "<u>The name of Cleopatra is not found on the Rosetta Stone, as is sometimes stated</u>."

That did not stop him, in the rest of his volumes, from

naming *Cleopatra* as one of two names that deciphered the texts of Rosetta Stone!

He/others even substituted Isis in the Egyptian Texts for 'Cleopatra'!!

9.5 THE EGYPTIAN THREE FUNCTION AND FORMS OF THE DECREE

The intent of the decree set on the Rosetta Stone is to set the promissory obligations of the community towards the Divine in order to be worthy of bestowed divine benefits. Such intent is provided on the middle and bottom registers. The top hieroglyphic register is an Invocation—a typical Egyptian (as well as other peoples') practice of invoking the name of the Lord, praising the Lord, etc., at the beginning of any/all actions.

Therefore, the three registers are three different parts of a whole.

It must be remembered that the decree on the Rosetta Stone is NOT bilingual [or trilingual], but written in three styles of writing. Therefore, trying to find a way to show correspondence between the three texts proved to be fruitless, as evident even by all conjectural translations by every/all Western academics.

<u>Top Register—Hieroglyphs—Invocation</u>

The top register consists of portions of the last fourteen lines of this register. Most of the lines are incomplete, both at the beginning and end, but such portions as are preserved are clear and quite legible. The remaining 14 lines of the hieroglyphic text of the Rosetta Stone is what remains from the original unknown number of lines.

Even in their intended misrepresentation of the hieroglyphic top register, Western academia admits that the 'nature' of the hieroglyphic text on such decrees are all the same—being a form of invocation.

Budge, in his book *Rosetta Stone*, Vol. 1, pages 160-161, states:

> "*but, in the broken state in which the lines are found on the Rosetta Stone, it is <u>impossible to put together anything like a connected translation of them</u>*"

As a result, Western academics have 'consulted' the hieroglyphics top register on other different decrees in different parts of the country such as the Damanhur Stele, Canopus Stele, inscriptions at the southern end of Egypt in Aswan, etc.

Budge, in his book, *Rosetta Stone*, Volume I, pages xi-xii, confirmed the similar intent of the top hieroglyphic lines in Egyptian documents:

> "*Because the hieroglyphic register is very much the same as found in many other similar steles, both the Stele of Damanhur and the Stele of Canopus, helped to explain those on the other, <u>the phraseology is in many cases identical</u>.*"

The point to be made here is that the intent of hieroglyphic text on the top register of such decrees is an 'invocation' using the metaphysical symbols of Egyptian hieroglyphs.

Middle Register—Cursive Style—Promises to Heavens

The text of the second register sets promises that will

be fulfilled by the public/community/country to please the divine forces—being ancestors and neteru (gods, goddesses). The writing style is therefore of the 'public' style, being cursive from right to left, the common running hand of the country.

This is consistent with Egyptian [depictions and otherwise] symbolism, where the right hand represents 'giving', 'offering' 'promising', etc. Some of the promised deeds shown in this Stele/Stone are:

- Protect the land and people as needed
- Protect and maintain canal systems
- Maintenance, restoration and upkeep of temples, shrines and alters
- Honors to be paid to neteru (gods/goddesses) and ancestors
- Observing public festivals of temples with rites. offerings and honors
- Observe festival processions with holy arks
- Provide prescribed offerings from the fruit of land and manufactured goods, sacrifices, etc.

[See *Egyptian Mystics* by Moustafa Gadalla for the significance of festivals in Egypt.]

Bottom Register—Uncial Style—Rewards from Heaven

The third and bottom register sets the heavenly rewards to the public in return for promises fulfilled that were set in the middle register. It is the Divine reward for sowing the seeds—so to speak. The uncials style that was performed by the Egyptian priests for religious writings is used here. While the middle register represents the public promising the divine—in cursive style from right to left—the divine rewards are written from left to right and in the Egyptian priestly style of uncials.

This is consistent with Egyptian [depictions and otherwise] symbolism, where the left hand represents 'receiving'.

9.6 SHAMELESSLY SUBSTITUTING 'GOD/GODDESS' FOR PTOLEMAIC 'KING/QUEEN'

Under the cover of claiming "conjectural translation", Western academia went wild. As their prime objective is to show the [European] Greeks as superiors and masters of Egyptians, they took the 'liberty' of translating terms on the Rosetta Stone such as 'our masters', 'nobles' and even 'neteru' (gods, goddesses) to mean "Ptolemaic kings/queens". Academics went even further, by putting 'Ptolemaic names' when the actual words/terms were just generic titles/epithets. This was an absolute strong-handed fabrication by Western academics who were desperate to elevate the [European] Greeks by any means!

The text on the Rosetta Stone reads:

"in the twenty-third year of the reign of HORUS-RA the CHILD, who hath risen as King upon the throne of his father, the lord of the shrines of NEKHEBET and UATCHET, the mighty one of two-fold strength, the beautifier of ..."

No name is mentioned of a 'Ptolemy'!

9.7 SELF-SERVING CONJECTURAL "DECIPHERMENT"

Earlier, we exposed some facts about the scandalous work of Western academia on the Rosetta Stone. Their sole intent was to steal from the Egyptians to attribute things to their likewise Europeans, the Greeks. A summary is:

> i. Confusing the facts about the place of its original location and falsely stating that the Decree was issued 150 miles south of its temple's permanent location.
>
> ii. Falsifying the date of the decree
>
> iii. Shamelessly changing of the word 'Priestly ' to "Greek"!
>
> iv. Scandalous cartouches "decipherment"
>
> v. Shamelessly substituting 'god/goddess' for a Ptolemaic "King/Queen"

In addition to all the points made above, other points need to be added in order to expose the scandalous work done on the Rosetta Stone by Western academia:

> 1. They picked Rosetta Stone despite the presence of several similar multi-style writing stelae which, according to Western academia, were dated prior to the Rosetta. Even more incredible is their claim that the prior similar Stones such as the Damanhur Stone/Stele, Canopus Stone/stele and references in Philae [in Aswan] were used to figure out the meaning of texts on the Rosetta stone!!!

2. They peppered the text with Greek names [repeating a name or two over and over again] despite the fact that the text itself—according to their own interpretation—did NOT include such names! They put Ptolemaic names in place of words such as "neter", "Lord", " Mighty", "Lord of Two Lands"?!

3. Their so-called "conjectural translations" are more than five-fold the length of the text shown on the Rosetta Stone itself—there was too much added and padded to serve academia's bad intentions. Conjectural translation provided academics a perfect smoke screen for making up things.

It is very important for colonial-minded Western academia to show the supremacy of the [European] Greeks as the masters of the non-European Egyptians and how these Egyptians paid homage to their Greek Masters. Such 'whitewash' has nothing to do with facts.

PART III : HOW THE ONE WORLD LANGUAGE BECAME THE MANY

Chapter 10 : The Beacon of The Ancient World

10.1 EGYPTIAN SETTLEMENTS THROUGHOUT THE WORLD

Herodotus, the father of history and a native Greek, stated, in 500 BCE:

> *"Now, let me talk more of Egypt for it has a lot of admirable things and what one sees there is superior to any other country."*

The superior Ancient Egyptian monuments are the physical manifestations of their superior cosmic knowledge, for, as stated in Asleptus III (25) of *Hermetic Texts*:

> *"...in Egypt all the operations of the powers which rule and work in heaven have been transferred to earth below...it should rather be said that the whole cosmos dwells in [Egypt] as in its sanctuary..."*

From Ancient Egypt, its language (among other things) spread throughout the world; for Egypt was the most prosperous, dominant, populous, and famed country in the ancient world, as affirmed by Diodorus, *Book I*, [31, 6-9]:

> *"In density of population Egypt far surpassed of old all*

known regions of the inhabited world, and even in our own day is thought to be second to none."

Superficially, Ancient Egypt seems isolated and distinct from the rest of the world, isolated by the deserts that hem in the narrow valley of the Nile. Yet, the Egyptians were in constant contact with other countries. Classical writers such as Plutarch, Herodotus, and Diodorus told how Ancient Egypt had peaceful colonies throughout the world. Diodorus of Sicily, in *Book I*, [29, 5], states:

"In general, the Egyptians say that their ancestors <u>sent forth numerous colonies to many parts of the inhabited world, by reason of the pre-eminence of their former kings and their excessive population;</u>"

Diodorus, *Book I*, [28, 1-4], tells of some Egyptian peaceful colonies that were reported to him in Asia and Europe:

"... a great number of colonies were spread from Egypt over all the inhabited world. To Babylon, for instance, colonists were led by Belus, who was held to be the son of Poseidon and Libya ...

... They say also that those who set forth with Danaus, likewise from Egypt, settled what is practically the oldest city of Greece, Argos, and that the nation of the Colchi in Pontus and that of the Jews, which lies between Arabia and Syria, were founded as colonies by certain emigrants from their country..."

By virtue of the eminence of the Egyptian colonists in Asia and Europe, they played a major role in each of the countries of their new settlements. Diodorus, *Book I*,

[28,6-7], discusses the significant role of the Egyptian settlers as rulers of these new regions:

> *"Moreover, <u>certain of the rulers of Athens were originally Egyptians</u>, they say. Petes, [called Peteus in Iliad 2.552.] for instance, the father of that Menestheus who took part in the expedition against Troy, having clearly been an Egyptian, later obtained citizenship at Athens and the kingship."*

Diodorus, *Book I*, [29, 1-5], also states:

> *"In the same way, they continue, <u>Erechtheus also, who was by birth an Egyptian, became king of Athens</u>... Erechtheus, through his racial connection with Egypt, brought from there to Athens a great supply of grain, and in return those who had enjoyed this aid made their benefactor king. After he had secured the throne he instituted the initiatory rites of Demeter in Eleusis and established the mysteries, transferring their ritual from Egypt... And their sacrifices as well as their ancient ceremonies are observed by the Athenians in the same way as by the Egyptians...*
>
> *... in charge of the more important religious ceremonies of Attica; the pastophoroi were those Egyptian priests who carried in processions small shrines of the gods. They are also the only Greeks who swear by Isis, and they closely resemble the Egyptians in both their appearance and manners."*

Herodotus [500 BCE] stated that he came from Halicarnassus, a Dorian town. He clearly stated the connection between the Dorians and Egypt in *The Histories*, Book 6, [Sections 53-55]:

> *[53]"... if one were to trace back, generation by generation, the lineage of Danaë the daughter of Acrisius, <u>the chiefs of the Dorians would turn out to be true-born Egyptians</u>.*
>
> *[55] Enough has been said about all this. Others have explained how and through what achievements <u>they became kings over the Dorians, despite being Egyptians</u>, and so I will not go into that. I will record things that others have not picked up."*

Herodotus, in [55], above, stated that such a fact was common knowledge at his time [500 BCE] and needed no elaboration.

Other connections between the Dorians and Egyptians were referred to several times by Herodotus, such as in *The Histories*, Book 2, [Section 91].

Lastly, it should be noted that Ancient Egyptian records (as well as records in other areas) have countless names of places in the world that are not recognizable in our present time. Names of places, ethnic groups, and countries keep on changing. The names of the European countries just 100 years ago, for example, are unrecognizable to most present-day Europeans. Eventually, when these records disappear a few centuries from now, the names of such countries will be totally unrecognizable.

In numerous locations in the world, there are references to tanned/brown-skinned people who provided enlightenment in regions throughout the world. They are described as:

1. Of "oriental" origin and characteristics.

2. Un-warlike people who settled peacefully among the local population.

3. Highly advanced in metallurgy, and have manufactured large quantities of metal products.

4. Highly organized and very talented in management.

5. Highly advanced in dry weather farming, irrigation, etc.

6. Experienced builders and artisans, and have built megalithic tombs, etc.

7. Very religious people who had Animistic beliefs.

The above descriptions can only apply to one country—Egypt. By combining oral traditions, ethno-history, and archaeological evidence (the dating of major settlements, tombs, mining activities, etc.) of various regions in the world, one can see that the civilized newcomers could have come only from the Nile Valley.

Immigration from Egypt occurred in several waves. It was closely related to events in Ancient Egypt. Some left in prosperous times to pursue business contacts. The majority left in stressful times.

[For more information about the Egyptian immigration

waves to sub-Sahara and interior Africa, read *Exiled Egyptians: the Heart of Africa*, by Moustafa Gadalla.]

[For more information about the Egyptian immigration waves to the Iberian Peninsula, read *Egyptian Romany: the Essence of Hispania*, by Moustafa Gadalla.]

10.2 ANCIENT EGYPT AND THE SEVEN SEAS

Transferring people, minerals, and goods between Ancient Egypt and other faraway places was much more extensive and common than is generally imagined. The seas were not barriers, but high roads for active international commerce. Traveling by water has been (and continues to be) the most effective, economical, and safest way to travel for both people and goods. Travel by land complements travel by water for major/large goods. The Ancient Egyptians had the means to travel the high seas with a large number of high-quality ships.

Ancient Egypt had the means, knowledge, material, and experience to transport people and goods by sea and land. The quality of the Ancient Egyptian ships were truly recognized and appreciated when the Khufu (Cheops) boat (4,500 years old) was found next to the Great Pyramid in Giza during the 1970s. That boat, now housed in a museum next to the Great Pyramid, is superior and much more seaworthy than Columbus' Santa Maria, the Mayflower, or the Vikings' ships. The physical evidence is clear that the Egyptians had the means to travel on the high seas.

The Ancient Egyptians had a large fleet, as evident from the huge quantities of timber that they had imported from Phoenicia. **All types of commercial and military vessels** were known more than 5,000 years ago, transferring goods to the northern shores of Britain, Ireland, and Europe. This was long before the 'Phoenicians' were recognized as seafarers in the 1st millennium BCE.

The Ancient Egyptians also had a naval fleet, the size of which varied according to defensive needs on the high seas during the different eras of Ancient Egyptian history. Special boats were built purposely for war. Herodotus and Diodorus both mentioned the fleet of long vessels, or ships of war, fitted out by the Egyptian Pharaoh Sesostris on the Arabian Gulf. They were 400 in number, and there is every reason to believe that trade, and the means of protecting it with ships of war, existed there at least as early as the 12th Dynasty, about 4,000 years ago.

[More details about Egyptian ships, harbors, navigation, etc. is to be found in two of Moustafa Gadalla's publications: *Ancient Egyptian Culture Revealed* and *Egyptian Romany: The Essence of Hispania*.]

10.3 ANCIENT EGYPT: THE WORLD ECONOMIC ENGINE

Egypt was the economical engine of the ancient world, in addition to its immense influence on all aspects of life throughout the world.

There were thriving trade activities throughout the ancient world. The Ancient Egyptians were responsible for the establishment of trading routes and trading centers throughout the world.

Archaeological evidence shows us that many thriving

cities/communities around the world have vanished. There is a direct correlation between the rise and fall of events in Egypt and the corresponding rise and fall of such "vanished" economical centers throughout the world. These trading centers and ancient prosperous regions—which some call "lost civilizations"—were vacated/shut down when Ancient Egypt fell prey to foreign invaders.

The following are three examples of such areas that lost their economical significance due to the demise of Ancient Egypt.

A. Moab – Diodorus, *Book I*, [28, 1-4], tells of an Egyptian colony at present-day Moab:

> . . . *that the nation of the Colchi in Pontus and that of the Jews, which lies between Arabia and Syria, were founded as colonies by certain emigrants from their country [Egypt]; and this is the reason why it is a long established institution among these two peoples* [Arabs and Jews] *to circumcise their male children, the custom having been brought over from Egypt.*

Archaeological evidence recovered from the above-mentioned region shows that this was a major trading center that was established and protected by the Ancient Egyptians. The famed Ancient Egyptian "Road of Horus" connected Egypt to Moab and beyond.

The Ancient Egyptian influence extended to all aspects of life there. When this prosperous center (as well as Egypt itself) was attacked by the Assyrians, Persians, and then the nomadic Arabs, it ceased to exist, and turned into a "ghost" center. [More about Moab in later chapters of this book.]

B. **Present-day Yemen and the United Arab Emirates** held a strategic location at the entrance of the Red Sea to the Indian Ocean. The archaeological evidence shows abandoned temples and ancient script that are identical to Egyptian shrines and script. It was from this region that the Ancient Egyptians imported a large quantity of incense and myrrh, which were necessary for all religious services. When the Ancient Egyptian temples were closed by foreign invaders, Yemen and their neighboring communities lost their main source of export, and thus these thriving communities became "ghost towns".

C. **The Iberian Peninsula** was the main source of several mineral ores for Ancient Egypt. The Portuguese coast was dotted with thriving ports to serve the heavy traffic along the "Tin Route", named after the tin mines in Galicia, Ireland, and Britain that were mined extensively to transport this material to the most populous and richest country in the ancient world—Egypt. All these thriving communities vanished and turned into "ghost towns" when Egypt became the victim of foreign invasion.

The rise and fall of events in Ancient Egypt correlated directly to events in the Iberian Peninsula [as detailed in *Egyptian Romany: the Essence of Hispania* by Moustafa Gadalla].

10.4 THE DOMINANT EGYPTIAN LANGUAGE

The Ancient Egyptian texts reflect the high culture of the Egyptian language and people. The German Egyptologist Adolf Erman, in his book *The Literature of the Ancient Egyptians* [page xxiv], wrote:

> *"As far back as we can trace it, the Egyptian language displays signs of being carefully fostered. It is rich in metaphors and figures of speech, a "cultured language", which "composes and thinks" for the person who writes."*

The British Egyptologist Alan Gardiner, in his book *Egyptian Grammar* [page 4], wrote:

> *"No less salient a characteristic of the language is its concision; the phrases and sentences are brief and to the point. Involved constructions and lengthy periods are rare, though such are found in some legal documents. The vocabulary was very rich. The clarity of Egyptian is much aided by a strict word-order..."*
>
> *"For pithiness of proverbs, oracles and sentences, no language can parallel with it.*
>
> *In axioms, maxims and aphorisms, it is excellent above all other languages.*
>
> *For definitions, divisions and distinctions, no language is so apt."*

Modern Western scholars affirm, explicitly and implicitly, the universal originality of the Ancient Egyptian alphabet (and language). In his book, *Literature*, pages xxxiv-v, the German Egyptologist Adolf Erman admits:

> *"The Egyptians alone were destined to adopt a remark-*

able method, following which they attained to the highest form of writing, the alphabet.."

Isaac Taylor showed how the Ancient Egyptian alphabet that spread eastward also spread westward to North Africa, when he also remarked, as per Petrie, in his book *Formation of Alphabet*, page 2, that:

"In many respects the Libyan agrees curiously with the South Semitic alphabets."

The British Egyptologist Gardiner tells us about the spread of the Egyptian language to Asia Minor and to Northwest and East Africa. In his book *Grammar*, Gardiner, on page 2, wrote:

"The Egyptian language is related, not only to the Semitic tongues (Hebrew, Arabic, Aramaic, Babylonian, etc.), but also to the East African languages (Galla, Somali, etc.) and the Berber idioms of North Africa."

From these groups of languages, other groups were created throughout the world on all continents, as will be demonstrated later in this book.

The British Egyptologist Petrie, in his book *The Formation of the Alphabets*, page 3, concluded:

"From the beginning of the prehistoric ages, a cursive system consisting of linear [letterforms] signs, full of variety and distinction was certainly used in Egypt."

Petrie has collected and tabulated alphabetical letterforms from pre-dynastic Egypt (early and late) and the 1st dynasty, 12th dynasty, 18th dynasty, 19th dynasty, Abu

Simbel, and Roman Egypt. Petrie also compiled (from several independent scholars) what appears to be alphabetical signs from Libya, Lydia, Lykia, Cyprus, Runes, Kabia, Northern Spain, Southern Spain, Nabathaea, Thamudite, Sabaea, Crete, Phylakopi, Lachish, Phoenicia, Thera Melos, Kornith, Athens, Elis, Halikarnassos, Pelasgic Italy, Faliscan, Etruscan, Oscan, and Latin. The earliest alphabetical inscriptions belong to the early prehistoric age of Egypt (probably before 7000 BCE), extending to the Greek and Roman Eras.

The main points are:

> 1. The monumental evidence shows that from the beginning of the prehistoric ages, a cursive system consisting of alphabetical letter-forms was certainly used in Egypt.

> 2. The quality of alphabetical forms are the best in Egypt. Elsewhere, it is of poor quality.

> 3. The number of alphabetical inscriptions in Ancient Egypt far exceeds the total number of all other countries combined.

> 4. All alphabetical inscriptions were present in Ancient Egypt since early pre-dynastic eras (over 7,000 years ago). The same exact letter-forms found all over various regions of the world is indicative of one source. There is no argument that these alphabetical letter-forms inscriptions are found in pre-dynastic Egypt, thousands of years before anywhere else.

> 5. Petrie collected letter-forms are clearly distin-

guishable in all styles of the Ancient Egyptian alphabetical writings, being cursive or uncials, which are also much older than all others.

10.5 THE EGYPTIAN MOTHER LANGUAGE OF ALL LANGUAGE FAMILIES

Because of Egypt's unique geographic location and her prominence as the most populous, literate, and richest country in the ancient world, the (Ancient) Egyptian language is considered to be the source of all other languages. Our focus in this edition will be on how the Ancient Egyptian language was the basis for at least three language families—Afro-Asiatic, Semitic, and Indo-European. In a later chapter, we will detail the Semitic Characteristics of the Ancient Egyptian language. The "Semitic family" provides the original and purest form of all languages.

Chapter 11 : Common Characteristics of Ancient Egyptian Alphabetic Writing System

The Egyptian language has had a natural organized comprehensive and coherent system to represent all the qualities of its tonal aspects which have been implemented in speech, poetry, singing, and musical performances.

A summary of the highlights of the most common characteristics of Egyptian [which were also extended to later Semitic] Alphabetic Writing are:

1. Ancient Egypt had 28 letters in their alphabet—just like later "Arabic"—with the same sound values. Hebrew uses the first 22 letters of the ABGD letters, but it is admitted that the riginal number was 28 letters.

2. Letters can each have up to four forms; as found exactly in later "Arabic":

>o Detached – the letter as it appears by itself, no letters joining to it either before or after.

o Initial – the letter as it appears when not preceded by a joining letter.
o Medial – the letter as it appears when there are joining letters both before and after the letter.
o Terminal – the letter as it appears when it is preceded, but not followed by joining letters.

3. Writing is normally from right to left. On some occasions the lines proceed alternately from right to left and from left to right. Cursive writing was from right to left—just like later Hebrew and "Arabic".

The orientation of the alphabet could be affected by a multitude of factors such as the type of material written on, or the position of the text in relation to figures or other texts, or the nature of the inscription, or the limitation of space that results in changing direction from horizontal to vertical, or vice-versa.

Egyptians utilized the writing surface configuration to the maximum. Therefore, some texts are written horizontally, others are vertically written, and some use both directions to fill a papyrus to the fullest available surface area. They may be written in columns (mostly from top to bottom) or in horizontal lines, which are sometimes to be read from left to right and sometimes from right to left. In some cases, they used a combination of horizontal and vertical for the same word and/or for the same sentence. This is/was in conjunction with their artistic variety in calligraphic writings, which were usually highly ornate.

4. There are/were two primary writing styles: the uncials and cursive which was/is ligatured following special rules

where some letters may be connected while others may not.

5. Rules of ligaturing different letters within a word were exactly like present-day "Arabic". Certain characters may be joined to their neighbors, others to the preceding one only, and others to the succeeding one only. The written letters undergo a slight external change according to their position within a word. When they stand alone or occur at the end of a word, they ordinarily terminate in a bold stroke; and when they appear in the middle of a word, they are ordinarily joined to the letter following by a small, upward curved stroke. With the exception of six letters which can be joined only to the preceding ones, the initial and medial letters are much abbreviated, while the final form consists of the initial form with a triumphant flourish. The essential part of the characters, however, remains unchanged.

6. There is/was no separation between words—words are never divided at the end of a line; the scribes preferring either to leave a blank space or to stretch out certain letters (hence called dilatable) in order to fill out the line.

The separation of groups of syllabic segments by a small vertical dividing mark was used for singing purposes

A scribe may mark the end of a clause or a phrase by prolonging horizontally the final stroke of a suitable letter.

7. Associated with the letters proper are a number of complimentary symbols which serve to modulate or regulate the voice in expressing a word or sentence, indi-

cated by signs placed above or below the consonant or long vowel that they follow.

As noted by all Egyptologists, the *"complete absence of phonetic complements is uncommon."*

The practice of indicating the pronunciation by writing furigana alongside the characters depends on the purpose of writing, the level of expected pronunciation accuracy, and who will be the expected reader. For example: you will not find it in newspapers, but you will find the supplementary phonetic symbols being used in varying degrees in some books, especially in religious texts and texts where musicality is essential, such as chanting, hymns, etc.

Not only do these phonetic notations have tonal function, but just as important, they have syntactical functions. In the Egyptian language, syntactical and tonal are one and the same.

The Phonetic Notations/Signs serve three functions:

a. Syntax: They provide information on the syntactical structure of the text. They divide verses into smaller units of meaning, a function which also gives them a limited but sometimes important role as a source for exegesis. This function is accomplished through the use of various conjunctive signs (which indicate that words should be connected in a single phrase) and especially a hierarchy of dividing signs of various strengths which divide each verse into smaller phrases.

The function of the disjunctive cantillation signs may be

roughly compared to modern punctuation signs such as periods, commas, semicolons, etc.

b. Phonetics: Most of the cantillation symbols indicate the specific syllable where the stress (accent) falls in the pronunciation of a word.

c. Music: The cantillation signs have musical value: reading the text with cantillation becomes a musical chant, where the music itself serves as a tool to emphasize the proper accentuation and syntax (as mentioned previously).

These symbols describe the features of a language above the level of individual consonants and vowels, such as prosody, tone, length, and stress, which often operate on syllables, words, or phrases —that is, elements such as the intensity, pitch, and germination of the sounds of a language, as well as the rhythm and intonation of speech. Although most of these symbols indicate distinctions that are phonemic at the word level, symbols also exist, for intonation, on a level greater than those of the word.

The forms of 'common writing' attempted to use a very simple visual code. For instance, the addition of a line, dot, or hooked curve modified the basic term with respect to gender, number, person, tense, voice, or other grammatical categories, depending on where it was placed (above, below, left or right, and so forth).

Such phonetic markings define the exact pronunciation far beyond the Western hysteria of "independent vowels". In the Egyptian tonal system, accommodations are made beyond a *fixed* vowel sound. The "vowel" sounds may be short or long, and are indicated by means of dots or dashes placed either above or below the consonants and, particularly for the long 'vowels', in conjunction with one of the weak letters. Besides these full 'vowels', there are also very short 'vowel sounds'—e.g. like that contained in the first syllable of the English word before—that were indicated likewise by combinations of dots and dashes, and represented very short vowel sounds.

8. Letter-forms were also used for other purposes such as numbers and musical notes.

In order to differentiate between a letter-form used for alphabetical writing and other such uses, the following "modifications" were utilized:

- Alphabetical letters in various positions—turning right, left, upside down or downside up.

- Added to letters were bars which were separate or incorporated into the body of the letter-form itself. Certain notes sometimes appear with a bar above them or through them (¥), signifying a portion of a natural note

- Individual musical notes were indicated by alphabets and each degree of the scale was represented by a letter of the alphabet, purely for musical instruments.

- Letters were used to signify the seven natural tones of the diatonic scale and each of the seven original notes of the scale was followed by two supplementary notes for smaller intervals, such as 1/4 1/3 3/8 tone—enharmonic notes.

– Additional signs and symbols were added for musical texts with/without accompanying musical instruments. [For such information, read *The Musical Aspects of The Ancient Egyptian Vocalic Language* by Moustafa Gadalla.]

Chapter 12 : Letterforms Divergence of World Alphabets From Its Egyptian Origin

12.1 THE APPARENT VARIATIONS OF LETTER-FORMS IN WORLD ALPHABETS FROM ITS EGYPTIAN ORIGIN

The most competent person to provide the best view on this matter is Petrie, who collected hundreds of alphabetical characters from different regions of the world over several millenniums. In his book *Formation of Alphabets*, Petrie wrote, on page 4:

> *"For the illiterate peoples [outside Egypt], they like small children don't appreciate the form and/or direction of a sign. So, he would <u>reverse both the forms of letters and the direction of writing, or later on only reverse the forms, while writing from left to right</u>. He had never been shown reversed writing, every example that he saw was normal; yet the reversal seemed not only unintentional, but so entirely immaterial to his mind, that he could hardly see any purpose in writing direct rather than reversed, the two were all one in idea.*

> *This same lack of sense of direction may often be seen in uneducated writing, where such letters as N, S, and Z are reversed."*

Petrie continues to sum it up:

> *"Much light is thus thrown on the treatment of [alphabetical letter-forms] signs in the early alphabets; they are turned up- side down, or tilted over one way or another, they are written reversed, and the direction of writing may be from either side, or each way alternately, as in the boustrophedon inscriptions. All of these variations were as nothing to the men who had not yet developed the sense of direction as' significant, and who thought only of the form in whatever position or reversal it might appear."*

In conclusion, we should consider that different handwritings (with different orientation) may appear to represent different alphabets. By taking the potential causes of 'apparent variations' into account, we can trace numerous scripts throughout the world to their origins—namely, the Ancient Egyptian alphabetical writings.

In summary, different related shapes of letter-forms are due to:

    a. Negligence in the orientation of letters.

    b. The slight four variations in a letter-form and the unique Egyptian ligaturing rules in cursive writing.

    c. Added vocalic markings on the fringe of a letter—sometimes separate other times touching the letter or embedded into the body of the letter-form itself.

d. Inability to recognize 'modified' letter-forms when they are used as numbers, musical notes, etc.

e. Quality of writing as affected by writing surfaces, devices and inks, the frequency of lifting the writing device to re-ink it, and carelessness in using inked instruments (e.g. too-thick and too-faint lines).

f. Level of ornamentation, varying in degree from plain simple to very calligraphic.

g. Confusing configuration/shape of closely shaped letter-forms—equivalent examples in English are confusing a and d, b and p, l and I, or E and F.

h. Writing confusion as a consequence of vocalic limitations/inability of some to pronounce certain letters as well as the phenomena of sound shifts — which will be discussed in a later chapter

12.2 OVERVIEW OF ARCHETYPAL 28 EGYPTIAN LETTER-FORMS AND DIVERGENCE INTO OTHER REGIONS

The British Egyptologist Petrie, in his book *The Formation of the Alphabets*, on page 3 concluded:

> *"From the beginning of the prehistoric ages, a cursive system consisting of linear signs, full of variety and distinction was certainly used in Egypt."*

Several references (as posted in the Selected Bibliography and Sources and Notes at the end of this book) were used to bring forth the list below. One of these references was *The Formation of Alphabets* by Petrie, who collected hundreds of alphabetical letter-forms from various region of [Ancient] Egypt that cover various eras. The collections extends from Pre-dynastic Egypt [before 5000 BCE] to the end of the "Roman" era. Some were uncials and others were ligatured. The Egyptian letter-forms were tabulated and compared (by Petrie) with similar inscriptions from numerous countries and regions in Africa, Asia and Europe. The Egyptian forms, as being by far the oldest, lead the way; followed by those from Asia Minor; followed by those found in the European countries. Petrie's tabulations leave no doubt that the Egyptian letter-forms were used by all such countries. Any apparent deviation from the Ancient Egyptian prototypal letter-forms are explained throughout this book, in several locations.

We will be showing here one or two of the basic Ancient Egyptian letter-forms. Two main cursive forms have existed since the 1st dynasty—one square/angular, and the other curved/rounded.

1st letter 'A/a' [numerical value 1]

As always, both square and round forms were found in Ancient Egypt long before their sparse appearance in any other region of the world:

> – **The square/angular form** is basically the same form as letter '**A**' with two equal legs; and has existed as such since at least the 1st dynasty, 5,000 years ago. A one-legged form in an upright position was also

in use, in some cases. It is this latter form that is presently used in "Arabic".

– The round [for cursive use] form is basically a rounded form of the top triangle of the form 'A' which looks exactly like present-day 'a'.

– A much simplified form was also used as an upright line with a tiny circle at the top/bottom of such a line. This form is found in present-day "Arabic" as well.

Western academics have been mistakenly identifying letter-forms from inscriptions worldwide as being letter-form(s) 'A/a'. The reason could be their unfamiliarity with certain cultural facts in Egypt, which result in:

– Q, G and A are confused since Egyptians pronounce 'Q' in their common speech in some locations of a word as A or G [hard].

– A/Y and '<u>A</u>.' are pronounced the same by non-Semitic peoples, and are confused in their alphabets, as a result.

– A, G,Y, N and S letter-forms are confused by academies; as admitted by Petrie.

EGYPTIAN UNIVERSAL WRITING MODES 127

. . .

2nd letter 'B/b' [numerical value 2]

As always, both square and round forms were found in Ancient Egypt long before their sparse appearance in any other region of the world:

> **– The square/angular form is basically** three sides of a square, which is to be found exactly in later years/centuries in the Hebrew 'beth'. The Ancient Egyptian open square form occurs later, in Arabia.
>
> **– The round [for cursive use] form is basically** the rounding and closing of top and bottom sides, giving the in-curving which starts the closed form, which is found in Ancient Egypt during the 12th dynasty and continued in Phylakopi, in the south Phoenician of Lachish, and in Arabia as well as in Greece. When 'b' becomes more cursive at the top, it provides the early form for 'B'. Further calligraphic ornamentation provided more rounding that result in shapes no different than present-day Latin's 'B/b'.

The letter-forms 'B' and 'b' came as result of incorporating calligraphic cursive rounding of the basic Egyptian letter-form as well as connecting lines to either/or previous/subsequent letters in a word. The same exact calligraphic cursive rounded forms are found in earlier Egyptian texts.

The "Arabs" continued using the same basic figures of the Ancient Egyptians. However, as a result of these Arabs butchering the Egyptian letter-form of letters 'B', 'Y', 'T/

t' and the 23rd letter 'Th', all four Arabic letters (being 'B', 'Y', 'T/t' and 'Th') looked the same. To distinguish between these "similar" shapes, the "Arabs" added two dots above the letter-form for the Arabic letter 'T'. They also added one dot below the letter-form for the Arabic letter 'B'; two dots beneath the letter-form (to distinguish it as the Arabic letter 'Y'); and three dots above the letter-form to distinguish it as the Arabic letter 'Th'.

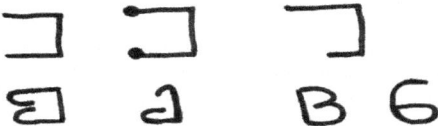

There was no distinction in Egypt between 'B' and 'P'. They are both the same letter (i.e., see the related words 'lips' and 'labial'—one with 'P' and its sister word with 'B').

Academia also confuses the Egyptian B/b (P/p) and R/r. The letter 'P' is actually a careless writing of 'b'—that became an "independent" letter, in the West!

. . .

3rd letter 'G/g' [numerical value 3] – The **hard G/g** is a guttural sound as in the English word 'frog'.

As always, both square and round forms were found in Ancient Egypt long before their sparse appearance in any other region of the world:

> – **The square/angular form** is basically an angle shape which continued to be used later by the "Arabs" who added a dot below the letter-form since the 10th Century CE.

- **The round [for cursive use] form** is basically an arc just like a short simple curve exactly like the Latin letter 'C' which has a 'K' sound that is closely related to the hard 'G' sound of the Egyptians.

The two forms (above) of the Egyptian examples are evidently the necessary prototype(s) both of the sharp angle and of the large curve which seem so diverse in the later alphabets.

Western academics have been mistakenly identifying letter-forms from inscriptions worldwide as being letter-form(s) 'G/g'. Some reasons could be their unfamiliarity with certain cultural facts in Egypt which result in:

- Letter-forms of the 3rd letter 'G' and the 11th letter 'K' are confused, since they come from same area in the human vocal system. Also both are very close in their Egyptian letter-forms.

- As noted by all studies such as those by Budge and Petrie, Egyptian letters that are aspirated and gutturals (such as G, H, 'H.', K, 'A.', Q, 'Kh' and 'Gh'), were mixed up and blended with similar, softer-sounding letters. The result was confusion by Western academics in identifying the appropriate letter-forms in the alphabets utilized in other regions of the world. That led to bad/wrong translations of texts and Western academics' usual contempt that "scribes made mistakes"(?!).

...

4th letter 'D/d' [numerical value 4]

As always, both square and round forms were found in Ancient Egypt long before their sparse appearance in any other region of the world:

- **The square/angular form** is basically the shape of a triangle and is one of the oldest and most generally – used forms. The same Ancient Egyptian angular letter-form continued to be used later by the "Arabs".

- **The round [for cursive use] form** is basically a cursive rounding of the triangle form.

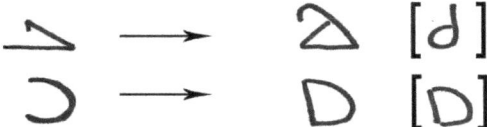

The 4th Latin [English] letter 'D/d'

-The shape 'd' is the rounded form of the angular Egyptian form.

-The shape 'D' is the same as the Egyptian rounded form with a line on its left side.

...

5th letter 'H/h' [numerical value 5] – The letter H/h—is one of four Egyptian letters with twin sounds/forms pronounced as 'Heh'. The other three letters are 'Waw' [6th letter], 'Mym/Mim' [13th letter] and 'Noon' [14th letter]. There are mystical reasons for such a peculiarity for these four letters. For detailed information refer to *Egyptian Alphabetical Letters of Creation Cycle* by Moustafa Gadalla.

As always both square and round forms were found in Ancient Egypt long before their sparse appearance in any other region of the world:

- **The square/angular form** is basically twin squares/triangles—top and bottom.

- **The round [for cursive use] form** is basically twin halves of a circle—top and bottom.

The same exact letter-forms are used in later "Arabic".

$$\boxminus \rightarrow [E] \quad [H]$$
$$\ominus \rightarrow [e] \quad [\epsilon]$$

The 5th Latin [English] letter is posted as 'E/e':

- The Latin letter-form 'E' is also basically the Egyptian square form being a twin square—top and bottom with an open right side.

- The Latin letter-form 'e' is also basically the Egyptian round [cursive] letter-form being a circle with a horizontal diagonal.

Western academics have been mistakenly identifying letter-forms from inscriptions worldwide as being letter-form(s) 'H/h'. Some reasons could be their unfamiliarity with certain cultural facts in Egypt, which result in:

- The 5th letter 'H' and the 8th letter 'H̲' are blended into each other as a singular aspirated 'H'. As a result the two letter-forms were confused by Western academics.

– There is also confusion by Western academics regarding the round letter-forms of Egyptian letters 'H' [5th letter] and 'T' [22nd letter] at the end of special ligatured cursive characteristics.

– As noted by all studies such as by Budge and Petrie, Egyptian letters that are aspirated and gutturals (such as G, H , 'H.', K, 'A.', Q, 'Kh' and 'Gh'), were mixed up and blended with similar, softer-sounding letters. The result was confusion by Western academics over identifying the appropriate letter-forms in alphabets utilized in other regions of the world. That led to bad/wrong translations of texts and Western academics' usual contempt that the "scribes made mistakes"(?!).

. . .

6th letter 'W/w' [numerical value 6] – The letter W is one of four Egyptian letters with twin sounds/forms pronounced as 'Waw'. The other three letters are 'Heh' [5th letter], 'Mym/Mim' [13th letter] and 'Noon' [14th letter]. There are mystical reasons for such a peculiarity with these four letters. For detailed information refer to *Egyptian Alphabetical Letters of Creation Cycle* by Moustafa Gadalla.

As always both square and round forms are found in Ancient Egypt long before their sparse appearance in any other region of the world:

- **The square/angular form** is basically a twin square—side by side [90 degrees opposite the orientation of the prior letter 'Heh'].

- **The round [for cursive use] form** is basically a twin half of a circle—side by side [90 degrees opposite the orientation of the prior letter 'Heh'].

The same exact letter-forms for 'Waw' are being used in later "Arabic", especially the rounded/cursive form. In singular use of this letter in a word, only the left half of the circle is utilized.

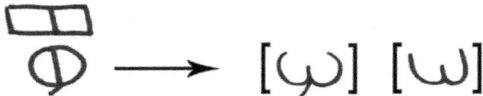

The 6th Latin [English] letter is posted as 'F/f':

- The twin nature of this letter is recognized as being 'Di-gamma' which means double/twin 'gamma' which is the 3rd letter of the Egyptian alphabet. As such this 'Waw' (being the 6th letter) is double the number 3 of the letter 'G'. Moreover, its Egyptian letter-form is the double/twin form of the letter-form for 'G'. By turning this twin/double form horizontally, it looks exactly like the Latin letter-form for the letter 'W/w'.

- In Latin/English and other tongues, the sound shift phenomena was, in effect, changing the sound 'waw' to 'vav', and from there to the sound 'F'. As such, the letter 'F' took the 6th place order of the Latin alphabets.

– The sound for 'F' occurs as the 17th letter in the Egyptian ABGD order.

...

7th letter 'Z/z' [numerical value 7]

As always both square and round forms were found in Ancient Egypt long before their sparse appearance in any other region of the world:

– **The square/angular form** is basically a two-bar z, linked by a stem—exactly like in present-day Latin/English.

– **The round [for cursive use] form** is basically a rounding arc.

The same letter-forms for 'Z' were used in later "Arabic" with slight modifications since the 10th Century CE. They turned the Ancient Egyptian form around and made it appear as the lower 1/4 arc of a circle. Such "modification" made the letter looks like the letter 'r'. They then added a dot above the "modified" form in order to distinguish it from the letter 'r', which has no dot.

$$\begin{matrix} Z \\ \supset \end{matrix} \longrightarrow \begin{bmatrix} Z \\ \dot{\subset} \end{bmatrix}$$

Western academics have been mistakenly identifying letter-forms from inscriptions worldwide as being letter-form(s) 'Z'. They are always confusing letters 'Z' [7th letter] with 'S' [15th letter], and 'Z' with 'r' [19th letter].

The 7th Latin [English] letter is posted as 'G/g':

The sound of 7th Egyptian letter 'Z' is relatively close to that of the 7th Latin letter of 'G' in its soft form as in the English word *angel*.

...

8th letter 'H.' [numerical value 8]

This letter-form were found in Ancient Egypt long before their sparse appearance in any other region of the world. There was no real distinction between a squared/angular and a rounded form. It was basically joined two unequal, parallel, vertical lines.

⌐⌐

Western academics have been mistakenly identifying letter-forms from inscriptions worldwide as being letter-form 'H.' As noted by all studies such as Budge and Petrie Egyptian letters that are aspirated and gutturals (such as G, H, 'H.', K, 'A.', Q, 'Kh' and 'Gh') were mixed up and blended with similar, softer-sounding letters. The result was confusion by Western academics in identifying the appropriate letter-forms in the alphabets utilized in other regions of the world. That led to bad/wrong translations of texts and Western academics' usual contempt that "scribes made mistakes"(?!).

Here is an example of such Western confusion; being that the 8th letter 'H.', and the 5th letter H are blended into each other as a singular aspirated 'H'. As a result, the two letter-forms were confused by Western academics.

Also, the 8th letter 'H.', and the 24th letter 'Kh' are very often confused with each other by non-Egyptians and later "Arabic"-speaking peoples, including Western academics. These two letters are/were always confused by Western academics in older inscriptions worldwide because they have the same letter-form with an additional dot/bar for the letter 'Kh'.

The 8th Latin [English] letter is posted as 'H/h':

As noted by all studies such as by Budge and Petrie, Egyptian letters that are aspirated and gutturals such as H., and H are blended into each other as a singular aspirated 'H'. As a result the two letterforms were confused by western academies.

...

9th letter 'T.' [numerical value 9]

As always both square and round forms were found in Ancient Egypt long before their sparse appearance in any other region of the world:

– **The square/angular form** is basically a square divided into upper and lower halves.

– **The round [for cursive use] form** is basically the rounding of the above square shape being a circle divided by its diameter, which is curiously enough the same shape for a *proclaimed* "Greek" letter[theta]. In Egyptian cursive writing the full circle was not drawn.

In the later "Arabic" alphabet, this letter maintained the same characteristics of the Egyptian cursive letter-form.

The 9th Latin [English] letter is posted as 'I/i':

The Egyptian 9th letter was deleted from the Latin/English alphabet because of their inability to pronounce it. This 9th Latin letter 'I' and the following Latin/English 10th letter 'J' are redundant in many European tongues!

...

10th letter 'Y' [numerical value 10]

As always both square and round forms were found in Ancient Egypt long before their sparse appearance in any other region of the world:

– **The square/angular form** is basically joined, two equal, inclined parallel lines.

– **The round [for cursive use] form** is basically the rounding of the squared/angular form above.

In cursive writing, when this letter occurs in the middle of a word, only one inclined line is used. Due to space limitations, the parallel lines may be shown as vertical and the angle of the horizontal ligaturing is shown as being inclined.

The later "Arabic" of the 10th Century CE ignored the inclination of the lines. As a result of these Arabs butchering the Egyptian letter-forms of letters 'B', 'Y', 'T/t' and its 23rd letter '<u>Th</u>', all four Arabic letters (being 'B', 'Y', 'T/t' and 'Th') looked the same. To distinguish between these "similar" shapes, the "Arabs" added two dots above the letter-form for the Arabic letter 'T'. Also added one dot below the letter-form for the Arabic letter 'B'; two dots beneath the letter for the letter-form to distinguish it as the Arabic letter 'Y'; and three dots above the letter for the letter-form to distinguish it as the Arabic letter '<u>Th</u>'.

Western academics have been mistakenly identifying letter-forms from inscriptions worldwide as being letter-form(s) 'Y'. Major Western academics' confusion occurs basically in two letter groups:

    i. Letters **A/Y** and '<u>**A**</u>.' are pronounced the same by non Semitic peoples .

    ii. Letters **A, G,Y, N** and **S** letter-forms are confused by academics, as admitted by Petrie.

The 10th Latin [English] letter is posted as 'J/j':

This 10th Latin letter 'J/j' is pronounced in many European regions, just like the Ancient Egyptians, as the sound 'Y/y'. Additionally, it is easy to see that the letter-form of the 10th Egyptian letter is the same as the Latin/English letters 'U'; and by adding a vertical line below 'U', it results in the letter 'Y'. All these letter-forms share the same sound.

...

11th letter K/k [numerical value 20]

As always, both square and round forms were found in Ancient Egypt long before their sparse appearance in any other region of the world. These form(s) continued unchanged when they were adopted by other regions of the world, such as in the Latin/European languages to the present times.

The letter-form here is associated with both the letters 'B' and 'G'. As such, the letter 'K' consists of a line added to the earlier associated letter-forms.

> **– The square/angular form** is basically a vertical line on the left of the 'G' letterform which makes it look exactly like the very same letter 'K' in Latin/English languages.

An additional horizontal line is added to the Egyptian 'B' letter-form. This and the above form are recognized and were adopted exactly in the later "Arabic" language.

> **– The round [for cursive use] form** is basically the rounding of the letterform(s) above.

Western academics have been mistakenly identifying letter-forms from inscriptions worldwide as being letter-form(s) 'K'. The 11th Egyptian letter 'k' and the third Egyptian letter 'G' have been confused by many in the field since they come from same area in the human vocal system. Also both are very close in their Egyptian letter-forms.

The 11th Latin [English] letter is posted as 'K/k':

Same form and order.

...

12th letter L/l [numerical value 30]

As always both square and round forms were found in Ancient Egypt long before their sparse appearance in any other region of the world:

> **– The square/angular form** is basically an upright vertical line—exactly as in Latin/English letter-form 'l'.
>
> **– The round [for cursive use] form** is basically an acute angled line—with/out rounding at its top/bottom—exactly as in the cursive forms of Latin/English letter-form 'l'.

The same letter-forms were adopted in the later "Arabic" language!

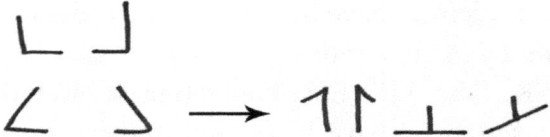

The 12th Latin [English] letter is posted as 'L/l':

Same form and order.

...

13th letter M/m [numerical value 40] – The letter M is one of four Egyptian letters with a twin sounds/forms pronounced as 'Mym/Mim'. The other three letters are 'Heh' [5th letter], 'Waw' [6th letter], and 'Noon' [14th letter]. There are mystical reasons for such a peculiarity with these four letters. For detailed information refer to *Egyptian Alphabetical Letters of Creation Cycle* by Moustafa Gadalla.

As always both square and round forms were found in Ancient Egypt long before their sparse appearance in any other region of the world:

> – **The square/angular form** is basically two equilateral triangles side by side—exactly like the shape of the later Latin/English letter 'M'.

> – **The round [for cursive use] form** is basically the rounded form of the above angular forms—exactly like the shape of the later Latin/English letter 'm'.

The same letter-forms were adopted in the later "Arabic" language!

Western academics have been mistakenly identifying letterforms from inscriptions worldwide as being letterform(s) 'M/m'. The 13th letter M, the Egyptian 21st letter Sh, and the Egyptian 15th letter S are confused by academics as admitted by Petrie. Such confusion is so unwarranted because of the distinct characteristics of these letter-forms.

The 13th Latin [English] letter is posted as 'M/m':

Same form and order.

...

14th letter N/n [numerical value 50] – The N/n is one of four Egyptian letters with twin sounds/forms pronounced as 'Noon'. The other three letters are 'Heh' [5th letter], 'Waw' [6th letter], and 'Mym/Mim' [13th letter]. There are mystical reasons for such a peculiarity situation with these four letters. For detailed information refer to *Egyptian Alphabetical Letters of Creation Cycle* by Moustafa Gadalla.

As always both square and round forms were found in Ancient Egypt long before their sparse appearance in any other region of the world:

- **The square/angular form** is basically exactly like the shape of the later Latin/English letter 'v'.

- **The round [for cursive use] form** is exactly like

the upside down shape of the later Latin/English letter 'n'.

The same rounded cursive letter-form was adopted in the later "Arabic" language with a dot added to it, which occurred at the beginning the 10th Century CE!

Western academics have been mistakenly identifying letter-forms from inscriptions worldwide as being letter-form(s) 'N/n'. The letter-form(s) for 'N/n' are confused by academies as admitted by Petrie, for letter-forms of the letter 'A', the third Egyptian letter 'G', the 10th Egyptian letter 'Y' and the 15th Egyptian letter 'S'.

The 14th Latin [English] letter is posted as 'N/n':

Same form and order.

...

15th letter S/s [numerical value 60]

As always, both square and round forms were found in Ancient Egypt long before their sparse appearance in any other region of the world:

> **– The square/angular form** is basically two horizontal lines of equal length, usually connected by a vertical/diagonal line. When the connecting line is diagonal, it gives the letter-form the image of a proclaimed "Greek" *Sigma*.

– The round [for cursive use] form is basically a rounded executed cursive form of the square/angular form.

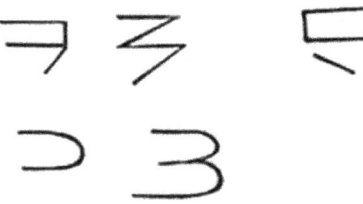

The "Arabs" confused the two interchangeable sounds of 'S' and 'Sh'. As a result, beginning in the 10th Century CE, they adopted the 21st Egyptian letter-form for the letter/sound 'Sh' and made it the letter-form for the "Arabic" letter 'S'. For the letter/sound 'Sh' the Arabs added three dots above the pointless Egyptian letter-form.

Western academics have been mistakenly identifying letter-forms from inscriptions worldwide as being letter-form(s) 'S'. Letter-forms for the 15th Egyptian letter 'S' have been confused by academics, as admitted by Petrie, for:

i. Letter-forms of the 21st Egyptian letter being 'Sh', as well as with the 13th Egyptian letter, being 'M'.

ii. Letter-forms of the 3rd Egyptian letter, being 'G' as well as with the 10th Egyptian letter (being 'Y'), as well as with the 14th Egyptian letter (being 'N').

The 15th Latin [English] letter is posted as 'O/o'. The letter 'S/s' comes later in the order of "their" alphabet.

· · ·

16th letter 'A.' [numerical value 70]

As always both square and round forms were found in Ancient Egypt long before their sparse appearance in any other region of the world:

> – **The square/angular form** is basically an acute-angled stem of the Latin/English letter 'y'. An alternate is to show a vertical stem but an acute ligatured line will be shown.
>
> In the middle of a word only the top 'v' shape is used. At the beginning of a word, the main letter-form is turned around 90 degrees in a horizontal position.
>
> – **The round [for cursive use] form** is basically the rounding form of the above square/angular form(s).

The "Arabs" continued using the same form except that they ignored the acute stem distinction and carelessly closed the open part of the top 'v' section. Such carelessness made the letter looks like the 28th Egyptian letter '**Gh**'. As a result, the "Arabs" in the 10th Century CE added a dot to the wrongly-closed form of this in order to distinguish it from the letter '**A.**'

As noted by all studies such as by Budge and Petrie, Egyptian letters that are aspirated (and gutturals such as G, H, H., K, 'A.', Q, 'Kh' and 'Gh') were mixed up and blended with similar, softer-sounding letters. The result was confusion by Western academics in identifying the appropriate letter-forms in the alphabets utilized in other regions of the world. That led to bad/wrong translations of texts and Western academics' usual contempt that "scribes made mistakes"(?!).

Western academics have been mistakenly identifying letter-forms from inscriptions worldwide as being letter-form(s) 'A.'. This guttural-sounding letter has always been confused by Western academics, as noted by Budge and Petrie, for the letter 'A/a' and/or the 10th Egyptian letter 'Y'.

Also, there is a similar confusion by Western academics between this guttural letter 'A.' and its guttural counterpart, the 28th Egyptian letter 'Gh', as explained above.

The 16th Latin [English] letter is posted as 'P/p':

The Egyptian 16th guttural-sounding letter 'A.' was dissolved into other easier sounds such as 'A' and 'Y', in Western tongues. Actually, there was no distinction in Egypt between 'B' and 'P'. They are both the same letter; i.e. they see the related words (lips and labial)—one with 'P' and its sister word with 'B'. To fill an empty space in the Latin/English alphabet order, a 'duplicate' letter 'P' became an "independent" letter in their alphabet!

...

17th letter F/f [numerical value 80]

As always both square and round forms were found in Ancient Egypt long before their sparse appearance in any other region of the world:

– **The square/angular form** is basically the angular form of letter 'B/b' turned 90 degrees—or, like the letter 'L' turned upside down—shaped like a walking cane.

– **The round [for cursive use] form** is basically the rounding of the top part of the square/angular form. Such rounding is located in the directional orientation of the writing script.

The "Arabs" continued using the same rounded cursive form except that they confused the form of this letter with the 19th letter 'Q/q' – the Egyptians made it face the opposite direction of writing [an example in English is the reversed letterforms 'p' and 'q']. As a result, the "Arabs" in the 10th Century CE added a dot to the top of the Egyptian letter-form for 'f' and two dots to their wrongly-oriented letter 'q'.

⌐ ⌐ ' ᒿ ᒿ ᕳ ᕵ F

Western academics have been mistakenly identifying letter-forms from inscriptions worldwide as being letter-form(s) 'F/f,' which resulted in them confusing these letter-forms for:

i. 'Q' and 'F' because of their similar shape—yet with a different orientation; as explained above.

ii. 'F' and 'L' because of their similarity in shape—yet with a different orientation; as explained above.

iii. 'F' and 'B/b' because of their similarity in

shape—yet with a different orientation; as explained above.

iv. A false distinction of a letter 'P', which the Egyptians never had in their language, as an independent letter. Such a sound was always considered a tonic shade of the Egyptian 2nd letter 'B'.

The 17th Latin [English] letter is posted as 'Q/q', which is found in the Egyptian alphabetical order as the 19th letter. As will be shown later herein, the Latin/English shapes of the 'Q/q' letter-forms are exactly the same throughout Ancient Egyptian history.

. . .

18th letter 'S.' [numerical value 90]

As always both square and round forms were found in Ancient Egypt long before their sparse appearance in any other region of the world:

– **The square/angular form** is basically the same as letter-form '<u>A.</u>' above except that the acute angled stem of the Latin/English letter 'y' is in the other direction. An alternate is to show a vertical stem but an acute ligatured line will be shown.

– **The round [for cursive use] form** is basically the rounded forms of the above square/angular form(s). The result is an upside down letter-form '<u>T.</u>'—the large top segment of a circle.

The "Arabs" continued using the same large top segment of a circle form.

Western academics have been mistakenly identifying letter-forms from inscriptions worldwide as being letter-form(s) 'S.' from Egyptian, which results in them confusing letter-forms of 'S.' with that of 'T.', 'A.', 'D.' and several others of sibilant and/or dental sounds.

The 18th Latin [English] letter is posted as 'R/r' which is found in the Egyptian alphabetical order as the 20th letter. As will be shown later herein the Latin/English shapes of the 'R/r' letter-forms are very closely related to these of the Ancient Egyptians.

. . .

19th letter Q/q [numerical value 100]

As always both square and round forms were found in Ancient Egypt long before their sparse appearance in any other region of the world:

– **The square/angular form** is basically a square or a triangle shape with a vertical stem.

– **The round [for cursive use] form** is basically the rounded forms of the above square/angular shapes.

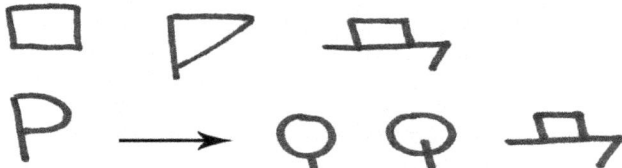

The "Arabs" continued using the same rounded cursive form, except that they confused the form of this letter with the 17th letter 'F/f' which the Egyptians made face the directional flow of writing [an example in English would be the reversed letter-forms 'p' and 'q']. As a result, the "Arabs" in the 10th Century CE added a dot to the top of the Egyptian letter-form for 'f' and two dots to their wrongly-oriented letter 'q'.

Western academics have been mistakenly identifying letter-forms from inscriptions worldwide as being letter-form(s) 'Q/q' ; confusing letter-forms:

i. 'Q' and 'F', because of them having similar shapes —yet with different orientation; as explained above.

ii. 'Q', 'G' and 'A' – possibly because Egyptians pronounce 'Q' in their common speech in some locations of a word, as 'A' or 'G' [hard as in the English word 'ego'].

iii. G, H, 'H.', K, 'A.', Q, 'Kh' and 'Gh' were mixed up and blended with similar, softer-sounding letters. The result was confusion by Western academics in identifying the appropriate letter-forms in the alphabets utilized in other regions of the world. That led to bad/wrong translations of texts and Western academics' usual contempt that "scribes made mistakes"(?!).

The 19th Latin [English] letter is posted as 'S/s' which is found in the Egyptian alphabetical order as the 15th letter. As in regard to the 19th Ancient Egyptian letter-form(s) 'Q/q', the Latin/English shapes of the 'Q/q' letter-forms are exactly the same as those of the Ancient Egyptians.

...

20th letter R/r [numerical value 200]

As always both square and round forms were found in Ancient Egypt long before their sparse appearance in any other region of the world:

- **The square/angular form** is basically an isosceles right-angled triangle.

- **The round [for cursive use] form** is basically the rounding of the two sides of the triangle that result in an arc presenting the lower 1/4 of a circle. For very cursive applications, the letter-form is reduced to a 45-degree inclined line.

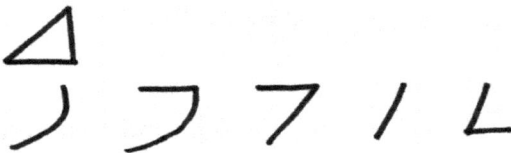

The "Arabs" continued using the same rounded cursive form of the Ancient Egyptians.

Western academics have been mistakenly identifying letter-forms from inscriptions worldwide as being letter-form(s) 'R/r' with a variety of other letters such as 'D/d', 'L/l', 'F/f' and 'Q/q'.

The 20<u>th</u> Latin [English] letter is posted as 'T/t' which is found in the Egyptian alphabetical order as the 22nd letter. As in regard to the 20th Ancient Egyptian letter-form(s) 'R/r,' the Latin/English shapes of the 'R/r' letter-forms are very closely related to these of the Ancient Egyptians'. The form 'r' is very much 1/4 of a circle and has the same general principle as the Ancient Egyptians. The form 'R' is basically a rounded form of the above Ancient Egyptian square/angular form, with an added vertical stem. Similar inscriptions of the very same 'R' shape are found in Ancient Egypt.

...

21st letter ' Sh' [numerical value 300]

As always both square and round forms were found in Ancient Egypt long before their sparse appearance in any other region of the world:

– **The square/angular form** is basically the shape of the letter 'E' turned 90 degrees.

– **The round [for cursive use] form** is basically a rounded form of the above square/angular form. In cursive writing, just the three vertical short lines without a horizontal connecting base are shown.

The "Arabs" confused the two interchangeable sounds of 'S' and 'Sh'. As a result, beginning in the 10th Century CE, they adopted the 21st Egyptian letter-form for the letter/sound 'Sh' and made it the letter-form for the "Arabic" letter 'S'. For the letter/sound 'Sh', the Arabs added three dots above the pointless Egyptian letter-form.

Western academies have been mistakenly identifying letter-forms from inscriptions worldwide as being letter-form(s) 'Sh'. The 13th letter 'M', the Egyptian 21st letter 'Sh', and the Egyptian 15th letter 'S' are confused by academics as admitted by Petrie. Such confusion is unwarranted because of the distinct characteristics of these letter-forms.

The 21st Latin [English] letter is posted as 'U/u':

See previous discussions on the Ancient Egyptian 6th and 10th letters (being 'W' and Y/y').

...

22nd letter T/t [numerical value 400]

As always both square and round forms were found in Ancient Egypt long before their sparse appearance in any other region of the world:

> – **The square/angular form** is basically the same as both common figures 't', mostly turned flat at 90 degrees, as well as the figure 'T', turned upside down.

> – **The round [for cursive use] form** is basically the cursive form of the above, sometimes without the typical short crossbar.

The "Arabs" continued using the same basic figure as the Ancient Egyptians. However as a result of these Arabs butchering the Egyptian letter-form of letters 'B', 'Y', 'T/t' and the 23rd letter 'Th', all four Arabic letters ('B', 'Y', 'T/t' and 'Th') looked the same. To distinguish between these "similar" shapes, the "Arabs" added two dots above the letter-form for the Arabic letter 'T'. They also added one dot below the letter-form for the Arabic letter 'B'; two dots beneath the letter for the letter-form to distinguish it as the Arabic letter 'Y'; and three dots above the letter for the letter-form to distinguish it as the Arabic letter 'Th'.

Western academics have been mistakenly identifying letter-forms from inscriptions worldwide as being letter-form(s) 'T/t', confusing its shape(s) with those of some other letters such as 'B/b', 'H' and 'Y/y'.

The 22nd Latin [English] letter is posted as 'V/v':

The sound for 'V' is closely related to several prime letters such as 'B', 'W' and 'F' and in the Egyptian alphabet is considered a variation of these three letters.

...

23rd letter 'Th' [numerical value 500]

The letter 'Th' is one of the last six letters in the Egyptian alphabet that has a sonic-twin letter in the top 22 letters. These last six letter-forms have the same letter-form of each primary letter, plus an added dot or a bar to distinguish each from its prime sonic-twin. Western academics have always confused such distinctions in these last six letters of the 28-letter alphabet.

Here the letter 'Th' is the sonic-twin of the prior letter 'T/t'.

As always, both square and round forms were found in Ancient Egypt long before their sparse appearance in any other region of the world:

> **– The square/angular form** is basically the same as the Egyptian letter 'T/t' above with a dot or a small cross or a tiny circle at the top of the letter-form.

> **– The round [for cursive use] form** is basically the rounding of the above.

The "Arabs" continued using the same basic figure as the Ancient Egyptians. However as a result of these Arabs butchering the Egyptian letter-form of the letters 'B', 'Y', 'T/t' and the 23rd letter 'Th', all four Arabic letters ('B', 'Y', 'T/t' and 'Th') looked the same. To distinguish between these "similar" shapes, the "Arabs" added two dots above the letter-form for the Arabic letter 'T'. They also added one dot below the letter-form for the Arabic letter 'B'; two dots beneath the letter for the letter-form to distinguish it as the Arabic letter 'Y'; and three dots above the letter for the letter-form to distinguish it as the Arabic letter 'Th'.

Western academics have been mistakenly identifying letter-forms from inscriptions worldwide as being letter-form(s) 'Th' by confusing it with several other Egyptian letter-forms for letters such as 'T/t'. 'T.', 'Y/y' and 'A/a'.

The 23rd Latin [English] letter is posted as 'W/w' which is the 6th Egyptian letter with the same shape, as discussed under the 6th Egyptian letter 'W/w' above.

...

24th letter 'Kh' [numerical value 600]

Letter 'Kh' is one of the last six letters in the Egyptian alphabet that has a sonic-twin letter in the top 22 letters. These last six letter-forms have the same letter-form of each's primary letter plus an added dot or a bar to distinguish each from its prime sonic-twin. Western academics have always confused such distinctions on these last six letters of the 28-letter alphabet.

Here the letter 'Kh' is the sonic-twin of the prior letter 'H.'

As always, both square and round forms were found in Ancient Egypt long before their sparse appearance in any other region of the world:

- **The square/angular form** is basically the same form as the letter 'H.' with a dot or a small dash line between the two primary vertical lines.

- **The round [for cursive use] form** is basically the same as above but sometimes the two primary vertical lines are connected forming an open angle with an additional dot or a short dash line in its middle.

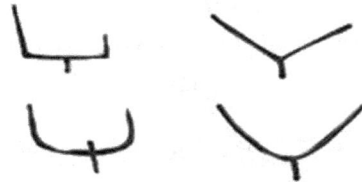

As noted by all studies such as by Budge and Petrie, Egyptian letters that are aspirated and gutturals such as G, H, 'H.', K, 'A.', Q, 'Kh' and 'Gh' were mixed up and blended with similar, softer-sounding letters. The result was confusion by Western academics in identifying the appropriate letter-forms in the alphabets utilized in other regions of the world. That led to bad/wrong translations of texts and Western academics' usual contempt that "scribes made mistakes"(?!).

The 24th letter 'Kh' and the 8th letter 'H.' are very often confused with each other by non-Egyptians and "Arabic"-speaking peoples, including Western academics. These two letters are/were always confused by Western academics in older inscriptions worldwide because they have the same letter-form, with an additional dot/bar for the letter 'Kh'. Also, Western academics confused this 'Kh' letter-form with those of Egyptian letter-forms for 'G/g' and 'Sh'.

The 24th Latin [English] letter is posted as 'X/x' which originally had the same exact sound as '**Kh**'.

· · ·

25th letter 'Dh' [numerical value 700]

Letter 'Dh' is one of the last six letters in the Egyptian

alphabet that has a sonic-twin letter in the top 22 letters. These last six letter-forms have the same letter-form as each primary letter, plus an added dot or a bar to distinguish each from its prime sonic-twin. Western academics have always confused such distinctions of these last six letters of the 28-letter alphabet.

Here the letter 'D̲h' is the sonic-twin of the prior letter 'D/d'.

As always both square and round forms were found in Ancient Egypt long before their sparse appearance in any other region of the world:

> – **The square/angular form** is basically the same as the 4th Egyptian letter-form 'D/d' with an additional dot/short bar.

> – **The round [for cursive use] form** is basically the same cursive letter-form 'D/d' with an additional dot/short bar.

The 25th letter 'D̲h' and the 4th letter 'D/d' are very often confused with each other by non-Egyptians and "Arabic"-speaking peoples, including Western academics. These two letters are/were always confused by Western academics in older inscriptions worldwide because they have the same letter-form with an additional dot/bar for the letter 'D̲h'. Also, Western academics confused this 'Dh'

letter-form with those of Egyptian letter-forms for 'G/g', 'H/ h', 'N/n' and 'Z.'.

The 25th Latin [English] letter is posted as 'Y/y', which is the 10th Egyptian letter with the same shape, as discussed under the 10h Egyptian letter 'Y/y' above.

...

26th letter 'D.' [numerical value 800]

Letter 'D.' is one of the last six letters in the Egyptian alphabet that has a sonic-twin letter in the top 22 letters. These last six letter-forms have the same letter-form as each primary letter, plus an added dot or a bar to distinguish each from its prime sonic-twin. Western academics have always confused such distinctions of these last six letters of the 28-letter alphabet.

Here the letter 'D.' is the sonic-twin of the prior letter 'S.'.

As always both square and round forms were found in Ancient Egypt long before their sparse appearance in any other region of the world:

– **The square/angular form** is basically the same as the 18th Egyptian letter-form 'S.' ,with an additional dot/short bar.

– **The round [for cursive use] form** is basically the same cursive letter-form 'S.' with an additional dot/ short bar.

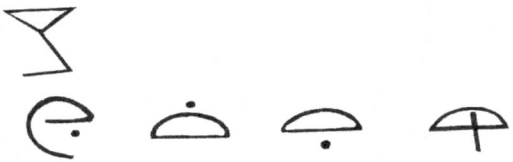

The 26th letter 'D.' and the 4th letter 'S.' are very often confused with each other by non-Egyptians and "Arabic"-speaking peoples, including Western academics. These two letters are/were always confused by Western academics in older inscriptions worldwide because they have the same letter-form, with an additional dot/bar for the letter 'D.'. Also, Western academics confused this 'D.' letter-form with those of Egyptian letter-forms for 'Y/y', 'A.','T.', and 'Z.', and several others of sibilant and/or dental sounds.

The 26th Latin [English] letter is posted as 'Z/z', which is the 7th Egyptian letter with the same shape, as discussed under the 7th Egyptian letter 'Z' above.

. . .

27th letter 'Z.' [numerical value 900]

Letter 'Z.' is one of the last six letters in the Egyptian alphabet that has a sonic-twin letter in the top 22 letters. These last six letter-forms have the same letter-form as each primary letter, plus an added dot or a bar to distinguish each from its prime sonic-twin. Western academics have always confused such distinctions of these last six letters of the 28-letter alphabet.

Here the letter 'Z.' is the sonic-twin of the prior 9th letter 'T.'

As always both square and round forms were found in Ancient Egypt long before their sparse appearance in any other region of the world:

– The square/angular form is basically the same as the 9th Egyptian letter-form 'T.' with an additional dot/short bar.

– The round [for cursive use] form is basically the same cursive letter-form 'T.' ,with an additional dot/short bar.

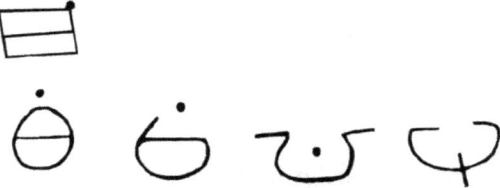

The 27th letter 'Z.' and the 9th letter 'T.' are very often confused with each other by non-Egyptians and "Arabic"-speaking peoples, including Western academics. These two letters are/were always confused by Western academics in older inscriptions worldwide because they have the same letter-form, with an additional dot/bar for the letter 'Z.'. Also, Western academics confused this 'Z.' with several others of sibilant and/or dental-sounding letters.

. . .

28th letter 'Gh' [numerical value 1000]

Letter 'Gh' is one of the last six letters in the Egyptian alphabet that has a sonic-twin letter in the top 22 letters. These last six letter-forms have the same letter-form as each primary letter, plus an added dot or a bar to distinguish each from its prime sonic-twin. Western academics have always confused such distinctions of these last six letters of the 28-letter alphabet.

Here the emphatic letter 'Gh' is the sonic-twin of the prior letter 'A.'.

As always both square and round forms were found in Ancient Egypt long before their sparse appearance in any other region of the world:

– **The square/angular form** is basically the same as the 16th Egyptian letter-form 'A.' with an additional dot/short bar.

– **The round [for cursive use] form** is basically the same cursive letter-form 'A.' with an additional dot/short bar.

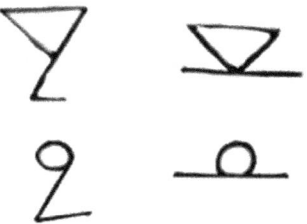

As noted by all studies such as by Budge and Petrie, Egyptian letters that are aspirated and gutturals such as G, H, 'H.', K, 'A.', Q, 'Kh' and 'Gh' were mixed up and blended with similar, softer-sounding letters. The result was confusion by Western academics in identifying the appropriate letter-forms of the alphabets utilized in other regions of the world. That led to bad/wrong translations of texts and Western academics' usual contempt that "scribes made mistakes"(?!).

The 28th letter 'Gh' and the 16th letter 'A.' are very often confused with each other by non-Egyptians and "Arabic"-speaking peoples, including Western academics. These two letters are/were always confused by Western academics in older inscriptions worldwide because they have the same letter-form with an additional dot/bar for the letter 'Gh'. Also, Western academics confused this 'Gh' letter-form with those Egyptian letter-forms for 'A/a', 'D/d', 'Y/y', and 'S.'

[For the mystical aspects of the 28 letters of the Egyptian alphabet, read *Egyptian Alphabetical Letters of Creation Cycle* by Moustafa Gadalla.]

Chapter 13 : Sound Divergence of World Alphabets From Its Egyptian Origin

There are basically two factors that have caused the variant dialects/languages of the world from its original one-world language—being the Ancient Egyptian:

i. Writing variations of the letter-forms and their orientations

ii. Systematic sound variations

In the previous chapter, we showed the divergence in writing of the original Egyptian letter-forms. In this chapter, we discuss the sound divergence of world alphabets from their Egyptian origin.

13.1 THE SYSTEMATIC SOUND VARIATIONS [SOUND SHIFTS]

From the earliest days of comparative philology, it was noticed that the sounds of related languages corresponded in apparently systematic ways. The most famous of these "sound shifts" were worked out by Jacob Grimm in 1822, and have become known as "Grimm's Law".

The circular relationship between these correspondences is a major feature:

G → K → X → Gh → G

Kh → K → Kh

T → Th [as in 'thin'] → Dh [as in 'the'] → D → T

P → F (Ph) → Bh → B → P

Other examples are:

- M is often exchanged for N.
- M often becomes B.
- B → V
- D → T Such as we find the name Mohammed being pronounced Mehmet in Turkish.
- K or C may be pronounced as 'G'.
- Z may be pronounced 'Ts' (using an emphatic 's' like the English word 'false').
- F → P
- R and L are often confused.
- Gl is often exchanged with Dl.
- H may be added or dropped at the end of a word.
- D may be dropped at the end of a word.
- S may be used instead of Sh.
- W may be G, Th may be F.

- W may be V.
- <u>Th</u> [as in 'three'] may be F

As an example of this phenomenon of sound shift, a person's name can still be recognized in vastly different sounds, such as Santiago/San Diego/San Jacob and Saint James. Jacob/Jack/Jaques/James are one and the same name, which exemplifies the phenomenon of sound shift.

Another simple example is: Michael, Mikhael, Miguel, Miqael, etc., which, despite being the same name, varies only in one sound in the middle of the name. One can imagine that a variation in two and even more sounds in the same word/name will make the changed name/word sound like a totally different name/word.

In addition to the numerous variations of sound shifts, many people have tendencies to reverse the letters (consonants and/or vowels) of a word. As a result, we end up with what appear to be totally different words.

13.2 CAUSES AND EFFECTS OF SOUND DIVERGENCE FROM ITS EGYPTIAN ORIGIN INTO OTHER WORLD ALPHABETS

i. The phenomenon of sound shift [explained earlier]

ii. Inability/'laziness' to pronounce some groups of letters such as guttural sounds. In the Egyptian Language as the Mother of all Semitic languages, there are two whole classes of guttural sounds which are foreign to European speech. These are, first, the so-called linguals or gutturo-dentals; and secondly, the guttural breaths or faucal sounds. How many letters were/are affected depends on the region of the world. Some sound values are recognizable for English speakers, others for German speakers, others for Spanish speakers, etc. A few examples will be shown throughout the book.

Budge in his book, *Egyptian Language*, page 27, wrote:

> *"The transliteration to remove or modify the gutturaux sounds which exist in the Ancient Egyptian language and miss in the Western languages. So the original gutturaux sounds which characterize the Ancient Egyptian language were sacrificed and disappeared in the current writing."*

Isaac Taylor in his book *The History of the Alphabet* states on page 81:

> *"In the Greek alphabet the Semitic semi-consonants (A, W, Y) and guttural breaths (H & A.) became vowels; aspirated mutes and <u>additional vowels were evolved</u>; and the <u>sibilants underwent transformation.</u>"*

Taylor continues:

> *"Five Primitive vowels were formed out of the breaths and semi- consonants, letters which even in Semitic languages tend to lapse into the cognate vowel sounds. The three breaths, aleph, he, and 'ayin, lent themselves readily to this process, <u>losing altogether their character of gutturals</u>, and sinking into the fundamental vowels, alpha, espsilon, and o-micron."*

Taylor continues:

> *"The semi-consonant yod, which had the sound of the English y or the German j, lapsed easily into the cog-*

> *nate vowel sound of iota. Analogy would lead us to expect that waw, the other semi-consonant, would similarly weaken into the vowel u. The Greek u-psilon does not, however, occupy the alphabetical position of the Waw, but comes among the new letters at the end of the alphabet."*

On page 280 of the same book, Isaac Taylor writes:

> *"The six Greek vowels, alpha, epsilon, eta, iota, omicron, and upsilon, were developed out of aleph, he, cheth, yod, 'ayin, and vau. In Armenian, Georgian, and Mongolian, a similar result has been attained in very nearly the same way."*

iii. The effect of persons'inability to pronounce some [Ancient] Egyptian letter sounds resulted in making two letters sound the same [such as Z and Z̲.], for some peoples. This resulted in eliminating apparent "duplicate" sounds from the "new alphabet"!

Isaac Taylor, in his book *The History of the Alphabet,* states, on page 81:

> *"In the Greek alphabet ... and the sibilants underwent transformation."*

iv. As discussed earlier, each letter may have several phonemes [shades of the same sound] that modulates because of the influence of either/both the sound value(s) of the letter prior/post of a particular letter. In some "languages", some phonemes took on a life of their own and became "independent" letters.

Chapter 14 : Cavalier Designations of New Languages

In the previous Chapter 13, we showed the sound divergence of world alphabets from their Egyptian origins. In the prior Chapter 12, we showed the divergence in writing of the original Egyptian letter-forms. In this chapter, we will review the cavalier designations of "new" languages in the world by Western academics. Between languages, the nations listed all speak fairly closely related Slavic languages.

14.1 REWARDING A NEW LANGUAGE FOR EACH HISTORICAL "WINNER"

It has been said that history is "written" (more correctly dictated) by the winner(s) of the latest conflict. In other words, *"Might is Right"*. But since they have the might, they declared themselves also to be "right"!

Geoffrey Sampson notes that "script follows religion"such as in the case of Eastern European languages. Russians, Bulgarians, and Serbs use Cyrillic; while Poles, Czechs, and Croats use Roman, and the division coincides with that between the Eastern Orthodox and the Western Catholic churches. It has nothing to do with differences between languages, the nations listed all speak fairly closely related Slavic languages.

Here are a few examples of how a conqueror is always awarded a new language to "recognize" its identity!

> 1. When the Roman Empire was established, a new language was awarded to them and they called it "Latin".
>
> 2. When the nomadic Arabs invaded and forced Islam on peoples, they declared the creation of an "Arabic" language.
>
> 3. During the later stages of the Moors' grip on Iberia, Castille became a dominant power in the north, and was the center from which the Reconquest of the peninsula was launched. The religious zealotry that followed the Reconquest included linguistic "purification". We are told that as the Reconquest was succeeding in moving south, Romance languages "emerged"—how "poetic"!

The so-called "emergence of Romance languages" in Iberia was similar to what happened in Turkey about a century ago, where their leader, Mustafa Kemal Atatürk, after losing the Ottoman Empire in WWI, wanted to sever ties with the East by abandoning the "Arabic" alphabet for a "Latin" alphabet. His action did not change the Turkish language. He merely wrote the same spoken language in a different alphabet and a different direction (left to right), which, incidentally, complicated their writing system. The same thing could be said of the "emergence of the Romance languages" – i.e. there was no change in the spoken languages, but merely a change to a "European" form of writing.

14.2 FABRICATING "NEW" LANGUAGES FROM EGYPTIAN SCRIPTS

The biggest linguistic piracy of Ancient Egyptian script is what is called "Greek". To add insult to injury, Western academia declared that the Egyptians adopted "Greek" alphabetical letter-forms —and they called this 'adoption' "Coptic"!!!

Similar linguistic piracies apply to the so-called "Arabic" and all these "languages" that were created from adopting/stealing Ancient Egyptian writing styles and their associated calligraphic forms, as explained earlier.

The European colonial powers rushed their academicians to their victimized countries—like Egypt—to steal the objects as well as the subjects of their civilized victims. As a result, all papyri that looks similar to later Greek and Roman writings were hauled away to European (and American) cities as being Greek and Latin/Roman. It fulfilled their desperate need to hype the status of like-Europeans.

The greatest Western intellectual heist from Egypt is commonly known as the 'Anastasi collection'. In the nineteenth century, Jean d'Anastasi (1780?- 1857), believed to be Armenian by birth, succeeded in bringing together large collections of papyri from Egypt; among them, sizable magical books, some of which he said he had obtained in Thebes. The collections he shipped to Europe were auctioned off and bought by various libraries: the British Museum in London, the Bibliothaquc Nationale and the Louvre in Paris, the Staatliche Museen in Berlin, and the Rijksmuseum in Leiden.

Such a heist is being called "findings" by Western academics and were credited to non-Egyptians despite their source of being deep inside Egypt, in present-day Luxor (Thebes).

A large body of such a heist was cavalierly credited to the Greeks by the colonial Western academics, and they called them "The Greek magical papyri". They contain a variety of magical spells and formulae, hymns, and rituals. These academics fabricated dates for such papyri from the second century BCE to the 5th century CE. Date fabrications follow in the same shameless way, as described in an earlier chapter about the Rosetta Stone. More about this heist in a chapter about the "Greek" language, later in this book.

PART IV : THE PRIMARY LINGUISTIC CHARACTERISTICS OF THE EGYPTIAN LANGUAGE

Chapter 15 : The Primary Linguistic Characteristics of The Egyptian Language

15.1 THE FOUR DISTINCTIVE PILLARS OF A LANGUAGE

The categorization of languages in the world by Western academic linguists, based on the lexicostatistic process, is inadequate for distinguishing or proving the grouping of language families. Other aspects that an analyst must consider in linguistic studies are: grammar, syntax, and mode of expression (style and literature). These four pillars (lexicography, grammar, syntax, and mode of expression) differ in emphasis (as to their importance) according to the different degrees of usefulness which they possess for conveying the intended meaning of speech.

The first and most important of the four pillars of a language is grammar, since it gives a clear indication of the basic principles used in expressing various intended meanings. Grammar is more important than lexicography, since ignorance of grammar is very harmful to mutual understanding. This is not the case with lexicography.

Syntax is the orderly or systematic arrangement of words as elements in a sentence to show their relationship to one another, since word order in a sentence indicates the intended emphasis. Syntax also deals with the organization and relationship of word groups, phrases, clauses, sentences, and sentence structure.

Lastly, it should be emphasized that the written form of a language does not necessarily concur with the origin and/or the categorization/classification of language families, such as the example given in an earlier chapter about the change of form in the Turkish language. In other words, seeing a text written in the "Latin" alphabet does not necessarily mean that the language of the text is "Latin" either in or outside Europe.

15.2 THE EGYPTIAN PROTOTYPAL INTERCONNECTED LEXICON, GRAMMAR AND SYNTAX

Long before the so-called Semitic forms of writing ever existed outside Egypt, the Ancient Egyptian writing system had a complete grammatical system, which was later adopted, almost exclusively, by other people in the Middle East. To have the same exact grammar is to have the same exact language—the Ancient Egyptian language—the one language that the Bible refers to. Here are the main points of the Ancient Egyptian grammar that are found in later "Semitic languages/dialects" as well as Greek and Latin; as will be shown in later chapters of this book.

1. Ancient Egyptian (and Semitic) grammar distinguishes three parts of speech: nouns, verbs, and particles.

   i. **Verb:** meaning and time (past—present—future)

   ii. **Noun**: concept/symbol/personal name (static)—timeless

   iii. **Article:** such as on, off, by, with, and, if, etc.

What would be called adjectives, adverbs, and pronouns in other languages are considered nouns in Ancient Egyptian [and later, Semitic] language families.

2. The Verb Tree—Roots—Two Stems—Three Branches/ Classification—Two Conjugations

Verbs are arguably the most important words in sentences because they indicate exactly what happens.

In the Ancient Egyptian language [as in other later Semitic languages], **verbs (like nouns) are derived from a three-letter root** which is a stem verb that contains the semantic core that signifies a certain general concept, such as K-T-B for writing.

It should be noted also that all Ancient Egyptian stem verbs consist of only 3 radicals. Ancient Egyptian stem verbs appear to foreigners as consisting of 2, 3, 4 & 5 consonants. True understanding will reduce all apparent forms to three-letter stem verbs.

The Ancient Egyptian language is a well-structured language where **words are formed from roots** by the addition of (unwritten) vowels, prefixes, infixes, or suffixes according to certain fixed patterns. For example, using the radicals H. -S-B, which refers to the basic concept of "reckoning/calculation", it is theoretically possible to derive as many as 14 new verbs and scores of nouns.

Both the tri-consonantal root verb (and its rich derivatives) and the varied sounds of vowels that change the grammatical character of the word make this language very poetic, powerful, expressive, energetic, and easy for everyone to compose poetry, puns, word plays, etc.

> – Ancient Egyptian language has **two model stem verbs** to express an action or a state of being of a given subject—one for instantaneous tenses and the other for habitual and continuous tenses.

> – **Verb Classification /basic groups**—For the sake of convenience, verbs are commonly classified into 3 groups [active, passive and reflexive] distinguished by the character of their 'stem' or 'theme'. The groups are generally classified into 7 basic groups/structures consisting of: 3 active structures, 3 passive ones, and 1 reflexive structure. Each verb group conjugates in a certain way.

> Details of such a system are beyond the scope of this book.

3. *Conjugation of Verbs*

The Ancient Egyptian language is a synthetic language with a moderate to high degree of inflection, which shows up mostly in verb conjugation.

Conjugation is the variation of the form of a verb by the

voice, mood, tense, number, and person which are identified.

There are two conjugations for all verbs:

– one for the instantaneous and the completed (or perfect) tenses and

– the other for the habitual and continuous tenses.

Conjugation is effected by means of prefixes, infixes, and suffixes, all added to the stem. The prefixes consist of the augment and reduplication, the infixes of the tense character and mood vowel, and the suffixes of the person endings.

Verbs undergo conjugation [inflection] according to the following categories:

i. **Tenses**

ii. **Moods:** indicative, subjunctive and imperative.

iii. **Voices:** 3 active, passive and reflexive.

i. TENSES OF VERBS 3 (8 categories)

The tenses of the verb tell when something is done in relation to now and/or another action. They also indicate the time when the action takes place. When speaking of verbs and time, we use the word 'tense'. There were, in the Ancient Egyptian language, three aspects: continuous, instantaneous, and completed. As each division of time comprises three different stages, there were also three representative tenses for each division of time: an effective, durative, and completed tense.

The three basic tenses were past, present, and future. Not all actions fit neatly into those three categories, however. Sometimes actions start in the past and continue into the present, and they may go on into the future. Each tense generally retained its relationships of time, grade (present, past, future), and kind (mere occurrence, duration, completion) through all three moods, generally also through both verbal nouns. Therefore, Egyptians have had **8 paradigms, as follows:**

THE PAST TENSES

1. (Aorist). It shows that something happened in the past.

2. (Pluperfect/past perfect). It shows that something was completed before something else happened.

3. (Imperfect). It shows that you were doing something continuously or habitually, in the past.

THE PRESENT TENSES

4. (Present tense). It shows that you are doing something now; you have started something in the past and are finishing in the future; or you are continuously or habitually doing something now.

5. (Present perfect). It shows that you have done something in the past and, at the time of speaking, the action is completed.

THE FUTURE TENSE

The future is nothing else than the present transferred

to a time to come. Hence, we have an effective future, a durative future, and a completed future or future perfect.

6. (Future continuous). It shows that something will happen in the future either continuously or habitually.

7. (Future simple). It shows that something will happen in the future without continuity or habitualness.

8. (Future perfect). It shows that, at sometime in the future, a future action will be in the past.

Verb conjugation also show both:

– Number: singular or plural.

– Person Endings—verb has separate person endings for the voices, as well as for the primary and secondary tenses.

Person: first, second or third.

– Distinction: familiar or respectful.

ii. Moods

Moods show in what situation an action occurs. The mood of verb is the form a verb takes to show how it is to be regarded (e.g.: stating a fact, expressing an opinion, a command, a wish, an uncertainty; or asking a question).

In addition to the various tenses, verbs can exist in three moods:

– **indicative**—for stating facts

– **subjunctive**—for stating possibilities, conjectures, "what if," what someone else said, thought or believed

– **imperative**—for stating commands

iii. Voices

The voice of a verb describes the relationship between the action (or state) that the verb expresses and the participants identified by its arguments (subject, object, etc.). Voice tells us whether the subject of a sentence is the actor or is acted upon. There are three types [active, passive and reflexive]:

– **Active Voice**: When the subject is the agent or doer of the action, the verb is in the active voice.

– **Passive Voice**: When the subject is the patient, target or undergoer of the action, the verb is said to be in the passive voice.

For example, in the sentence:

The cat ate the mouse.

The verb "ate" is in the active voice, but in the sentence:

The mouse was eaten by the cat.

The verbal phrase *"was eaten"* is passive.

- Active voice example: *John ate the whole pie!*
- Passive voice example: *The whole pie was eaten by John*

– **Reflexive [middle] Voice**: The subject is performing the action on him- or herself, making the object of the verb the same as the subject.

I wash myself. – myself is the object of wash

4. Two Genders

In the Ancient Egyptian language (followed later in other Semitic languages), two genders, masculine and feminine, are distinguished for nouns, adjectives, and also verbs. Masculine nouns have no special ending. The feminine forms are regularly derived from the masculine by adding the suffix 'at/et' at the end of the word, for singular forms. In the spoken language, the letter 't' is usually silent.

5. Three Numbers

The number of nouns and adjectives are three: singular, dual, and plural (each for feminine and masculine), with the same suffix endings as in present-day "Arabic".

6. Pronouns

A pronoun designates the person speaking (I, me, we, us), the person spoken to (you), or the person or thing spoken about (he, she, it, they, him, her, them).

A personal pronoun is a pronoun that refers to a particular person, group, or thing. Each of the pronouns in English (I, you, he, she, it, we, they, me, him, her, us, and them) comprises a set that shows contrasts of person, gender, number, and case. In the Egyptian language, a pronominal paradigm consists of 12 forms: In singular and plural, the 2nd and 3rd persons differentiate gender, while the 1st person does not. In the dual, there is no 1st person, and only a single form for each 2nd and 3rd person. Traditionally, the pronouns are listed in the order 3rd, 2nd, and 1st.

Personal pronouns are exactly the same in Ancient Egyptian as in "Arabic" (and Hebrew).

In addition to personal pronouns, the Egyptian language also utilized the enclitic forms of the pronoun.

Enclitic forms of the pronoun are the same in Ancient Egyptian and later Semitic languages.

7. Types and Structure(s) of Syllables

Ancient Egyptian language [as was copied exactly in later "Arabic"] has two basic types of syllables: short and long. Short syllables have the form consonant plus short vowel, and are followed by a short consonant vowel in the next syllable. Long syllables have a consonant plus either a long vowel or a short vowel, followed by one long consonant or by two short consonants. Long syllables take approximately twice as long to say as do short ones, and this gives the Ancient Egyptian language [the same is true in "Arabic"] a characteristic "stacatto" rhythm.

The syllable structure is such that there may be clusters of two (but not of three) consecutive consonants. A cluster of two consonants at the beginning of an utterance will be preceded by an auxiliary vowel.

8. Syntax/Word Order/Sentence Types

As detailed in an earlier chapter, the cantillation signs in the Egyptian language serve three functions: syntax, phonetics ,and musical value, to emphasize the proper accentuation and syntax.

In English, the position of the nouns tells the listener what role the nouns play. Hence, the strict rule of SVO (subject-verb-object) does not apply to the Ancient Egyptian language. Depending on the word order, an emphasis may arise for an idea in the sentence and, of course, the positions of adverbs can change the meaning of the sentence.

SENTENCE TYPES—There are two basic types of sentence in Ancient Egyptian (and other Semitic) languages: verbal and non-verbal. A highly generalized representation of these two basic types carries no emphasis and follows neutral word orders as follows:

- **Verbal sentence**: VSO. This is the order most commonly used to express a new idea in the conversation.

- **Nounal sentence**: SVO

More complex sentences, and sentences that appear to deviate from these patterns, can easily be explained as transforms of them. The syntactical position of words is not tied down to fixed and definite rules, as is the case with English and other modern languages. Therefore, a sentence like *the father loves his son* may be expressed in Ancient Egyptian, accordingly, as the stress lies on this or that word.

There were rules regarding word order to indicate the intended emphasis.

In addition to the two basic word orders above, there are four more orders (SOV, OSV, OVS, and VOS), and the last idea in the sentence is the most emphasized. Verbally, the emphasis may be changed due to the raising of the speaker's voice [loudness].

If the object does not exist, the order of VS is more likely than SV.

In direct and indirect question clauses introduced by **interrogative** adverbs (interrogative pronouns plus prepositions), SVO, VSO and VOS are all neutral. Typically, the verb comes immediately after the interrogative word.

In direct and indirect questions clauses introduced by interrogative pronouns in which the interrogative words are the subject or object of the verb, the verb must stand immediately after the interrogative pronoun.

PART V : OUT OF EGYPT—DIFFUSION PATTERNS TO ASIA AND AFRICA

Chapter 16 : Hebrew and Moses of Egypt

Next, we discuss the diffusion patterns of the Ancient Egyptian vocalic/spoken and alphabetical writing forms into surrounding neighbors in Asia, starting with the Hebrews as a member of the Semitic language family.

16.1 MOSES AND WRITING

Isaac Taylor in his book *The History of the Alphabet*, Volume 1, page 145, wrote:

> *"Before the Hebrews went down into Egypt the art of writing was unknown to them: when they came out of Egypt they possessed it."*

On page 149 of the same book, Volume 1, Isaac Taylor wrote:

> *"It will be observed that the names of the Semitic letters are without exception consistent with the suggested origin of the alphabet in the [Nile] Delta."*

Ancient tradition ascribed the authorship of the Pentateuch [the first five books of the Old Testament] to Moses:

> *"Then the Lord said to Moses, 'Write this on a scroll as*

> *something to be remembered and make sure that Joshua hears it ..."*

According to the Bible, the Pharaoh who was killing Hebrew children to keep the Egyptian purity accepted baby Moses into his residence and as a result Moses was adopted and brought up and educated in Egyptian surroundings.

Later, we learn that after killing an Egyptian, Moses escaped into Sinai and hid among *Hebrew* tribes. After spending about 25 years hiding in the wilderness, fearful for his life, the biblical Moses began the preparation for a comeback. Strangely enough, his fear for his life was totally gone, and he was not worried about confronting the Pharaoh!

Below is shown one of the countless numbers of Proto Sinaiatic scripts that are just no different than the letter-forms found in the populated areas of Egypt.

Moses did not need any help to communicate directly with the Egyptian Pharaoh and his Court—for all spoke the same language of Egypt!

16.2 MOSES AND MOAB

The account in the Old Testament of the failure of Moses to reach the Promised Land, his death and his burial in an unmarked grave is another curious episode.

We are told initially that, when his followers complained of thirst, Moses used his rod to smite a rock and bring forth water. It was called "the water of Meribah"—a location in the north-center of Sinai, south of Canaan. It was this action that would later haunt him.

Some time later, when the Israelites were camped on the banks of the Jordan, near Jericho and opposite Canaan, Moses learned, according to the Book of Deuteronomy, that he was to be denied the opportunity to cross the river, no matter how hard he pleaded:

> *"I pray thee, let me go over, and see the good land that is beyond Jordan, that goodly mountain, and Lebanon. ... the Lord said ... speak no more unto me of this matter ... thou shalt not go over this Jordan".* [Deuteronomy 3:25-7]

Later in the Book of Deuteronomy, we have an account of the actual death of Moses. The Lord said to him:

> *"Get thee up into this mountain Abarim, unto Mount Nebo, which is in <u>the land of Moab</u>' 'that is over against Jericho; and behold the land of Canaan, which I give unto the children of Israel for a possession: And die in the mount ... Because ye trespassed against me among the children of Israel at the waters of Meribah-Kadesh, in the wilderness of Zin ... thou shalt not go thither*

unto the land which I give the children of Israel. [32:49-52]

In the next chapter we will present more details about the Egyptian colony of Moab and its central influence in the diffusion of the Egyptian alphabetical writing system into Asia.

16.3 THE TWO WRITING FORMS [OLD & NEW!]

So what form of writing did Moses, who spent his life in Egypt use? Logic and evidence points to Ancient Egyptian. Isaac Taylor, in his book *The History of the Alphabet*, volume I, page 145, writes:

> "*The internal evidence points to the same conclusion. The forms of the Semitic letters were not derived from the monumental hieroglyphics, but from the cursive Hieratic*".

It is also worth repeating that the British Egyptologist Alan Gardiner in his book *Egyptian Grammar*, page 3, stated:

> "*The entire vocalic system of Old Egyptian may indeed be proved to have reached a stage resembling that of Hebrew or modern Arabic*"

For the sacred writings, the uncial style—just like Ancient Egypt—was used, which was "revived" in the 20th Century to become the "Hebrew" language as the sole style of the newfound state of Israel in 1948. Here again, a "distinctive" language is being awarded to a "new" state!

It is, however, recognized that while the "uncial" style

was/is used for sacred scripts, there was another cursive script with rounded alphabetical forms that was used for non-religious scripts, same as in the Egyptian traditions. It was decided by the powers-to-be to forgo this style in modern times.

Modern Hebrew references therefore speak of two styles—the Early Hebrew, and the Classical (or Square) Hebrew—Archaic and traditional—being the rounded/circular cursive and the uncial/square styles.

The word 'Hebrew' comes from Egyptian "Apiru", which means 'to express/come across'.

Assembled below are the inscriptions most "proclaimed" as being "Hebrew", from various locations in the Palestine/Israel region. It is obvious that such letter-forms are found exactly in Ancient Egypt long before, during, and after the times of such inscriptions. For reference to letter-forms in Ancient Egypt, refer to Chapter 12 of this book, as well as Petrie's book, *Formation of Alphabet.*

Below is the "Hebrew" Gezer 'Calendar', 10th Century BCE.

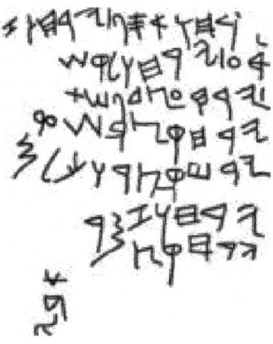

Below is the "Hebrew" inscription from Siloam tunnel, Jerusalem, c. 700 BCE.

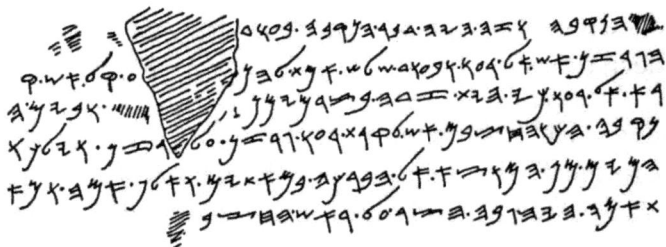

Below are mason marks found in Samaria

Below are mason marks found in Megiddo

Below are mason marks found in Lachish

Shown below are inscribed ostraca from Ahab's palace [both sides]

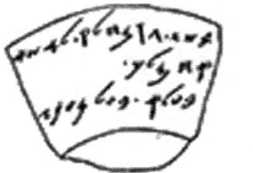
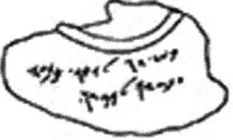

To sum up the sameness of the "Hebrew" writing system to the [Ancient] Egyptian system, as outlined in the Chapter 11 of this book:

1. The same configuration of the alphabet and in the same order ABGD. The same letter-forms were present in Egypt much earlier than Moses, and are consistent with letter-forms in Egypt utilizing various writing tools and surfaces; as was also evident in Petrie's work.

2. Present-day Hebrew consists of 22 alphabetical characters. It is recognized among Hebrew linguists that the original alphabet was 28 letters and that the missing six letters were in use in the past. These last six letters in the Egyptian alphabet have a sonic-twin letter in the top 22 letters. Therefore, these last six letter-forms have the same letter-form of each's primary letter, plus an added dot or a bar to distinguish each from its prime sonic-twin. Western academics have always confused such distinctions in these last six letters of the 28-letter alphabet.

3. The same orientation as in [Ancient] Egyptian alphabetical writing system: i.e. written from right to left.

4. Two styles—uncials and cursive/ligatured.

5. The same phonetic markings [including vowel sounds] are written as dots and dashes under the text. Different combinations of dots and dashes signify different types of vowel sounds, which are used

in scriptures, children's books, and also poetry when exact vocalization is needed for liturgical and musical texts.

6. The vocalic values of some letters have been changed in accordance with the phenomenon of 'sound shift' when some particular letters are hard to pronounce by certain particular groups of people.

16.4 SAMENESS OF EGYPTIAN PROTOTYPAL INTERCONNECTED LEXICON, GRAMMAR AND SYNTAX

The "Hebrew Language" complies exactly with all the linguistic characteristics of the much older Ancient Egyptian language which was detailed in Chapter 15 of this book. Such include (but are not limited to) the Ancient Egyptian prototypal interconnected lexicon, grammar, and syntax. These include the significance of verbs, verb roots, verb stems, verb classes and structures, the conjugation scheme for verbs, and Egyptian prototypal etymology/lexicon and word formation/derivation from a three-letter root (which signifies a certain general concept) into numerous patterns through the use of intermediate vowels and prefixes, infixes and suffixes, etc.; in addition to types and structures of syllables as well as syntax, word order, and sentence types.

Affinities and characteristics of the Ancient Egyptian language are described by Egyptologist Alan Gardiner in his book *Egyptian Grammar*, on page 2:

> *"**The Egyptian language** is related, not only to the Semitic tongues (**Hebrew**, Arabic, Aramaic, Babylonian, etc.), but also to the East African languages (Galla,*

Somali, etc.) and the Berber idioms of North Africa. Its connection with the latter groups, together known as the Hamitic family, is a very thorny subject, but the relationship to the Semitic tongues can be fairly accurately defined. In general structure the similarity is very great; <u>Egyptian shares the principal peculiarity of Semitic</u> in that its word-stems consist of combinations of consonants, as a rule three in number, which are theoretically at least unchangeable. Grammatical inflection and minor variations of meaning are contrived mainly by ringing the changes on the internal vowels, though affixed endings also are used for the same purpose."

In this chapter we have discussed diffusion patterns of the Ancient Egyptian vocalic/spoken and alphabetical writing forms into surrounding neighbors in Asia, starting with the Hebrews as members of the Semitic language family. In the next chapter, we'll continue discussing diffusion patterns of the Ancient Egyptian vocalic/spoken and alphabetical writing forms into other surrounding neighbors in Asia.

Chapter 17 : The Ancient Egyptian Hegemony of Asiatic Neighbors

17.1 THE EGYPTIAN SETTLEMENT AT MOAB

Diodorus, in *Book I*, [28, 1-4], tells of an Egyptian settlement at present-day Moab:

> "... *that the nation of the Colchi in Pontus and that of the Jews, which lies between Arabia and Syria, were founded as colonies by certain emigrants from their country [Egypt]; and this is the reason why it is a long established institution among these two peoples* [Arabs and Jews] *to circumcise their male children, the custom having been brought over from Egypt.*"

Recovered archaeological evidence from the above-mentioned region shows that it was a major trading center that was established and protected by the Ancient Egyptians. The famed Ancient Egyptian "Road of Horus" connected Egypt to Moab and beyond.

There was a gap of some considerable length with no records of writings whatsoever in this area until the Moabite Stone, now dated to the 9th century BCE, was found. The "Moabite stone" is a very rare find in this vast region.

The text, in its present condition, contains 34 lines; of which 27 are perfectly preserved. The following 7 lines are in an increasingly bad condition, and the end has been lost. The letters are unmistakably Egyptian alphabetical letter-forms.

Below are the Moabite stone inscriptions from Dibon [Jordan] c.850 BCE:

Another rare but interesting find came from Balu, in Moab, which is dated to about the twelfth century BCE. The inscriptions on one side [as shown below] are those of the Ancient Egyptian uncial writing style; which also looks exactly like the predominant writing style found in South Arabia [described in Western references as "South Semitic"].

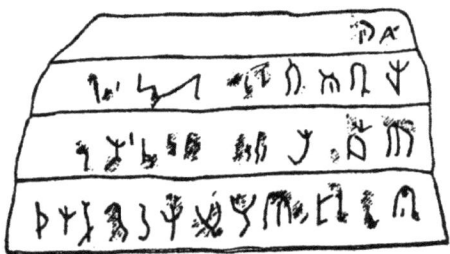

The other side shows the cursive ligatured rounded style.

A comparison table of Sinaitic and South-Semitic signs will be shown later in this chapter, when dealing with Southern Arabia, which again will show no difference in scripts found there than in Egypt itself.

17.2 FALSE DESIGNATIONS OF VARIOUS ALPHABETS IN NORTH ARABIA [NABATEAN, ARAMAIC AND UGARITI]

The Moab region was a part of this vast area of North Arabia that was designated by the general name of "Nabathean", which extended between the Red Sea and the Euphrates, as per the writings of Josephus. This whole region was broken up into a number of petty warring states. It was by no means a significant region.

One of the prime strategic centers of this region was

Petra, where a few inscriptions have been found in the so-called "Nabathean alphabet". However, after all the hoopla, Western academia admits that: *"**A large number of inscriptions in the same alphabet have also been obtained from rocks in the [Egyptian] peninsula of Sinai**".*

Assembled below are the inscriptions most "proclaimed" as being "Nabathean" scripts from this vast region.

Below are 5 lines of the inscriptions of Ahiram, from Byblos in the late 11th Century BCE:

Below is a part of the Namara inscription dated 328-9 CE

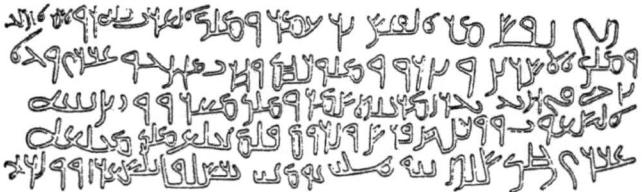

And again, the very same alphabetical characters have been in use in the most prominent country in the region, being Egypt, as shown in the monumental work of Petrie's Formation of the Alphabets and several locations throughout this book.

Aramaic Promoting—According to the Bible, the infant Jesus escaped with his mother to Egypt. They stayed there until he was called upon by his Father (**"Out of Egypt have I called my son".**) Immediately, Jesus appeared as a mature man, speaking and communicating with people of all classes. We have here Jesus speaking the same exact language as the people of Palestine, even though he spent all his previous life in Egypt. The conclusion should be that there was no distinction between the vocalic language in Ancient Egypt and Ancient Palestine!

Isaac Taylor, in his book *The History of the Alphabet,* Volume I, page 259, admits:

> *"... we are mainly dependent on documents of Egyptian origin ... Egypt supplies the materials for the history of the Aramean alphabet during the important period of transition between the 4th and the 1st centuries BCE".*

Several Egyptian papyri that came from southern Egypt were cavalierly designated by Western academics as "Aramean Papyri". Such Papyri follow the same exact typical Egyptian system, with its unique ligaturing rules in cursive writing.

Isaac Taylor, in his book *The History of the Alphabet,* Vol. I, page 269, admits:

> *"The Egyptian papyri sufficiently prove that from the beginning of the 2nd century BCE, if not earlier, the Aramean alphabet was that which was ordinarily used by Jews resident in Egypt; and there is no reason to suppose that at this period the alphabet of Palestine*

> *differed in any respect from the Aramean alphabet used in the neighboring lands."*

Below is the only major item that has been proclaimed by Western academia to be that of an "Aramean alphabet". It came from Bar-Rakkab.

And again, the very same alphabetical characters have been in use in the most prominent country in the region (being Egypt), as shown in the monumental work of

Petrie's Formation of the Alphabets and in several locations throughout this book.

The Ugaritic Writing Records show a "cuneiform" form of writing that employs simple lines, strokes, and dots, which is a necessarily adaptive way to write on clay tablets which do not tolerate curves.

Western academics agree that the Ugaritic alphabetical letter-forms resemble:

> 1. The Sumerian or Accadian letter-forms ["syllabary"] in a striking resemblances. Some forms are identical and others very similar, as **though they were derived from the corresponding symbols by turning them around 90 degrees or by dropping superfluous strokes**, and so on.

Accadian		Ugaritic		Phoenician		Accadian		Ugaritic		Phoenician	
𒀀	a	⊢—	d	K ⸸	'	𒈠	ma	⊢⊣	m	ʼ)	m
𒂊	e	⊨	ḏ,ḍ			⊢⊣	na	⊢⊢—	n	ϟϟ	n
𒌋	u	𒀭	ú			𒅀	ša	𒅀	s		
𒁉	bi	𒉿	ḇ	99	b	𒌍	se	𒅎	ṣ	𐤕	s
𒄀	gi	T	g	1ⸯ	g	◀	ḫa	◀·	ʿ	o	ʿ
𒁕	da	𒌅	d	◇◁	d	𒉺	pa	⊨	p	))	p
𒄭	ḫa	⊨	h	∃⅂	h	𒁀	ṣa	𒀭	ṣ	ᴚ	ṣ
𒉿	wa	⊢⊢	w	ΥΥ	w	𒋗	šu	𒆪	ž		
𒅎	za	𐠊	z	I I	z	𒋡	qa	⊢⊣	q	ϙ	q
𒄩	ḫa	𒁇 / 𒁀	ḫ / ḥ	ЯB	ḫ,ḥ	𒌨	ur / ra	⊢—	r	𐤓𐤓	r
𒋾	ṭi	⊢⊢	ṭ	⊕	ṭ	𒊭	ša	𒐋	š		
𒅀	ya	𒅀	y	ᴣ⁊	y	𒋗	šu	★	ṣ́	W	š
𒅗	ka	⊢⊣	k	∨	k	𒁲	ṭi	⊢—	ṭ	+	t
𒇻	lu	𒁐	l	∟ʟ∟	l	𒂵	ga	⊢⊣	ġ		

Writing surface [clay vs. stone vs. papyrus vs. leather, etc.] and tools provide an apparent difference in letter-forms, which do not lead to different alphabets!!

Writings on clay will be devoid of curves, and as such, letter-forms with curves will be slightly modified on clay using dots, lines, and dashes.

2. The letter-forms found in both North and South Arabia, especially when allowance is made for the fact that the former are impressed in clay while the latter are incised in stone.

3. The Sinaitic alphabetical cursive inscriptions on the one side and with the letter-forms found in South Arabia. They all agree that resemblances can indeed

be traced between the Sinaitic and Ugaritic letter-forms, in their general appearance.

Below is a comparative table for the first 22 letters of the Alphabet — "Early Phoenician","Moabite", "Hebrew 6th Century BCE", "Early Aramaic", "Late Aramiac", "Palmyrene Aramaic", "Monumental Nabataean Aramaic" and "Square Hebrew Printed".

	Early Phoenician	Moabite	Hebrew Ostraca (6th Century BC)	Early Aramaic	Late Aramaic Papyri	Palmyrene Aramaic	Monumental Nabataean Aramaic	'Square' Jewish/ Hebrew Printed
ʼ	⊀	⊀	⟊	⊀	⋉	⋉	⌐ʟ	א
b	◁	⅃	⅁	⅁	⌐	⌐	⌐	ב
g	⌐	1	⌐	1	⌐	⋋	⋋	ג
d	◁	◂	◂	4	⅂	⌐	⌐	ד
h	≡	⌐	⪇	∄	⌐	⋊	⋏	ה
w	Y	Y	⌐	Y	⌐	?	⌐	ו
z	I	⌐	⌐	I	⌐	⌐	⌐	ז
ḥ	⊟	⊟	⊟	⊟	⌐	⌐	⌐	ח
ṭ	⊗	⊙	⊙	⊕	⌐	⌐	⌐	ט
y	⌐	Z	⌐	⌐	⌐	⌐	⌐	י
k	⌐	⌐	⌐	⌐	⌐	⌐	⌐	כ
l	⌐	⌐	⌐	⌐	⌐	⌐	⌐	ל
m	⌐	⌐	⌐	⌐	⌐	⌐	⌐	מ
n	⌐	⌐	⌐	⌐	⌐	⌐	⌐	נ
s	⌐	⌐	⌐	⌐	⌐	⌐	⌐	ס
ʿ	○	○	○	○	⌐	⌐	⌐	ע
p	⌐	⌐	⌐	⌐	⌐	3	⌐	פ
ṣ	⌐	⌐	⌐	⌐	⌐	⌐	⌐	צ
q	⌐	⌐	⌐	⌐	⌐	⌐	⌐	ק
r	⌐	⌐	⌐	⌐	⌐	⌐	⌐	ר
š	W	W	W	W	⌐	⌐	⌐	ש
t	×	×	×	×	⌐	⌐	⌐	ת

EGYPTIAN UNIVERSAL WRITING MODES 209

And again, the very same alphabetical characters have been in use in the most prominent country in the region (being Egypt), as shown in the monumental work of Petrie's Formation of the Alphabets and several locations throughout this book.

17.3 FALSE DESIGNATIONS OF SOUTH ARABIAN ALPHABETS

Southern Arabia had an important strategic position in international trade when Ancient Egypt was the economical engine of the ancient world. Present-day Yemen and the United Arab Emirates held strategic locations at the entrance of the Red Sea to the Indian Ocean. The archaeological evidence shows abandoned temples and ancient script that are identical to Egyptian shrines and scripts. It was from this region that the Ancient Egyptians imported a large quantity of incense, myrrh, and frankincense, which were necessary for all religious services. When the Ancient Egyptian temples were closed by the foreign invaders, Yemen and their neighboring communities lost their main source of income and thus these thriving communities became "ghost towns".

There is abundant evidence that Arabia Felix was an active international trade juncture with a strong Ancient Egyptian presence. Egyptian records from several Egyptian pharaohs are found in the region, such as Tothomoses III in the 17th century BCE and again in the 8th and 7th centuries BCE.

The building styles of the temples/shrines in Southern Arabia are distinctively Egyptian, with recessed walls/niches and "false doors/windows" like those in hundreds of tombs in Giza, Saqqara, etc., as well as all Egyptian temples such as the Hatshupsut Temple in Luxor.

Similarly, in Yemen and at a much later date, we find the closest parallels in full-size architecture are the false stone windows in the peristyle hall of the Marib Temple. These windows are recessed to a depth of 10 cm, and are carved to resemble wooden lattice-work. The Timna Temple (c. 6th Century BCE) in Yemen is another good example of the use of such recesses. As also is the practice in Ancient Egypt, relief sculpture was commonly carved on recessed panels and stelae.

Yemen was the great central mart between Egypt (as the richest country in the ancient world) and India. For a prolonged period, this lucrative traffic was in the hands of the Sabeans and was the main source of their proverbial wealth. The trade between Egypt and Yemen began as early as 2300 B.C., and that between Yemen and India was established not later than 1000 B.C. Their ports were frequented by trading vessels from all places; from the Red Sea and the Persian Gulf to the coast of Africa and especially from the mouth of the Indus River.

Sabaeans are the most prominent name associated with this region. Sabaean means "lion" in the Egyptian language. One of the most significant depictions in Yemen is a young lady standing on top of a lion. The very same depictions have been in Ancient Egypt for thousands of years, and the depiction is that of the netert [goddess] Kadesh/Qadesh. Qadesh is ordained and described in Ancient Egyptian texts as the Beloved of Ptah. It is therefore that we find the very same depiction here from Memphis more than 4,000 years ago—and we find similar depictions in Yemen, at the southern end of the Red Sea, in later times.

South-Arabian writing records again point to Ancient Egypt's alphabetical writing style as the source. While Western academics will not confess to this obvious conclusion, they have no problem agreeing with G.R. Driver in his book *Semitic Writing*, page 123, which states:

> *"About the same time also, a form of script was introduced into South Arabia which had affinities with the Old Phoenician script, but with script forms closely analogous to this became widely prevalent throughout the south and center of the Arabian peninsula, where they remained in normal use down to the 5th century A.D."*

Isaac Taylor showed how the Ancient Egyptian alphabet that spread eastward also spread westward to north Africa when he also remarked, as posted on page 2 of Petrie's book *Formation of the Alphabet*, that:

> *"In many respects the Libyan agrees curiously with the South Semitic alphabets."*

So here we go again, admitting similarities, affinities, etc.

between north, central, and south which are all connected to "old Phoenician script" which, as shown throughout this book, is a fabricated name for the Ancient Egyptian alphabetical writing which has been in use for thousands of years prior to the rise of these areas of the world. These regions collapsed and "vanished" when Ancient Egypt lost its power and became a colony of the Arab Moslem invaders.

The four most commonly recognized old scripts in this region are Sabaean or Himyaritic [including Haramitic]; Minaean [Madhabian]; Qatabanian; and Haddramitic. These four scripts were older than post-Islam "classical Arabic".

The Sabean or Himyaritic [Haramitic] has been obtained from numerous inscriptions found near Aden and in other parts of southern Arabia. The spotty locations of all such inscriptions and their estimated dating show Ancient Egypt as their origin; and that that they were duplicated in such Asiatic regions in geographical lines from Egypt to Sinai and then to these Asiatic regions.

The Egyptian Source of the South Arabia Alphabetical Letter-forms—In addition to the obvious sameness of the letter-forms found in South Arabia as compared to the same writing forms in Ancient Egypt during and earlier in time than that found in South Arabia, such sameness is further evident from the following facts:

> 1. The South-Semitic alphabetical letter-forms are basically Egyptian uncials with incorporated vocalic markings; as opposed to the mostly-Egyptian cursive

style that is found in the inscriptions in Northern Arabia.

2. The general aspect of the script is square and monumental. This unique style is found in earlier numerous Egyptian papyri and monuments throughout Egypt, including the mining sites in Sinai, earlier than the so-called "Proto-Sinaitic inscriptions" estimated as being from 1300 BCE.

3. The Egyptian origin of both these unique, vocalized, marked uncials and the Egyptian cursive style are both found in the inscription from Balu, which proves the existence of a form of this unique style in the Ancient Egyptian settlement of Moab at about the twelfth century BCE.

4. The discovery of inscriptions at Safa, in the neighborhood of Damascus, has supplied another intermediate link between these unique vocalized marked uncials found prominently in Southern Arabia and the Egyptian cursive style found prominently in Northern Arabia.

5. Similar inscriptions of these Egyptian vocalized, marked uncials are found near the tip of the Gulf of Aqaba around the 8th/7th centuries BCE.

Below is a comparative table of Sinaitic and South Semitic signs — Sinai, Byblos, Balu, Ur, and South Semitic:

Sinai	Byb-los	Balû	Ur	{Minaean Sabaean} Lihyânian	South Semitic - Arabian Thamûdean	Safâitic	Value
ʊ ʊ	א א	ʰ		ʰ	▽ ʊ ▽	ʰʰ ʰ ⊃ ϫϫ I⊦	ϰ I ϰ ϰ ϰ ϰ	'
⊂ ⊃	ϭϭϭ	ո	ŋ	ո	ոʊ	ոո ϽϿ	ϰ(⊃⊂∪ո	b
∟ ⊥	ϡ∖	⊿	ɾ ϡ	⊐	⊐	◻ ο	∧ ո ο	g
◀ ‿	⊲⊲	Ϸ .	▷⊲	ǁ	ϸ ϸ ϸ	ʤ ʤ ɟ ─ ─	⟨⟩⊢ⵏ⟨⊦	d
∢ ϒ	─	ϒϒ ϒJ		ᴍ	ᴍ⩟⩡	⊤ ⊥ ϒ ⟑	⊤⊥⟨⟩	đ
	⥛	ϒ		ϒϒ	⟩⟩⩛	ϒ⊥ ϒϒ ʰ	ϒ⅃⎮ɼ⅃∟	h
	ϒ			⊕	⊕⟡⩢	⊕⊖⊟⥼⊛⥈⊟⊝	ⵉ⊝⊛⊕⊙	w
≖ ⊦	ɪ⫟		⏀	ɪ	ϰ ⊦	⊤ ⊓	⊤	z
⩌⩌ ⩌	⪽	⩿		⪽ϒ	∧ ∧ ∧	⩌ ⩌ ɜɜ ⪧ ⩛ ⩙	{⩓⩛⩌ ⋺⋹⋖}	ẖ
⩜	─		⋌	ϒϒϒ	⫝̸ ⫝̸ ⊿⋋ ⫝̸	⨯	⨯	ṭ
		⩍		⬜	⬜	⧣ ⩎ ⫝̸ ⩎ ⋺	⥄ ⩎⩎ ⫝̸ ⫝̸ ⫝̸ ⫝̸⫝̸	y
				⫷⊦		⫷⊦⫷⊦	⨐⨐⨐⨐⨐⨐	ḏ
	⫞		ϙ	ʄ	ϟ ϟ	ϟⵉ ϟⵈ	⨐⨐⥓⨐⨐⨐⨐	y
	⩛	⫟	⋂ϙ⋂	⋂	⩗ ⩘	⋂⋂⨅⋂ ⋂⋂⩗⊿	⨐⨐⥄⥀⥀⥈	k
⨐⥀	⫒⫒⫒	⫟	⋃∧	⊣	⨐⨐⨐	⨐⨐⥀ ⋉⊤⨐⩛⅃	⨐⅃⫟⫞	l
	⫟	⩌	0	⨐⨐⅃⨐	⩊⊃⩗⩊	{⨐⩊ ⊃ο ⋒⩎}	⊚⊛⩊⩊⨐ϒ⋀	m
⨐	ϟϟ		⊮⩯⩎	ϟϟ	⫟⊦⫟	ϟϟϟϟ⨐ⵉ'	⋅	n
⨆	⫡		⋂	⋂	⩎ϖ⩛⥈	⩎⩎ ⊂ ⊐	∧ ⩗⊂⊐	s'
⊖	ο			ο	ο ο	ο ⋅ ⋮	⋅ ⊖ ⌢ ⋅	ʿ
	─	⪡		⊓	⫝̸ ⫟	⫟ ⩘	⨐ ⨐ ⨐	ġ
	⨒		⊖⊖	⊖◇	⊖ⵉⵉⵉ	⊓⊓⋿⊋⋿⫟	{⨐⨐⩇⨐⩇}	p, f
⧗	⧖			ϒ⩎⩛	⩎⩎⩛⩗⩎	⩗⋱⅃⅃⋶⊥⋶⊕	⨐ⵉⵉ⩗⋉	ṣ
	─		ⵏ		⅂	⨐⨐ ⨐⨐⨐⫝̸⨐⫝̸⫝̸	⨐ ⫝̸ ⧣	ḍ
	ϙ			⧩	⧩⧩	ϙ	⧩⧩	q
	⋂		( )	⟩⫞	⟩⟩	⟩⟨	⫝̸⫝̸⊃⊂	r
⊔⫟	⨐	⨐		⨐	⨐	⨐⨐⥓⨐⅃⅃	⨐	š
⨯ ⨁	⨯⨁			⨯	⨯	⨯ ⨁	⨯ ⨁	t
⩛ ⊖	─		⨐	⨐	⨐⨐⨐	⨐	⨐⨐⨐⨐⨐	ṯ

6. The estimated dating of the inscriptions in South Arabia proper appears around 500 BCE to 600 BCE, and it continued to be used until around 600 CE.

7. Western academics claim that the Sabaean "alphabet" has 29 letters. It is only 28 letters, as two of the presumed 29 letters are a variation of a same letter. Such 'variation' occurs exactly in the Ancient Egyptian [and later "Arabic"] alphabet.

8. Based on no facts whatsoever (and circulated as such by Western academics), it was wrongly stated

that the order of the letters in Southern Arabia do not follow the ABGD sequence/order.

There is no single evidence to support such a variance. No evidence was ever presented, and no reasons and/or rationale for a non-ABGD sequence was given by Western academics.

9. Other inscriptions that were found in Southern Arabia are of the typical Egyptian cursive style. However, such cursive scripts are rarely mentioned by Western academia as in order to highlight the uncials style in a prominent light!

10. Variations in forms—as mentioned several times before—occurs for many reasons, such as from writing surfaces, writing tools, subject matter, level of the inscriber/writer's knowledge, etc.

Shown below is a table with two columns — South Arabian letters (column 1) formal and (column 2) cursive.

Shown below a recovered South Arabian inscription:

And again, the very same alphabetical characters have been in use in the most prominent country in the region (Egypt)—as shown in the monumental work of Petrie's *Formation of the Alphabets* and in several locations throughout this book.

11. This unique Egyptian uncial style that is found prominently in the Southern Arabia's Sabaean region was also a contemporary relative of the same style that was found further to the north for writing down the Thamudic, Lihyanite, and Safaitic inscriptions using the same 28-letter alphabet. Below is the "Sabaean alphabet":

H 𐩱 ᐋ ᑎ ? ▥ Ψ 𐩻 Φ 𐩢 Ψ ᐈ ᐃ ᑎ ᐅ
X ᑎ 8) ♦ 𐩧 ◇ ○ 𐩧 𐩻 𐩯 ᑎ 𐩨 ᒪ

12. This unique Egyptian uncial style that is found prominently in the Southern Arabia's Sabaean region was also used across the Red Sea in Ethiopia, where it changed its name, being the classical Ethiopic (**Ge'ez**).

So Western academics go round and around, naming a "separate" alphabet to any insignificant group/region of their choice; but always ending by saying how similar to each other such "separate" alphabets are! Again and again, it is a distinction without a difference!

17.4 "ARABIC": THE STOLEN EGYPTIAN LANGUAGE

The rise and unexpected sweeping success of the Islamic forces in the 7th century CE prompted the need to write the Koran. The Moslem Arabs scrambled, after the sudden rise and success of their forces, to have the Koran printed. They utilized the existing Ancient Egyptian cursive style that was commonly used in northern Arabia, and tried to make an independent language out of it.

The (Koranic) Arabic language tried to look different from its Ancient Egyptian source by re-arranging the order of the ABGD alphabet to a, b, t, th, etc., which caused them more problems. Other Semitic languages, like Hebrew, maintained the same order of the ABGD alphabet.

It was and is a pathetic attempt to give a form of identity to a new "religion" by awarding them with a "new" language. With the exception of a few changes in letter-forms and adding plenty of dots, it remains the Ancient Egyptian language in every and ALL regards. More analysis of letter-forms in Ancient Egypt as compared to present letter-forms can be found in Chapters 12 and 23 of this book. This twisted Arabic script survived and continues to survive only because it is the only permitted language for the Koran and prayers for the Moslems. The fate of "Arabic" is connected to the fate of Islam.

Despite such attempts, the British Egyptologist Alan Gardiner, in his book *Egyptian Grammar*, page 3, stated:

> "**The entire vocalic system of Old Egyptian may indeed be proved to have reached a stage resembling that of Hebrew or modern Arabic**"

As for other pillars of a language such as grammar, syntax, etc., it remains exactly like the Ancient Egyptian language.

The British Egyptologist Alan Gardiner, in his book *Egyptian Grammar*, page 2, stated:

> "**The Egyptian language** *is related, not only to the*

> Semitic tongues (Hebrew, <u>Arabic</u>, <u>Aramaic</u>, Babylonian, etc.), but also to the East African languages (Galla, Somali, etc.) and the Berber idioms of North Africa. Its connection with the latter groups, together known as the Hamitic family, is a very thorny subject, but the relationship to the Semitic tongues can be fairly accurately defined. <u>In general structure</u> the similarity is very great; Egyptian shares the principal peculiarity of Semitic in that its word-stems consist of combinations of consonants, as a rule three in number, which are theoretically at least unchangeable. Grammatical inflection and minor variations of meaning are contrived mainly by ringing the changes on the internal vowels, though affixed endings also are used for the same purpose.

The "Arabic Language" complies exactly with the all linguistic characteristics of the much older Ancient Egyptian language which was detailed in Chapter 15 of this book. Such include (but are not limited to) Ancient Egyptian prototypal interconnected lexicon, grammar, and syntax such as the significance of verbs, verb roots, verb stems,, verb classes and structures, the conjugation scheme for verbs, and Egyptian prototypal etymology/lexicons and word formation/derivations from a three-letter root (which signifies a certain general concept) into numerous patterns through the use of intermediate vowels and prefixes, infixes and suffixes, etc.; in addition to types and structures of syllables as well as syntax/word orders and sentence types.

And just like Ancient Egyptian writings, so-called "Arabic" employs two primary scripts with several calligraphic variations which continue to be used extensively for various purposes:

> 1. Easy to read—called "Bassri" is legible and clear—and hence, "Bassri" means "vision/eyesight", with rounded forms. This style has nothing to do with any particular city/geographic location.
>
> 2. Easy to write—called "Kufii", which means "hand", which also has nothing to do with any particular city/geographic location. It is written with angular forms.

There is no religious distinction in Islam for using uncials to write religious matters. However, some early writings were made in the uncial style.

And it should not come as a surprise that all academics agree that the oldest specimens of the two styles [Bassri and Kufi] in the "new Arabic" are two Egyptian passports of the year 700 CE and a private letter, also written in Egypt, dated in the year 670 CE.

To say that Egyptians speak and write "Arabic" is totally false and illogical. It is the other way around—the "Arabs" have long ago "adopted" and continue to speak and write EGYPTIAN.

17.5 DISTINCTION WITHOUT A DIFFERENCE [SAME WRITING SYSTEM & LINGUISTICS]

G.R. Driver, in his book *Semitic Writing*, page 119, sums up the geopolitical situation of this large Asiatic region east of Egypt that extended from Turkey to the Indian Ocean:

> *"This whole region was broken up into a number of petty warring states."*

In order to provide "historical relevance" to irrelevant regions/peoples, Western academia was/is eager to "grant" an identity to each of their favorite groups/regions by "granting" each of them a distinct alphabet! The objective is to give each of these groups a "historical relevance". So we hear of "distinctive" alphabets called *Moabite, Nabataene, Aramaic, Hebrew, Arabic*, etc.

Yet, the fact remains of the pre-existence of all these "numerous alphabets" in Ancient Egypt prior to their sparse presence in such Asiatic regions, as shown in several locations in this book.

To sum it up, apparent variations are due to one or more of the following very simple reasons:

> 1. Writing surface [clay vs. stone vs. papyrus vs. leather, etc.] and tools provide apparent differences in letter-forms that do not lead to different alphabets!!

> Writings on clay will be devoid of curves, and as such, letter-forms with curves will be slightly modified on clay using dots, lines and dashes.

> 2. Present-day fonts [typefaces] in Latin/English/European languages show very different letter-forms. Such differences are not called "different alphabets" despite the fact that present differences are more distinct than letter-forms found in the old

inscriptions in North and South Arabia and in-between.

3. Each Egyptian [and, later, "Arabic"] letter has had up to 4 forms—an uncial form and 3 possible slight variations depending in the letter's position in a cursive writing of a word—initial, middle, and end.

4. Too much is made of the number of letters in an alphabet. Western academics ignored a dot in 6 of the 28-letter alphabets, and thus concluded an alphabet to be of only 22 letters and not the [standard] 28 letters. Also, sometimes they thought that it was more than 28 letters by mistaking a ligatured two-letter as being a single letter; or counting various orientations of the same letter as several letters; or considering an embedded vocalic mark within a letter as a new letter.

5. Some scripts have vocalic notations, while others have none. As stated earlier, the use of such signs is generally limited to a specific purpose—religious, musical, and the like. Western academia grossly misunderstood its purpose and usages, assigning an independent script for those with signs and a different script to those that do not have them. In other cases, they considered such vocalic notations to be signs of "progression/development"!!!

6. Ignorant/careless changes in the orientation of letter-forms by turning them round 90 degrees or by dropping superfluous strokes.

7. There is no distinction between the four pillars of

the language—including etymology- for all parts of this region.

The British Egyptologist Alan Gardiner, in his book *Egyptian Grammar*, on page 3 stated:

> "*The entire vocalic system of Old Egyptian* may indeed be proved to have reached a stage *resembling that of Hebrew or modern Arabic*"

Affinities and characteristics of the Ancient Egyptian language were described by Egyptologist Alan Gardiner in his book *Egyptian Grammar*, on page 2:

> "*The Egyptian language is related, not only to the Semitic tongues (Hebrew, Arabic, Aramaic, Babylonian, etc.), but also to the East African languages (Galla, Somali, etc.) and the Berber idioms of North Africa. Its connection with the latter groups, together known as the Hamitic family, is a very thorny subject, but the relationship to the Semitic tongues can be fairly accurately defined. In general structure the similarity is very great; Egyptian shares the principal peculiarity of Semitic in that its word-stems consist of combinations of consonants, as a rule three in number, which are theoretically at least unchangeable. Grammatical inflection and minor variations of meaning are contrived mainly by ringing the changes on the internal vowels, though affixed endings also are used for the same purpose.*

The facts remain as outlined above: that ALL such "alphabets" are one—being the Ancient Egyptian alphabet— and that the four pillars of the Egyptian language are the same pillars of all these languages *manufactured* by Western academia.

Chapter 18 : The African Connections

18.1 THE TRADITIONAL "IMMIGRANTS" GE-EZ LANGUAGE [DEAD OR ALIVE?!].

Long ago, movements and mercantile relations were very common between the peoples of Southwest Arabia on the west side and the coastal shores of Abyssinia/Greater Ethiopia on the west side of the Red Sea.

It is, however, claimed by Western academia that from the south of Arabia, some of the Sabaeans crossed over into the African coast sometime early in the first millennium BCE; for they only had to cross the Straits of Bab el-Mandeb in the Red Sea to be based in the northern part of the Ethiopian plateau.

It is also claimed that the "new settlers" somehow abandoned their identity of being Sabaeans and instead called themselves Ghe'ez, *"the emigrants"* , their language being 'Lisana Ghe'ez', *"the speech of the emigrants."*

Because "Ghe'ez" means "emigrants", Western academia looked for immediate neighboring lands as the source.

Despite the lack of evidence, academics keep on repeating that they came from Yemen, across the Red Sea!

It is not worth the effort in this book to defend the obvious: that the emigrants/settlers came directly from Egypt. In this book, we will follow the account that the African settlers came from South Arabia—despite this being arbitrarily presented by Western academics—because it will lead us back to Ancient Egypt as the source, no matter how much Western academics want to ignore the role of Ancient Egypt.

Western academics gave two different names for the language in both places, despite their concurrence that they are one and the same! As such, the script in South Arabia is commonly known as "Sabaean", and it is called "Ghe'ez"/"Ge'ez" for the coastal shores of Abyssinia/Greater Ethiopia!

The traditional Ge-ez writing system mirrors that from South Arabia, on the other side of the Red Sea. In fact, a great number of southern Arabian inscriptions have been discovered in many places in the north of Ethiopia and the south of Eritrea – that is to say, in the province of Tigré, identical with what once was Aksum, as attested to by the 500 monumental Sabaean inscriptions.

The earliest Ethiopic/Abyssinian inscriptions—like their counterparts across the Red Sea—were written in a purely consonantal/uncial script. Each consonant/uncial was slightly modified by the use of vocalic markings. This alphabet is still used today, modified, to write in the modern Ethiopian languages.

Below is the Sabaean alphabet:

Below is the Ge-ez alphabet, which has the very same letter-forms and sound values in Sabaean and Ancient Egypt.

And all the above looks exactly the same as shown below from an Old Abyssinian inscription from the second half century, CE:

In order for Western academics to establish a new identity for this African region, they want us to believe that these Sabaeans who emigrated across the Red Sea to Africa have made major changes to their own form of writing! They further claimed that it was either a gradual transformation of the southern Semitic writing or the deliberate work of an individual!

In comparison, no such suggestions can be made for British people emigrating across the whole world to Canada, Australia, or New Zealand (that these British immigrants have drastically changed their native English language), because such suggestions are totally outlandish!

Here are the main outlandish claims of changes to the African emigrants' writing system:

> 1. The early form of Ge'ez was basically written from right to left, and on occasion was written in boustrophedon (the cause for the reverse orientation of some letters in Ethiopic), which is writing in alternate lines in opposite directions, as from left to right and then from right to left on the next line, and then left to right on the next line, and so on.

> Later, to distinguish itself from the other Semitic writings [why, who, when?], the form of left to right *prevailed*.

> 2. It is also claimed that these new Sabaean emigrants used only 24 alphabetical characters [out of the 28/29 alphabetical characters] from their own Sabaean writing system in their "renamed language" of Ge'ez. Western academics do not make any sense, in addition to not being factual. Would they expect British emigrants to Australia to forgo some of their English language's letters?!!

3. Ge'ez inscriptions are found—just like other locations—with (and others, without) vocalized markings. Again and again, Western academivs assign a *"new and improved language"* for uncials with vocalized markings!!

As explained earlier, vocalic markings in the archetypal Egyptian language were used extensively in religious and poetic writings where the exact pronunciation is mandatory. So, if Ge-ez writings are used for religious writing scripts, then they naturally include extensive vocalic markings. This feature does not make it a separate language from a script with a little or only a few of such vocalic markings!

The Ge'ez texts are almost completely ecclesiastics in nature. Today Ge-ez remains as a liturgical and worship services language used by both the Christians of Ethiopian Orthodox Tewahido Church and the Beta Israel Jewish community of Ethiopia.

In summary, the overly-hyped differences between Semitic Sabaean/South Arabia and Ethiopic Ge'ez—and by extension, Ancient Egyptian alphabetical writings—is a distinction without a difference. And in all matters of etymology, grammar, syntax, etc. – that what makes a language a language – there is absolutely no difference whatsoever between Sabaeans, Ge-ez and the [Ancient] Egyptian language.

18.2 AMHARIC—A RESHUFFLED GE-EZ

Consistent with Western academics' practices of "awarding" a new-named language (here, Amharic) for a new religion [Christianity], Western academics fabricated two steps in order to reach their objective:

> 1. The South Arabian immigrants [Ghe-ez] modified their own native language [Sabaean] to be called 'Ge'ez, just like that! "The *Sabaean language is dead, Long live Ge'ez*"!
>
> 2. When Christianity took over Ethiopia, a quick reshuffle of Ge'ez led them to declare Amharic as the NEW language, and Ge'ez was *dead*! Sort of – since it continues to be used in the Ethiopian Church! We are told to forget about Ge'ez, which academics declared a dead language. We have now the new and improved Amharic—*Ge'ez is dead. Long live Amharic*!

How has Ge'ez been replaced with Amharic when, in the same breath, Western academics admit that Ge'ez has been and continues to be the liturgy language of Ethiopian Orthodox Tewahedo Church?!

A few academics tell us that at about the year 1300 CE, a family from the province of Amhara obtained possession of the throne, and the Ghe'ez language has been replaced, in the court and capital of Gondar, by Amharic!

However, the vast majority of Western academics tells us that the Ethiopic Amharic script developed from the script of Ethiopia's classical language, Ge'ez, was derived from Sabaean script!

To break the chord of its Semitic/Egyptian origin (or, more accurately, to deny and eliminate the real source so as to call it the "evolution" of Sabaean into Ge'ez), some childish, irrelevant changes were claimed to take place, such as:

1. Orientation of writing from right to left changed to left to right.

2. The Semitic [Egyptian] sequence/order of letters changed from the ABGD sequence to an erratic and unexplained order. Such was also the case in awarding a new renamed language ("Arabic") to the new "religion", Islam, which reshuffled the ABGD order so that the "new" language appears distinct!

3. Names/words related to some letters were changed. The vast majority stayed the same. This is incredibly erratic, since such names/words related to the alphabetical letters will be like saying "D" for "Door", while others may say "D" for "deer". We do not have two different letters "D" because it was identified by two different objects!

4. After saying that the Ge'ez used only 24 letters of its original Sabaean 28/29 letters, Western academics declared that seven more letters were added to the 'shortened' 24-letter alphabet to make up the "new" Amharic alphabet! Shear nonsense!

The so-called six/seven "new" letters in the Amharic were already present in the Sabaean/Himyaritic alphabet, as admitted by Western academics. A case of absent-minded Western academics!

This is exactly the case with the last six letters in the Egyptian alphabet that have a sonic-twin letter in the top 22 letters. These last six letter-forms have the same letter-form of each's primary letter plus an added dot or a bar to distinguish each from its prime sonic-twin. Western academics have always confused such distinction of these last six letters of the 28-letter alphabet.

In Amharic, these letters are constructed on the same principle by the addition of an upper bar or a crossbeam.

All such Western academic confusion is self-inflected, for they neglected to notice that the "missing/added" seven letters have always been there.

5. The Apparent variations in the number of letters in the alphabet in the Ethiopic case, as compared to the original 28 Ancient Egyptian alphabets, is the result of considering a phoneme of the archetypal letters as a separate letter—i.e. in some "languages", some phonemes took a life of their own and became "independent" letters.

The fact remains that all sound values of the Ethiopian alphabet are present exactly in the [Ancient] Egyptian alphabet. The fact remains that present-day Ethiopian/Eritrean and Egyptian sounds exactly the same. Such affinities do not even exist in Egypt's immediate neighboring countries.

6. Western academics declared that this new and improved Amharic incorporated vocalic diacritics into the letters by adding strokes to the consonant, following somewhat regular patterns by means of the addition of small appendices to the right or the left of the basic character, above or down, shortening or extending one of its main outlines, and by other differentiations.

This is not new, and was used in earlier writings both in South Arabia, by Sabaeans, as well as by the new immigrant Geez—not to mention much earlier, in Ancient Egypt itself.

Western academics are always eager to "declare" a new language. For Western academics, the absence/presence of vocalic diacritics mean two different languages or 'an evolution' of a 'primitive' language. As explained throughout this book, the use and extent of use of such vocalic marks depends on the nature of the text.

7. There is no distinction between north and south Arabia or Ethiopic—all letter-forms found in this Afro-Asiatic regions are also found in Ancient Egypt, pre-Hyksos Papyri.

8. This new and improved Amharic or Ge-ez or Sabaean "languages/scripts" complies exactly with the all linguistic characteristics of the much older Ancient Egyptian language which was detailed in Chapter 15 of this book. Such include (but are not limited to) the Ancient Egyptian prototypal interconnected lexicon, grammar, and syntax, such as the significance of verbs, verb roots, verb stems,, verb classes and structures, conjugation scheme for verbs, and Egyptian prototypal etymology/lexicons and word formation/derivations from a three-letter root (which signifies a certain general concept) into numerous patterns through the use of intermediate vowels and prefixes, infixes and suffixes, etc.; in addition to types and structures of syllables as well as syntax/word orders and sentence types.

->> **In conclusion, any distinction between the Semitic Sabaean/South Arabia and Ethiopic Ge'ez and its reshuffled Amharic [shown below]—and, by exten-**

sion, Ancient Egyptian alphabetical writings—is a distinction without a difference.

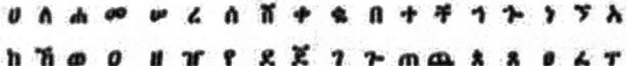

18.3 THE DIRECT EGYPTIAN-ETHIOPIC CONNECTIONS

a. Blue Nile: Egypt's Life Line

Egypt is (and was) one of the most arid areas in the world. More than 90% of Egypt consists of desert area. Only about 5% of the vast country is inhabited, along the banks of the Nile and its branches. This fertile Nile Valley is a strip, 7-9 miles [11-15 km] wide.

The Nile flows through Egypt from south to north. That's because the country slopes downhill toward the Mediterranean Sea. North of Cairo, the Nile splits into several tributaries that constitute the delta—a wide green fan of fertile countryside some 6,000 square miles [15,500 sq km] in area.

The River Nile in Egypt received (and continues to receive) 90% of its water during a 100-day flood period every year, as noted by Herodotus in *The Histories*, [2, 92], where he states:

> "... the water begins to rise at the summer solstice, continues to do so for a hundred days, and then falls again at the end of that period, so that it remains low throughout the winter until the summer solstice comes round again in the following year."

The floodwaters of the Nile come as a result of the rainy season in Ethiopia, which erodes the silt of the Ethiopian highlands and carries it towards Egypt along the Blue Nile and other tributaries. No appreciable amount of water arrives to Egypt via the White Nile that starts from Central Africa. No silt is carried by the White Nile—hence the name "white" means clear.

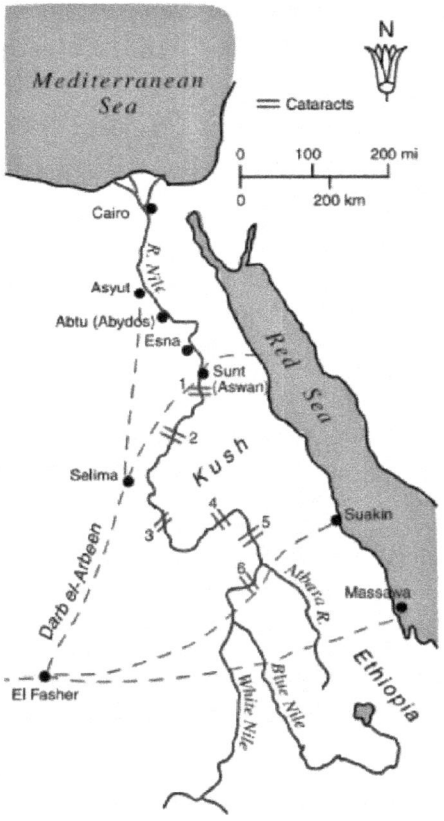

The muddy seasonal rushing water of the Blue Nile provides both water and soil nourishment to the farmlands.

Since time immemorial, there were very special relationships between Egypt and Ethiopia; for whatever happened/happens in Ethiopia has had unspeakable consequences on Egypt and the Egyptians. Well-coordinated efforts were maintained through treaties to ensure the uninterrupted flow of the muddy waters from the highlands of Ethiopia to Egypt proper and in between.

The most important part of the Ancient Egyptian calendar was the total awareness of the rainy season in Ethiopia. The Eve of the 11th of the Ancient Egyptian month of Ba-oo-neh (18 June) is called "Leylet en-Nuktah" (or the Night of the Tear Drop), as it commemorates the first drop that falls into the Blue Nile to begin the annual flood season.

This ancient festival was particularly welcomed by the Egyptian peasants all along the Nile Valley. Diodorus of Sicily tells us how the husbandmen indulged in recreations of every kind, and showed their gratitude to God for the benefits of the inundation. According to Heliodorus, it was one of the principal festivals of the Egyptians. Libanius asserts that these rites were deemed of so much importance by the Egyptians throughout the land, that unless they were performed at the proper season, and in a becoming manner, by the persons appointed to this duty, they believed that the Nile would refuse to rise and inundate the land. [Read *Ancient Egyptian Culture Revealed,* by Moustafa Gadalla, for more information about flood control and water management in Ancient Egypt.] The lands between Ethiopia and Egypt proper were always under the control of the Ancient Egyptians. Several projects were built and maintained by the Egyptians to control and manage the water for the benefit of all in Egypt proper and the lands between it and Ethiopia. [For additional details about Egyptian involvements in securing and managing the incoming waters of the River Nile outside the Egyptian borders, read *Exiled Egyptians* by Moustafa Gadalla.]

b. Punt Land and Ancient Egypt—Ancient Coastal Trade Connections

There were also contacts, in ancient times, by sea; along the Red Sea, the most popular of which was the famed Punt Expedition, as portrayed in Hatshepsut's [1490 to 1468 BCE] Commemorative Temple on the west bank of Luxor (Thebes). The walls there depict the naval expedition that she dispatched to the legendary land of Punt. Plants, animals, and produce are captured in the carvings, with graphic realism.

All evidence point to Punt as being Ethiopia or Somaliland.

Punt was always referred to in the Egyptian texts as a "Holy Land".

While the setting of the scene in Hatshepsut's temple is unmistakably African, there are numerous geological, racial, and botanical un-African matters in these supposedly-realistic friezes. Semitic and African races are shown together, or in adjacent scenes, to show that immigration to such coastal and interior areas are found prior to when Western academics considered the Ghe'ez as immigrants from South Arabia. These depicted Semitic peoples are very Egyptian; which should come at no surprise, considering the prominent status of Ancient Egypt as well as the Egyptian need for securing floodwater sources from Ethiopia.

But Hatshepsut (1490 to 1468 BCE) was not the first Egyptian pharaoh to communicate with the Greater Ethiopian region. There are documentations of several, much earlier expeditions and contacts with the settlers of Punt; one of which was during the reign of Pepi II (2246-2152 BCE), who wrote to the expedition's leader Herkhuf, as was proudly reproduced on the outside wall of Herkuf's tomb:

"... Your letter stated that you have brought a dancing dwarf of the neter (god) Bes, like the dwarf which the treasurer, Bawardede, brought from Punt in the time of Asosi [a king of about a century before this time].

The casual, matter-of-fact reference to Punt is unmistakable.

c. The Oneness of Ethiopic and Egyptian Church

The religious connection between Ancient Egypt and Punt of Greater Ethiopia continued when Christianity became a world religion. Throughout the Christian era, the Ethiopian Church was an integral part of the Egyptian Orthodox Coptic Church, with its base in Alexandria, Egypt. The Metropolitan (abuna) of the Ethiopian Church would be an Egyptian clergyman named by the Patriarch of Alexandria, with such allegiance continuing for almost 2,000 years until 1945, as a consequence of Italy's defeat in the Second World War.

d. Same People in Two Religious Camps

Ghe'ez means 'emigrant'. It is reasonable to consider there was direct immigration from Ancient Egypt in this strategic location of most importance to the welfare of the Ancient Egyptians (not to mention how all early historians spoke of Ancient Egyptian settlements throughout the world). This is not to forget their special relationship with this region, as documented most famously in Hatshepsut's era in her Temple on the western bank of the Nile River at Luxor; as well as the affinities of the Ethiopian Church (being a branch of the Egyptian Orthodox Church).

Ghe'ez [emigrants' language/script] has been and continues to be the liturgy language of the Ethiopian Orthodox Tewahedo Church.

Ethipoia and Egypt were destined to be a Siamese Twins which were separated by two religions—Egypt (becoming predominantly Moslem) and Ethiopia (becoming predominantly Christian). Eretria broke off Ethiopia, since it is predominantly Moslem.

At the end of the day, they are all the same people speaking extremely similar-sounding tongue(s) using the same Ancient Egyptian calendar in their very ancient festivities that adopted Christian "names" in Ethiopia and Moslem "names" in Egypt for the very same festivities.

18.4 EASTERN AFRICAN LANGUAGES

The British Egyptologist Gardiner tells us about the spread of the Egyptian language to Asia Minor and to

Northwest and East Africa. In his book, *Grammar*, Gardiner, on page 2, wrote:

> "<u>The Egyptian language</u> *is related, not only to the Semitic tongues (Hebrew, Arabic, Aramaic, Babylonian, etc.), but also to the <u>East African languages (Galla, Somali, etc.)</u> and the Berber idioms of North Africa.*"

Other languages throughout Africa are beyond the scope of this book. [More information about this and other related subjects are found in *Exiled Egyptians: The Heart of Africa*, by Moustafa Gadalla.]

Chapter 19 : From Egypt To India and Beyond

In the previous chapter we discussed diffusion patterns of the Ancient Egyptian vocalic/spoken and alphabetical writing forms into Greater Ethiopia and the east African regions.

In this chapter we discuss diffusion patterns of the Ancient Egyptian vocalic/spoken and alphabetical writing forms into India; both from sea and land; and further diffusion beyond India.

19.1 FROM EGYPT VIA YEMEN TO THE INDIAN SUB-CONTINENT

Yemen served as an intermediate location between Egypt (as the richest country in the ancient world) and India (as the source of medical plants not native to Egypt). The Ancient Egyptian Medical Papyrus commonly known as "Eber's Papyrus", alone, contains 876 remedies and mentions 500 substances used in medical treatments.

For a prolonged period this lucrative traffic was in the hands of the Sabaeans and was the main source of their proverbial wealth. Yemeni ports were frequented by trading vessels from all parts; from the Red Sea, the Persian Gulf, the coast of Africa, and especially from the mouth of the Indus River, as far back as 2300 BCE.

There was therefore ample opportunity for the transmission to India of the Sabaean writing system which is actually an Egyptian system in whole and in part. It is to this very period that the origin of the 'Indian alphabet' has been assigned.

19.2 THE TWO PRIMARY INSCRIPTION STYLES IN THE INDIAN SUB-CONTINENT

Egypt had intercourse directly with the Indian subcontinent and other coastal regions in between. In addition, there were contacts by land between Egypt and the northern regions of the Indian subcontinent.

Western academics keep talking about *two alphabets* in India, a northern and a southern one. At the end of the day, they admit that they are only different in style! Both styles are found in both north and south India, as found from the incredibly sparse number of inscriptions in this vast subcontinent. All agree that the art of writing was incompatible with the Indian culture. There is no doubt that the found inscriptions are of non-Indian source(s).

The *two alphabets* exhibit such structural resemblances and such agreement in the forms of the individual letters, that they can only be two styles of a singular alphabet—the Sabaean/Ethiopic/Egyptian one.

Isaac Taylor, in his book *The History of the Alphabet*, Vol. 1, page 357, states:

> *"Most of the resemblances between the Ethiopic and old Indian alphabets may, however, be sufficiently explained by their <u>descent from a common source</u>".*

Such a common source is Egypt, where styles of writing were found earlier and were much more abundant; and where writing was an essential pillar of its culture and civilization.

Such writing styles were employed in India in the middle of the 3rd century BCE. Viewing the "Asoka alphabet" of India shows its clear Egyptian origin, via the Sabaeans. The Brahmi-derived scripts are based on the same scripts that had vocalic diacritics "written" by adding strokes to the consonant following somewhat regular patterns.

The two primary inscription styles in the Indian subcontinent are:

a. Mostly Southern Uncial Style

The mostly Southern style is recognized by Western academics as being of Semitic origin, and is always compared and related to Southern Arabia's "alphabet".

Isaac Taylor, in his book *The History of the Alphabet*, Volume 1, page 318, writes:

> *"A very superficial examination will suffice to show that the Asoka alphabet, though it offers hardly any appreciable resemblance to any of the North Semitic alphabets, agrees in a very remarkable way with the general type of the alphabets of the South Semitic family.*
>
> *The common characteristics of the Indian and South Semitic alphabets are their monumental style, the direction of the writing, the vocalization, and the retention of the primitive looped and zigzag forms".*

> *"The general aspect of the Sabean inscriptions agrees so remarkably with those of Asoka that the resemblance cannot fail to strike the most careless observer. In both alphabets the letters are symmetrically constructed out of combinations of straight lines and arcs of circles. Hence the writing is rigid, regular, and monumental, all slanting and cursive forms being absolutely excluded".*

As noted by Taylor, the resemblances between the forms of the Arabian and Indian letters are quite conclusive.

Taylor also noted that the above style was not only limited to India, but is found in Sri Lanka and other Asiatic regions.

b. Mostly Northern Cursive Style

The mostly Northern style is recognized by Western academics as being of *Semitic origin,* and is always compared and related to Northern Arabia's "alphabet". The earliest findings of such a style is dated at 7th century BCE. The main recognized features of such a style are:

– It follows the ABGD sequence of letters.

– It is consonants writing, which means that each letter represents a consonant. Vowels following a consonant are inherent or are marked by diacritics.

– It has three prime vowels, being A, W/O/U — the same as the three prime Egyptian vowels.

– It is a cursive style of writing, with a slanting form.

– Its letters are ligatured according to the Egyptian system, where not all letters in a word can be joined. This phenomena is not understood by Western academics, who look at two ligatured letters as being *"conjunct consonants"* and, as a result, they call such writing system *"consonant clusters"*.

– It was originally written from right to left.

– the same style of inscriptions are also found in Afghanistan and Western Pakistan.

Since it is suggested that this Semitic cursive style came by land from the Middle East, all regions in between Indian subcontinent and the Middle East followed the same exact Egyptian [*Semitic*] system.

–>> The two styles are both from Egyptian ["Semitic"] origin and are always compared and related—by Western academics—to the Southern and Northern Arabian "alphabet(s)". As discussed in details earlier in Chapter 17 of this book, both styles [erroneously called "alphabets', by some] are one singular alphabet written in different styles, and both were used simultaneously—each for a particular purpose and/or limitations of writing tools and surfaces that dictated the various styles. At the end of the day, all agree that the very same styles of the same alphabet were used in abundance in Ancient Egypt long before its use in other parts of the world.

19.3 THE APPARENT LARGE NUMBER OF INDIAN LETTERS

The subject of the number of letters in a particular alphabet as compared to the original archetypal [Ancient] Egyptian alphabet was covered in detail in a previous chapter of this book. Here, we provide special additional attention to the reasons for the large number of the Indian alphabet's 42 letters, as compared to the prime [Ancient] Egyptian's 28 letters.

While the prime [Egyptian] alphabet consists of 28 letters and their applications in the Sabaean, and "alphabets" are mistakenly numbered as 29 letters by Western academics, a much larger number of letters is claimed in the Indian "alphabet" (forty-two characters, of which thirty-three are consonants and nine are vowels).

Careful studies show that this large number can be reduced to the prime [Egyptian] 28 letters. Studies have shown that:

> 1. The four Indian nasals are manifestly differentiations of a single letter, corresponding to the Semitic nasal sound of N as a result of grammatical pronunciation paradigms.
>
> 2. In similar manner, the eight Indian cerebrals and dentals resolve themselves into three primitive types corresponding to the three Egyptian/Semitic dentals.
>
> 3. Four aspirated consonants are also, evidently, of secondary origin.
>
> 4. The nine Indian vowels are all variations of the three primary vowels A, Y & W, reflecting variations in the length/duration of each vowel—being short, long and muted.

5. Counting what is called by Western academics as *"consonant clusters"*—ligatured two or three consonants—as an *alphabetical letter*!!

Deducting from the forty-two letters those which are obviously of secondary origin, twenty-eight characters are left to be identified with the twenty-eight letters of the prime [Egyptian] Semitic alphabet.

19.4 PUNJAB—BOTH STYLES TOGETHER

Assuming that the Sabaean alphabet was introduced into India as early as the 6th century BCE, in the 3rd century BCE (when epigraphic evidence first becomes available) the two alphabetical styles, spreading from different and remote centers, came into contact, actually overlapping each other (to some extent) on the eastern frontier of the Punjab.

That the Southern style [Asoka] of alphabetical writings had, at this time, gained possession of the more extensive region may indicate a certain priority in date; its earlier development implied by the dating of found inscriptions.

The point of contact of the two writing styles is the region of Punjab, where they must have overlapped. A few coins with the two writing styles were proven to predate any Greek presence proclaimed in the region, as is indicated by the character of the art.

Thus, the geographical and chronological conditions present no difficulties to the hypothesis of a derivation source of the Indian alphabet. The two writing styles exhibit such structural resemblances, and such agreement in the forms of the individual letters, as to bring the suggested origin (within the bounds of reasonable probability) to no place other than the richest and most influential country in the ancient world (Egypt), with its unmatched literary traditions with letter-forms that were in Egypt thousands of years before all others.

19.5 INDIA & FAR EAST

It has been claimed that, over the course of a millennium, the adopted Indian [Brāhmī] writing system developed into numerous regional scripts, commonly classified into a more rounded India group and a more angular India group. Nothing has really changed, since we find the consistent use of two styles of writing as having been initiated in Ancient Egypt.

The chief vernacular alphabets of the Indian family constitute four well-marked groups—the Pali, the Nagari, the Dravidian, and the "Malay—occupying distinct geographical regions. The Nagari alphabets prevail in the north of India and the Dravidian in the south; while the Pall type is confined to Ceylon and the regions beyond the Ganges, and the Malay to the islands of the Asiatic archipelago.

It will be observed that this classification of alphabets is essentially coincident with the great lines of linguistic and ethnologic demarcation. The Pall alphabets are used for the isolating tongues of Burma, Siam, and Pegu; the Nagari for the inflectional speech; and the agglutinative languages of the Dravidian and Malay races are expressed by ancient alphabetic types, distinct but not unrelated.

It is more than mere accident that the Pall script, which represents the old Indian alphabet of Asoka in the line of most direct descent, should now prevail only in lands beyond the confines of ancient India.

Chapter 20 : From Egypt to The Black Sea Basin [Georgia and Armenia]

In this chapter, we discuss diffusion patterns of the Ancient Egyptian vocalic/spoken and alphabetical writing forms into the Black Sea countries, with emphasis on the case of the eastern countries of the Black Sea, Georgia and its inland neighbor of Armenia.

20.1 AFFINITIES OF LANGUAGES FROM CENTRAL ASIA TO THE BLACK SEA

For the sake of continuation from the previous chapter, where we tied the Egyptian archetypal origin to the alphabetical letter-forms in northern India, Afghanistan, etc., here we continue to show further affinities between these regions and those of the Black Sea. The comparative chart below between Aramean, Pehlevi, Indo-Bactrian, Armenian and Georgian shows the unmistakable affinities between such "alphabets".

Yet, a direct connection existed between Ancient Egypt and the Black Sea region, as will be explained next.

20.2 ANCIENT EGYPTIAN SETTLEMENTS IN THE BLACK SEA BASIN

Egypt was the most dominant, populous, and famed

country in the ancient world, as affirmed by Diodorus, *Book I*, [31, 6-9]:

> *"In density of population Egypt far surpassed of old all known regions of the inhabited world, and even in our own day is thought to be second to none".*

Classical writers such as Plutarch, Herodotus, and Diodorus told how Ancient Egypt had peaceful colonies throughout the world. Diodorus of Sicily, in *Book I*, [29, 5], states:

> *"In general, the Egyptians say that their ancestors sent forth numerous colonies to many parts of the inhabited world, by reason of the pre-eminence of their former kings and their excessive population;"*

Diodorus, *Book I*, [28, 1-4], also tells of some peaceful Egyptian colonies that were reported to him in Asia and Europe:

> *... a great number of colonies were spread from Egypt over all the inhabited world. To Babylon, for instance, colonists were led by Belus, who was held to be the son of Poseidon and Libya ...*

> *... They say also that those who set forth with Danaus, likewise from Egypt, settled what is practically the oldest city of Greece, Argos, and that the nation of the Colchi in Pontus and that of the Jews, which lies between Arabia and Syria, were founded as colonies by certain emigrants from their country...*

Herodotus, Pliny The Elder, and many others concurred and affirmed, in some detail, the Ancient Egyptian settlements and influence in this eastern and southern region of the Black Sea Basin. Archaeological evidence is also in total concurrence; details of which are beyond the scope of this book, with its focus on languages.

It is worth noting that the Armenian and Georgian calendar is the traditional Sothic calendar of [Ancient] Egypt. It was used in Old Armenia even before the arrival of Christianity.

20.3 PRE-EXISTENCE OF "ARMENIAN/ GEORGIAN" ALPHABETS IN ANCIENT EGYPT

Isaac Taylor, in his book *History of the Alphabet*, pages 235-7:

> *"The <u>Armenian</u> and <u>Georgian</u> must also be regarded as isolated alphabets, as they are only known from manuscripts of comparatively late date, though they exhibit survivals of very primitive forms."*

Also, we read, in *The Myth of Egypt and its Hieroglyphs* by Eric Iversen, page 99:

> *"The German divine Andreas Acoluthus (1654-1704), who had studied Armenian and come to the conclusion that <u>Armenian was derived directly from the language of Ancient Egypt</u>, a theory which he professed himself able to prove by irrefutable etymological evidence".*

From the Table of the Armenian and Georgian alphabets shown above, it will be seen that the Georgian alphabet has preserved, almost unimpaired, the archetypal Ancient Egyptian [ABGD Semitic arrangement], while in Armenian, though the order of the letters has been to some extent disturbed, the primitive names have, in several cases, been preserved with so little change as to admit identification.

20.4 VOCALIC LIMITATION OF ARMENIAN/ GEORGIAN TONGUE VIS-À-VIS ITS NUMBER OF ALPHABET

Apparent variations in the number of alphabetical letters in the "Armenian/Georgian languages" as compared to the prototypal original 28 Ancient Egyptian letters are mainly the result of:

i. the phenomenon of sound shift [explained earlier]

ii. the inability/'laziness' to pronounce some groups of letters. In the Egyptian language as the Mother of all Semitic languages, there are two whole classes of guttural sounds which are foreign to European speech. These are, first, the so-called linguals or gutturo-dentals; and secondly, the guttural breaths or faucal sounds.

See more details on similar circumstances in the Greek tongue as shown in Chapter 21 of this book.

iii. While each letter may have several phonemes [shades of the same sound of a letter that depends/ modulates because of the influence of either/both the sound value(s) of the letter prior/post of a particular letter and therefore subject to its/their sound value(s)]; in some "languages" some phonemes took a life of their own and became "independent" letters.

See more details on similar circumstances in the Greek tongue as shown in Chapter 21 of this book.

20.5 SAMENESS OF ANCIENT EGYPTIAN ALPHABETICAL WRITING SYSTEM IN LATER "GEORGIAN & ARMENIAN LANGUAGES"

The Armenian/Georgian scripts follow EXACTLY the same DISTINCTIVE Egyptian writing characteristics as were stated in Chapter 11, being:

1. Each alphabetical letter can have up to four forms, being: detached/uncial, initial, medial and terminal.

The claimed "Armenian/Georgian texts" follow such distinctive phenomenon. However, such was/is unknown to Western academics, who could not figure it out and therefore considered them as "errors", in such texts!

2. Writing, in the so-called "Armenian/Georgian" scripts, as agreed by all Western academics, is normally from right to left. On some occasions, the direction is Boustrophedon (plough-wise); that is to say, the lines proceed alternately from right to left, and from left to right.

It should be noted that the ancient forms of the Armenian and Georgian letters which are given in the Table have been copied from the oldest known codices in the Bibliotheque Nationale at Paris. They have also been reversed – these scripts being written from left to right, instead of from right to left – as is the case with the other alphabets to which they have to be compared.

3. Just like the Ancient Egyptian writing system, proclaimed "Armenian/Georgian" writings have/had two primary styles: the uncials and cursive.

The Georgian alphabet has two distinct forms, the civil and the ecclesiastical. The oldest alphabet now confined to liturgical use is a square and monumental uncial alphabet of thirty-nine letters called the Khutsuri or 'sacerdotal' (from the word Khutsi, a 'priest'). The other style is the cursive rounded script of forty letters, used for ordinary purposes.

The Khutsuri does not differ very greatly from the ancient forms, from which both alphabetical styles are descended.

4. They followed the unique Ancient Egyptian ligaturing rules of connecting the different letters within a word. Certain characters may be joined to their neighbors, others to the preceding one only, and others to the succeeding one only.

20.6 LINGUISTIC CHARACTERISTICS WITH THEIR ANCIENT EGYPTIAN ROOTS

The "Armenian/Georgian Languages" comply exactly with the all linguistic characteristics of the much older Ancient Egyptian language which was detailed in Chapter 15 of this book. Such includes but is not limited to the Ancient Egyptian prototypal interconnected lexicon, grammar and syntax, such as the significance of verbs, verb roots, verb stems,, verb classes and structures, the conjugation scheme for verbs, and Egyptian prototypal etymology/ lexicon and word formation/derivation from a three-letter root (which signifies a certain general concept) into numerous patterns through the use of intermediate vowels and prefixes, infixes and suffixes, etc.; in addition to types and structures of syllables as well as syntax/word order and sentence types.

Their grammatical structures are incredibly consistent with the Ancient Egyptian alphabetical language. Differences, if any, are reflective of Western academics' frenzy to establish "a new identity" and nothing more. Any "stated" differences are basically differences without distinctions.

PART VI : OUT OF EGYPT—DIFFUSION PATTERNS TO EUROPE

Chapter 21 : Greek: A Shameless Linguistic Heist

21.1 THE EGYPTIAN SETTLERS AND KINGS OF GREECE

As stated earlier, it is a historical fact that Ancient Egypt was the most (if not the only) literate and civilized country in the ancient world. Additionally, Egypt was the most powerful (economically) and the most populated country. Classical writers such as Plutarch, Herodotus, and Diodorus told how Ancient Egypt had peaceful settlements throughout the world.

Diodorus of Sicily, in *Book I*, [29, 5], states:

> *"In general, the Egyptians say that their ancestors sent forth numerous colonies to many parts of the inhabited world, by reason of the preeminence of their former kings and their excessive population..."*

Diodorus, *Book I*, [28, 1-4], also tells of some peaceful Egyptian settlements that were reported to him in Asia and Europe:

> *... a great number of colonies were spread from Egypt over all the inhabited world. To Babylon, for instance,*

> *colonists were led by Belus, who was held to be the son of Poseidon and Libya . . .*
>
> *. . . They say also that those who set forth with Danaus, <u>likewise from Egypt, settled what is practically the oldest city of Greece, Argos</u>, and that the nation of the Colchi in Pontus and that of the Jews, which lies between Arabia and Syria, were founded as colonies by certain emigrants from their country. . .*

By virtue of the eminence of the Egyptian colonists in Asia and Europe, they played a major role in their new settlements. Diodorus, *Book I*, [28,6-7], discusses the significant role of the Egyptian settlements as rulers of these new regions:

> *"Moreover, <u>certain of the rulers of Athens were originally Egyptians</u>, they say. Petes, [Called Peteus in Iliad 2. 552.] for instance, the father of that Menestheus who took part in the expedition against Troy, <u>having clearly been an Egyptian, later obtained citizenship at Athens and the kingship</u>.*

Diodorus, *Book I*, [29, 1-5], also states:

> *"In the same way, they continue, <u>Erechtheus also, who was by birth an Egyptian</u>, became king of Athens. . . . Erechtheus, through his racial connection with Egypt, brought from there to Athens a great supply of grain, and in return those who had enjoyed this aid made their benefactor king. After he had secured the throne he instituted the initiatory rites of Demeter in Eleusis and established the mysteries, <u>transferring their ritual from Egypt</u>. . . And their sacrifices as well as <u>their*

> *ancient ceremonies are observed by the Athenians in the same way as by the Egyptians...*
>
> *... in charge of the more important religious ceremonies of Attica; the pastophoroi were those Egyptian priests who carried in processions small shrines of the gods. They are also the only Greeks who swear by Isis, and they closely resemble the Egyptians in both their appearance and manners."*

Herodotus [500 BCE] stated that he came from Halicarnassus, a Dorian town. He clearly stated the connection between the Dorians and Egypt in *The Histories*, Book 6, [Sections 53-55]:

> [53] *... if one were to trace back, generation by generation, the lineage of Danaë the daughter of Acrisius, the chiefs of the Dorians would turn out to be true-born Egyptians.*
>
> [55] *Enough has been said about all this. Others have explained how and through what achievements they became kings over the Dorians, despite being Egyptians, and so I will not go into that. I will record things that others have not picked up.*

Herodotus, in [55] above, stated that such a fact was common knowledge in his time [500 BCE], and needed no elaboration.

Other connections between the Dorians and Egyptians were referred to several times by Herodotus, such as in *The Histories*, Book 2, [Section 91].

The Ancient Egyptian neteru [gods, goddesses] were

adopted as deities in Greece and elsewhere throughout the Mediterranean Basin and beyond. Herodotus, in *The Histories*, Book 2 [2-8], wrote:

> *"The names of nearly all the gods came to Greece from Egypt."*

This makes sense because there were no language barriers between these Ancient Egyptian settlers and kings in these European countries or in religious and mundane daily activities because they all adhered to the language of the most influential and literal—being Egyptian. Common sense dictates common sense.

The found inscriptions in such countries, despite being very sparse, affirm that there were no linguistic differences in Egypt and such countries.

21.2 GREEKS AS EMPLOYED SECURITY GUARDS IN EGYPT

Egyptians are renowned worldwide as un-warlike people who can't (and won't) fight. The European presence in Egypt began when the Assyrians marched into Egypt and conquered the country as far as Luxor (Thebes), during the 7th century BCE.

In 654 BCE, the Egyptian Psammatichus, from Sais, hired Greek (Ionian and Carian) mercenaries to drive the Assyrians out of Egypt. The Egyptians allocated tracts of land as a base/garrison for the foreign troops to use while they were fighting the enemy. Herodotus wrote about these facts in *The Histories*, Book Two [154]:

> *"The docks and ruined houses of their first home, where*

they lived before Amasis moved them to Memphis, were still to be seen in my day."

21.3 GREEK MERCENARIES AND THE ABU SIMBEL INSCRIPTIONS

Isaac Taylor, in his book *The History of the Alphabet*, page 5, states that the "Greek" alphabet first appeared thousands of miles away from Greece and deep inside Egypt, beyond the southern end of its populated green Nile Valley:

> *"<u>The first absolutely firm standing ground in the history of the Greek alphabet</u>, and consequently in the history of our own, is furnished by a monument which appertains, not to Hellas, or to any of the numerous seats of Hellenic culture, but to the Nubian desert, a region so remote as to be almost beyond the confines of ancient civilization. At Abu Simbel, or as it used to be more correctly called, at Ipsambul."*

Isaac Taylor, in his book *The History of the Alphabet,* again on page 9, states:

> *"We have therefore at Abu Simbel nine records which may claim to be the earliest Greek inscriptions in existence to which any positive date can be assigned."*

Below is The Abu Simbel record; as shown in all references

ΒΑΣΙΛΕΟΣΕΛΘΟΝΤΟΣΕΣΕΛΕΦΑΝΤΙΝΑΝΨΑΜΑΤΙΧΟ
ΨΑΥΤΑΕΓΡΑΨΑΝΤΟΙΣΥΝΨΑΜΜΑΤΙΧΟΙΤΟΙΘΕΟΚΛΟΣ
ΕΠΛΕΟΝΗΔΘΟΝΔΕΚΕΡΚΙΟΣΚΑΤΥΠΕΡΘΕ ΥΙΣΟΠΟΤΑΜΟΣ
ΑΝΙΗΑΛΟΓΛΟΣΟΣΔΘΤΕ ΠΟΤΑΣΙΜΤΟ ΑΙΓΥΠΤΙΟΣ ΔΕΑΜΑΣΙΣ
ΕΓΡΑΦΕΔΑΜΕΑΡΧΟΝΑΜΟΙΒΙΧ ΟΚΑΙΠΕΛΕΡΟΣΟΥΔΑΜΟ

It is obvious that such letter-forms are found exactly throughout Ancient Egypt long before, during, and after the times of such few inscriptions—as shown in the monumental work of Petrie's Formation of the Alphabets and in several locations throughout this book.

Here are some other background facts about these bogus *"Greek"* inscriptions:

> 1. The referenced inscription consists of five lines of writing, among several other records that appear to be inscribed by different people in different times.

> 2. With no evidence whatsoever, Western academics declared that the inscriptions are related to a military mission of Greek and Carian mercenaries who were in the service of Psammetichus, an Egyptian king from the twenty-sixth dynasty, and it must therefore date from the 7th century BCE, or from the beginning of the 6th.

> Neither the name of the Pharaoh nor a calenderial month/year are mentioned in the inscriptions, as is the case with ALL Ancient Egyptian records/documents.

> 3. Western academics claim that these few inscriptions were made *"to record that a military mission undertook an exploration, sailing on to Kerkis, where they found navigation stopped by the second or Great Cataract. On their return they halted at Abu Simbel, and left there this record of their journey."*

This whole statement is made up by Western academics, and the text itself does NOT indicate anything about a "military mission"!

4. If there was a military mission, Western academics do not deny that, as is always the custom, such a military mission is accompanied by a scribe from the king. It is the Egyptian scribe who records events—which makes the inscriptions Egyptian.

The letter-forms of said inscriptions are simply Egyptian!

21.4 PRE-EXISTENCE OF THE PROCLAIMED "GREEK" ALPHABETICAL LETTER-FORMS IN ANCIENT EGYPT

All the proclaimed "Greek" letter-forms were found in abundance throughout Ancient Egypt LONG time before the Greeks, as shown clearly in Petrie's *Formation of the Alphabets* and as shown in different locations throughout this book. More tables will be presented in this chapter to show the sameness of letter-forms in Ancient Egypt much earlier than the Western-proclaimed "Greek".

That the "Greek" alphabet is of Egyptian [later Semitic] origin is undisputed. The sequence of the letters, their graphic forms, and their names have no semantic value in Greek and are strictly Greek pronunciations of the Egyptian [later Semitic] letter names.

Isaac Taylor, in his book *The History of the Alphabet*, Vol. 1, page 74:

"Not only do the names of the Greek letters [Alphabet]

thus testify to a Semitic origin, but the arrangement of the characters proves that they were handed over in the form of a complete alphabet by the Semites to the Greeks".

Western academics want us to believe that Greek came from the Semitic "Phoenician" alphabetical letter-forms. Even if we accept Western academia's claim of a Phoenician source of the "Greek" alphabet, all evidence proves that the "Phoenicians" adopted the Egyptian writing system 100%. Indirectly or directly, Ancient Egypt is the source of the "Greek" alphabet.

Other classical writers also stated that Egypt was the original source of alphabet, as explained in the following quotation from Isaac Taylor's book, *The History of the Alphabets*, Vol. I [pg. 83]:

"Eusebius has preserved a passage from the alleged writings of the so-called Tyrian historian Sanchuniathon, from which we gather that <u>the Phoenicians did not claim to be themselves the inventors of the art of writing, but admitted that it was obtained by them from Egypt. Plato, Diodorus Siculus, Plutarch, Aulus Gellius, and Tacitus, all repeat the same statement</u>, thereby proving how widely current throughout the ancient world was the opinion that the ultimate origin of letters must be sought in Egypt. It may suffice to quote the words of Tacitus, who says, 'Primi per figures animalium Aegyptii sensus mentis effingebant; (ea antiquissima monimenta memoriae humanae inpressa saxis cernuntur) et litterarum semet inventores perhibent. Inde Phoenicas, quia mari praepolle-

bant, intulisse Graeciae, glorimque adeptos, tanquam reperirint quae acceperant." Tacitus, Ann., xi. 14.

Below are Early "Greek" inscriptions from a vase found in Athens; followed by four rock-cut inscriptions from Thera, as per Gelb [exactly like AE letter-forms]

Assembled below are the most "proclaimed" inscriptions as being "Greek" from various locations in Greece.

It is obvious that such letter-forms are found exactly in Ancient Egypt long before, during, and after the times of such few inscriptions. For reference to letter-forms in Ancient Egypt, refer to Chapter 12 of this book, as well as Petrie's book, Formation of Alphabet.

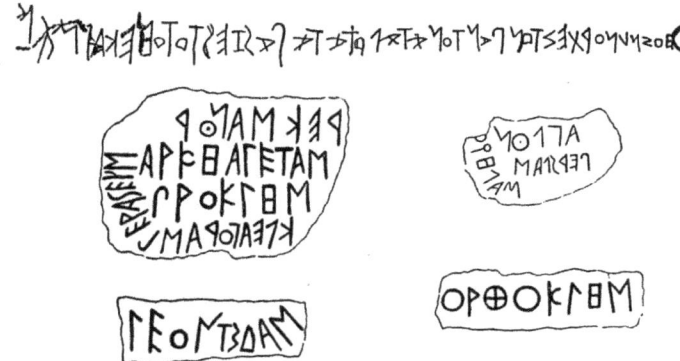

A claimed "Original Greek" text:

Below is Early Greek alphabets in 7 regions:

	Athens	Crete	Thera	Naucratis	Corinth	Melos	Naxos	
א	∀ ∀ ⋋ ⋌ ⋏ ⋏ ⋏ ⋏ ⋏	∧ ∧ ∧ ∧ ∧ ∧	∧ ∧ ∧ ∧ ∧	∧ ∧ ∧	∆ ∆ ∧ ∧ ∧ ∧ ∧ ∧	∧ ∧ ∧	∧ ∧ ∧ ∧	α
ב	B B	⅂ ß ∧ ɑ	ꓱ ꓱ		ᴎ ᴎ	ꓶ ꓶ	כ	β
ג	⌐ ∧	⌐ ∧ ∧	⌐ (⌐ ⌐ ⌈		⟨ ⟨ ⎴	⌐	∧	γ
ד	∆	∆ ∆ ∆	∆	⊂	∆	∆	∆ ∆	δ
ה	⅂ ⅂ ∃ ⌐ ⌐ ⌐ ∃ E	⅂ ⅂ ⅂ ⌐ ⅃ ∃ E ᴇ ᴧ ⅂ ⅂	⅂ ⅂ ⅂ ⅃ ⅂ ⅂ E ꞓ E	ɛ ɛ	⅂ ⅂ B B ꓑ ⅂ ∃ E	E	⅂ ⅂ Ǝ	ε
ו		⅂ ⅂ ⅂ ⅂ ⊤ ⅂ ⅂ ⌐ ∧ ∧	F		⅂ ⅂ ꓑ F			F
ז	I I	I			I			ζ
ח	B	B H ꞍH	B	ᗏ		H N	B B O	η
ט	⊕ ⊕ ⊙	⊙ ⊕ ♦	⊙ ⊙	⊕	⊕ ⊙	⊙	⊙	θ
.	⌐ ɩ	ᶻ ᴤ ᶻ ᴦ ɔ	ɔꓤᶻᴤᶻ ᶻꓤᴤ⌐	ɩ	ᶻ ᴤ ɩ	ɩ	ɩ	ι
כ,ך	ꓘ ꓘ ꓘ ꓘ	ꓘ ꓘ ꓘ ᐸ ꓘ ꓘ ꓘ ꓗ	ꓘ ꓘ ꓘ ꓘ Ƴ ᴇ K	К	ꓘ ꓘ ꓘ ꓘ ꓘ	K K	ꓘ ꓘ	κ
ל	⌐ ∟ ∟ ⌐ ⌐	⌐ ⌐ ⌐ ⌐ ∟	⌐ ⌐ ⌐ ∟	∧	⌐ ⌐ ∟	∧ ∟	⌐ ⌐	λ
מ,ם	⌐ ⌐ m m m	⌐ ⌐ ⌐ ⌐ᴡᴡ	⌐ M M ⌐	ᴍ M	⌐ M M	M M M M M	⌐ M	μ
נ,ן	⌐ ᴎ ᴎ ꓤ N N N N	⌐ ⌐ ⌐ ᴎ ᴎ	⌐ ⌐ ꓤ ꓤ	N	⌐ ⌐ ᴎ N N	N N N N N	⌐ ⌐ ⌐	ν
ס			⊤		⊤ ⊥	⊥	ɩ	ξ
ע	• ○ ○	○ ○ ◉ ○	° ○ ° ○	⟨	° ◉ ᴄ ᴄ		○	ο
פ,ף	⌐ ⌐ ⌐ ⌐	⌐⌐⌐⌐⌐ᴦ (⌐⌐ᴦᴦ	⌐ ⌐ ⌐ ⌐ ᴦ ᴦ ᴦ	ᴦ	⌐ ᴦ ᴦ ᴦ	⁄ᴦ ᴦ		π
צ,ץ		ᴍ	M M		M M	MᴍM	⋋	ϡ
ק		ꓑ	ꓑ ꓑ		ꓑ		ꓑ	ϙ
ר	⌐ ⌐ ⌐ ꓑ ꓑ ᴅ ʀ ʀ	⌐ ⌐ ⌐ ⌐ ꓑ ⌐ ᴅ	⌐ ⌐ ⌐ ꓑ	ᴅ	⌐ ꓑ ꓑ ᴅ ᴅ	ꓑ ᴅ ʀ ʀ	⌐ ⌐	ρ
ש	ᶻ ᶻ ᶻ ᶻ ᶻ			⟨		⟨	ᶻ ᶻ ᶻ ⟨	σ
ת	⊤ ⊤	⊤ ⊤ ⊤	⊤	⊤	⊤	⊤ ⊤	⊤	τ
ו	⋎ ⋎ ⊤ ∨ ∨	⋎ ⋎ ∨	⋎ ⋎ ⋎ ∨		⋎ ⋎ ∨ ∨	⋎ ∨		υ

Below is comparative chart of Greek and west Semitic writings:

AHIRÂM	RUEISEH	AZARBA'L	IEHIMELK	ABIBA'AL	ELIBA'AL	ŠAPA BA'AL	MEŠA°	ZINCIRU	CYPRUS	SARDINIA	GREEK OLD	GREEK LATE	LATIN
K	K	≮	K,ƙ	≮	≮	≮	≠	≮	≮	≮	⋎, A	A	A
9	9	9	9,9	9	9	1	9	9	9	9	9, 8	B	B
1			⌐	⌐	⌐	ʌ,1	1	⌐	⌐	⌐	1, ⌐	Γ	C (&G REFERENCE?)
⊿	⊲		⊿		⊿	⊿	⊲	⋀	⊿,⊿	⊿	⊿	⊿	D
⊀			⊀				⋾	1	⋶	⋶	⋾, ⋿	E	E
Y		Y	Y		Y	Y	Y	4	4	4	⋾, Y, V	(Y aruw)	F (&U,V,Y arw)
I		I	I		I	I	⊥	I	I		I	Z	(Z " w)
M	B	B	H,B		B	B	M	M		B	B	H	H
⊙						⊙	⊙	⊙		⊙	⊗, ⊙	Θ	
2	2	2	2		2	2	2	2	2	2	2, ⌐	I	I
⋎	⋎	⋎	⋎	⋎	⋎	⋎	𐝈	𐝈	X	⋎	1, ⋎	K	K
ℓ		ℓ	ℓ	ℓ	ℓ	ℓ	ℓ	ℓ	ℓ	ℓ	1, ⌄	Λ	L
$		$	$	$	$	y	⋎	y	$	\	⋎	M	M
'	\	'	'		)	\	7	⋏	\	\	\	N	N
╪		╪					╪	╪			王	王	(X " w)
O	O	O	O	O	O	O	O	O	O	O	O	O	O
7		7,7	)		7	>	7	7	7	7	7, 7	π	P
	h		λ	h			⊢	⊢		h	٩, H	(M)	
			φ			?	φ	φ	φ		φ, φ	(φ)	Q
⋀			⋀	⋀	⋀	⋀	⋀	⋀	⋀	⋀	⋀, P	P	R
w		w	w		w	w	w	w	w	w	⋟, ⋞, ⋞	Σ	S
+,X		+	×		✝	+	X	✝	✝	X	T	T	T
											Y,Φ,X,Y,Ω	U.V.X,Y,Z	

21.5 ROBBING AND POSTDATING EGYPTIAN SCRIPTS TO RENAME THEM AS "GREEK"

In order to rob Egypt of a script so as to call it "Greek", Western academic schemes began with confusing the issue about the Ancient Egyptian alphabetical writing system. The fact remains that the so-called "Hieratic" and "Demotic" scripts are nothing more than a single alphabetical system for non-religious writings. Western academia "colonized" the "Coptic" script that was used by the

Ancient Egyptians for their religious writings so as to accredit the [European] Greeks with a "new language".

The Western scheme regarding inventing a separate "Greek" language needed documents, and therefore they robbed Egyptian documents and then set ARBITRARY Dates to undated Egyptian texts so as to make them fit into their scheme to proclaim them as "Greek" texts. They went further, adding names of Ptolemaic "kings" when the text NEVER mentioned a name because, as always in Ancient Egypt, no calenderial date is ever mentioned, and Egyptians never mentioned the name of a sitting Pharaoh. Much more about the corruption and deceit of Western academics in this regard was explained earlier in Chapter 9: Multiple Writing Forms of The Rosetta Stone.

Isaac Taylor, in his book *The History of the Alphabet*, page 150, admits:

> **"The oldest extant specimens of Greek manuscripts have been <u>obtained from Egypt</u>."**

Thus, Egypt was the "rich" source of the proclaimed "Greek" scripts. The biggest portion of the Egyptian robbery to claim it as "Greek" came from the Anastasi collection of several THOUSANDS Egyptian Papyri from Egypt. [See Chapter 14 for more details.]

Here is another stunning admission of the Egyptian origin, from E.G.Turner, because one would have expected that, at minimum, the proclaimed "Greek" papyri came from areas that had had Greek presence. However, that was not the case, as admitted at least twice by E.G. Turner in his book *Greek Papyri: An Introduction*, on page 43:

> *"But the site of Alexandria has provided no papyri, nor has the ancient Greek foundation of Naucratis, to which Sappho's brother went trading. Nor has the purely Greek city of Ptolemais in Upper Egypt."*

E.G. Turner also states, in his book *Greek Papyri: An Introduction*, page 43:

> *"In Middle Egypt the number of places at which [Greek] papyri have been found are few in relation to the ancient populations of the area."*

Here is a summary of Western falsification scheme: After cavalierly proclaiming an Egyptian document as being "Greek", Western academics twist facts so everything must be reconciled towards that "Greek" end. As detailed in Chapter 9 of this book about The Rosetta Stone, a similar falsification scheme was used to make an Egyptian document into a "Greek" document. This corrupt and pathetic scheme has been used over and over again on hundreds of Egyptian documents, as follows:

1. Place of its original Location—Western academies made up a location and gave it a Greek-sounding name for emphasis, to camouflage its location as being an Egyptian site!

E.G. Turner, in his book *Greek Manuscripts of the Ancient World*, on page 21, says:

> *"The absence of criteria for determining the place at which a papyrus manuscript was written is a more serious impediment to knowledge than is commonly realized."*

2. Dating Falsehoods—This is very essential in their Western scheme to fabricate a date that falls within the short Ptolemaic era in Egypt.

It is worth repeating that ALL such Egyptian texts follow the very same limited information, only showing:

1. The day and month of lunar calendar.

2. The day, month and season of the solar/Sothic calendar

3. The reigning year of the sitting Pharaoh.

The year of the reign of a sitting Pharaoh only refers to the title of such a pharaoh and NEVER to his "name"—as is the case on the Rosetta Stone. Here again is another pathetic attempt by Western academia to insert a name of "Ptolemaic ruler" where the text clearly did NOT name such a person/king/ruler!!!

E.G. Turner, in his book *Greek Manuscripts of the Ancient World*, says, on page 21:

> *"In the ancient world the writers of private letters (to judge from those that survive on papyrus) for the most part did not put a date on their correspondence; similarly literary scribes; remain dateless"*

3. Shameless Change of the Word "Priestly" To "Greek"!

Calling the writing style "Greek" is a lie, for according to Budge himself, in his book *Rosetta Stone*, Volume 1, page 167, Budge admits:

> *"but when the allusion is to Greek, the word used is called is a very old one, and is in the dual, "H.aui-nebui"; the germ H. a-nebu, i.e. "lords of the north," er "lords of the marshes [in the Delta]" occurs in the pyramid Texts"*

Budge admits that the term used is found in the Pyramid Texts, three thousand years prior to the Greeks!!

Additionally, the Egyptian word does NOT say anything about 'marshes' or 'north'. It only and simply means 'Priestly' as translated as such hundreds of times from Egyptian documents of all eras by the very same Western academics!

The "Priestly" Style is the uncials style, as discussed earlier in this book. It is this 'style' that was dubbed the Egyptian "Coptic Style" that is found in Ancient Egyptian texts and documents a long time before the Greeks.

4. Shamelessly Substituting "god/goddess" for a Ptolemaic "King/Queen"

Under the cover of claiming "conjectural translation", Western academia went wild. As their prime objective is to show the [European] Greeks as superiors and masters of the Egyptians, they took the "liberty" of translating terms like "our masters", nobles and even neteru (gods, goddesses) to mean "Ptolemaic kings/queens". Academia went even further by putting "Ptolemaic names" when the words/terms were ALL generic titles/epithets!

The text reads, as per Budge's *Rosetta Stone* book, Volume 1, page 169:

> *"in the twenty-third year of the reign of HORUS-RA the CHILD, who hath risen as King upon the throne of his father, the lord of the shrines of NEKHEBET and UATCHET, the mighty one of two-fold strength, the beautifier of ..."*

No name is mentioned of a Ptolemy!

5. Self Serving Conjectural "Decipherment"

Under the cover of "conjectural translations", we find "translated texts" to be more than five-fold the length of text itself—too much added to serve western academies' bad intentions.

They peppered the text with Greek names [repeating a name or two over and over again] despite the fact that the text itself—according to their own interpretation—did NOT include such names. They put names whenever the text read "neter/god" "Lord," " Mighty," or "Lord of two lands."

Magical Papyri with Multiple styles of Writings—Hundreds of Ancient Egyptian magical papyri were proclaimed to be of "Greek" origin just because one of their multi-styles of writing may appear to look like the later "Greek uncials". Just because of a few lines in a document, the whole document was proclaimed to be "Greek"!! As stated earlier, multiple styles of language writing is common, even nowadays. The purpose of each style was explained earlier, in several places in this book. Here, we will present some additional highlights on this particular Western heist of Egyptian documents:

– All these Magical Papyri were found in Egypt. They contain a variety of magical spells and formulae, hymns and rituals.

– Not surprising, all these magical papyri were a part of the HUGE heist, the so-called Anastasi collection, whose origin was not Alexandria but hundreds of miles deep inside Egypt in the city of Luxor/Thebes. Just because the papyri contain uncials which the Greeks later adopted as their language, Western academics claimed it to be of the "Greco-Roman era". To double up on their assertion, they gave these papyri dates to correspond with their stolen items. Yet, as always is the case with these scripts/texts, not a single papyrus has a date on it. It was all fabricated by Western academics in this Greek heist of Egyptian texts/documents.

– The contents and methodology of these texts are overwhelmingly Egyptian. The material is completely Egyptian, and its origins are easily traceable in earlier Egyptian religious and magical literature. The methods used are, likewise, standard Egyptian practices. Egyptian divinities and Egyptian mythological references abound in these magical texts and go back to the earliest Egyptian religio-magic literature that goes as far back as the "Pyramid Texts" about 4,500 years ago. The Egyptian religion and rituals are evident, in whole and in part, throughout these magical papyri.

Funerary Stelae With Multi Styles of Writing—Hundreds of Ancient Egyptian funerary stelae in Egypt were proclaimed to be of "Greco Roman" origin just because one of their multiple styles of writing may appear to look like later Greek uncials. Just because of a few lines in a document, the whole document was proclaimed to be "Greek"!! As stated earlier, multiple styles of writing of a language is common even nowadays. Here are a few facts that make such stelae purely Egyptian:

> i. The scenes depicted on them are essentially connected with the allegory of Osiris, which are found more than 5,000 years ago in places like the *Egyptian Book of the Dead*.
>
> ii. The deities depicted on the stelae are all Egyptian, mainly: Osiris, Isis, Nephthys, Anubis, Horus, Hathor, Thoth, and other related aspects of these deities.
>
> iii. The name of the deceased is always introduced by the word W s i r n – "Osiris of" [an Egyptian theme that every deceased person is Osiris].
>
> iv. No calenderial date is ever given. This was not unknown to Aly Abdalla who, in his book [commissioned and dictated by British sources] *Graeco-Roman Funerary Stelae from Upper Egypt,* page xvii, "writes":
>
>> *"Dating has proved to be the most difficult task of all. This is due to several reasons.*
>>
>> *– The first is the absence of reference on the stelae*

> *to regnal years with names of emperors, or to persons otherwise identifiable.*
>
> *– The second reason is that the poor quality of carving does not readily allow comparison of the hair style of the deceased and other features with imperial sculpture or other portraits, as can be done in the case of painted mummy panels and masks.*
>
> *– The final reason is that the lack of any relevant detailed reports of the tombs themselves and of other objects found in these tombs makes it impossible to determine accurately the date of the tombs and therefore of the stelae."*

Yet these facts never stopped him from pleasing a European audience by making up dates any way so as to make these hundreds of monuments "European-Greco-Roman"! Aly Abdalla in his book [commissioned and dictated by British sources] *Graeco-Roman Funerary Stelae from Upper Egypt*, page 128, "writes" the following statements:

> <u>*"In the absence of a firm date on the stelae and of securely datable finds associated with the tombs from which the stelae have come, it is difficult to date individual examples".*</u>

Aly Abdalla, in his book [commissioned and dictated by British sources] *Graeco-Roman Funerary Stelae from Upper Egypt*, page 128, "writes":

> *– "It has proved impossible to classify the material*

into clear independent groups from which a chronological order can be established as a result of an analysis of stelae reported to have come from the same tomb. It seems as if individual tombs were used over several generations and as a result date classification by find spot is precluded".

<u>*– "The wider groups of scenes of presentation (excluding those with mummies), of offering, of adoration, of the deceased standing or of family scenes do not readily fall into datable units*</u>

<u>*– "The quality of the workmanship in the representation of the deceased does not allow dating from comparative study of hair style or dress as is possible with the painted mummy portraits or masks modeled in plaster".*</u>

<u>*"The wider groups of scenes of presentation (excluding those with mummies), of offering, of adoration, of the deceased standing or of family scenes do not readily fall into datable units."*</u>

Again: these admitted facts never stopped him from pleasing a European audience of making up dates any way so as to make these hundreds of monuments "European-Greco-Roman"!

21.6 VOCALIC LIMITATION EFFECTS OF GREEK TONGUE ON THE 28 PROTOTYPAL ALPHABETICAL LETTERS

The apparent variations in the number of letters in the proclaimed new "Greek alphabet" as compared to the prototypal original 28 Ancient Egyptian alphabetical letters are mainly the result of:

i. the phenomenon of sound shift [explained earlier].

ii. inability/"laziness" to pronounce two whole classes classes of guttural sounds which are foreign to European speech. These are, first, the so-called linguals or gutturo-dentals; and secondly, the guttural breaths or faucal sounds.

Budge, in his book *Egyptian Language*, on page 27, wrote:

> *"The transliteration to remove or modify the gutturaux sounds which exist in the Ancient Egyptian language and miss in the Western languages. So the original gutturaux sounds which characterize the Ancient Egyptian language were sacrificed and disappeared in the current writing."*

In other words, letter sounds not familiar to them were lumped together!

Isaac Taylor, in his book *The History of the Alphabet*, writes, on pages 81-82:

> *"In the Greek alphabet the Semitic semi-consonants (A, W, Y) and guttural breaths (H & <u>A.</u>) became vowels; aspirated mutes and <u>additional vowels were evolved</u>; and the <u>sibilants underwent transformation</u>".*

> *"Five Primitive vowels were formed out of the breaths and semi- consonants, letters which even*

> *in Semitic languages tend to lapse into the cognate vowel sounds. The three breaths, aleph, he, and 'ayin, lent themselves readily to this process, <u>losing altogether their character of gutturals</u>, and sinking into the fundamental vowels, alpha, epsilon, and o-micron."*
>
> *"The semi-consonant yod, which had the sound of the English y or the German j, lapsed easily into the cognate vowel sound of iota. Analogy would lead us to expect that waw, the other semi-consonant, would similarly weaken into the vowel u. The Greek u-psilon does not, however, occupy the alphabetical position of the Waw, but comes among the new letters at the end of the alphabet".*

Isaac Taylor, in his book *The History of the Alphabet*, Vol. I, page 280, states:

> *"The six Greek vowels, alpha, epsilon, eta, iota, omicron, and upsilon, were developed out of aleph, he, cheth, yod, 'ayin, and vau [waw].*
>
> *In Armenian, Georgian, and Mongolian, a similar result has been attained in very nearly the same way."*

iii. The combined effect of persons' inability to pronounce some [Ancient] Egyptian letter sounds resulted in a duplicate of an [easier] existing sound value of another letter [such as Z and Z., for some people]. This led the "new/adopted" language to eliminate the "duplicate" sound from its "alphabet".

Isaac Taylor, in his book *The History of the Alphabet*, writes, on page 81:

> *"In the Greek alphabet ... and the <u>sibilants underwent transformation</u>".*

21.7 SAMENESS OF ANCIENT EGYPTIAN ALPHABETICAL WRITING SYSTEM IN LATER "GREEK LANGUAGE"

The so-called "Greek" texts are stolen Egyptian documents. The analysis of Western academics of such stolen texts shows that the writing system of such texts cannot be anything but Egyptian system in every and all details. Western academics spent enormous energies to make it "distinctively Greek"; but their very own works confirm, without any doubt, that Greek language is a Western-created illusion.

Their own "complaints about scribes' errors", coupled with their ignorance of the peculiarities of the Ancient Egyptian writing system, affirm without a doubt a pan-Greek deceitful "house of cards."

E.G., Turner in his book *Greek Papyri: An Introduction*, says, on page 43:

> *"It may seem platitudinous to insist that even to a good <u>scholar the language of his texts will be a considerable obstacle to ready understanding of them</u>. They will contain words not found in any dictionary, technical and colloquial expressions that have to be worked out analytically, names and places not previously recorded. Above all, common words may wear an unfamiliar, almost unrecognizable look because they are*

<u>misspelled</u>, or because they are represented by a spelling that makes them approximate to the pronunciation of the Hellenistic and Roman period."

The incredible arrogance is a sign of ignorance, contempt and denial.

E.G. Turner, in his book *Greek Papyri: An Introduction*, on page 93:

> *"The manuals of paleographers tell us that it was the task of professional copying-houses to 'proof-read' their texts; ... But several of our surviving papyrus manuscripts, and especially those which are beautifully written, contain such serious un-noted errors that it is clear their 'proof-reading' was of a summary, superficial kind, if done at all.*

Western academics have had a difficult time dealing with and explaining the writing system that they proclaimed to be "Greek". There is a very simple reason for such confusion by Western academics, which is that such scripts follow EXACTLY the same DISTINCTIVE criteria as in the Ancient Egyptian [and later, Arabic] linguistic system. All such proclaimed Greek cursive writings are 100% EGYPTIAN. We follow here the same distinctive points stated in Chapter 11, being:

1. Letters—having up to 4 forms.

2. Orientation—right to left, left to right, and both.

3. Two styles—uncials and cursive/ligatured.

4. Cursive's connectivity/ligaturing rules.

5. No space between words—no word separation.

6. Reading/diacritic/phonetic/accent/cantillation marks/signs.

1. Letters—having up to 4 forms

Ancient Egyptian alphabetical letters can each have up to four forms: detached/uncials, initial, medial and terminal.

The claimed "Greek texts" follow such distinctive phenomenon. However, such was/is unknown to Western academics, who could not figure it out and therefore considered such slight variations in each letter-forms as "errors".

E.G. Turner, in his book *Greek Papyri: An Introduction*, on pages 58-59, says:

> *"Misspellings due to vowel contaminations of this character are encountered frequently in literary texts as well as in documents: their presence or absence in a literary text is a pointer to the degree of education of the scribe, not necessarily to the quality of the underlying text. In private letters and documentary texts such misspellings, combined with unusual consonantal values, can produce words baffling to the eye, but which may give up their meaning to the ear."*

Herbert C. Youtie, after showing several particular examples of those who "translated" texts that assumed/asserted that it is "Greek", wrote in his book *The Textual Criticism of Documentary Papyri, Prolegomena*, on page 46:

> *"Of the twenty-four letters of the alphabet, not one has*

escaped confusion with one or more other single letters or groups of letters. For seven of them the substitutions range from 20 to 37; for eleven more, from 11 to 19; for the remaining six, which are the aspirated stops and the double consonants, from 1 to 8. <u>*The alphabet as a whole has given rise to 371 equivalences*</u>*. And to these may be added the 39 instances in which entire groups of letters have been replaced by other groups".*

Herbert C. Youtie followed up his above-mentioned stunning findings on the following page of his book *The Textual Criticism of Documentary Papyri, Prolegomena,* on page 47:

"This is a striking count for material drawn from fewer than 250 texts.

The number of letters and combinations of letters mistaken one for another would certainly rise if the texts were doubled or tripled."

Herbert C. Youtie, in his book *The Textual Criticism of Documentary Papyri, Prolegomena*, page 47:

"One might therefore be tempted to think that the inability of editors to distinguish the characteristic forms of letters comes close to total incompetence."

Herbert C. Youtie, in his book *The Textual Criticism of Documentary Papyri, Prolegomena*, page 48:

"Numerals give editors almost as much trouble as the alphabet, and naturally so because for the most part they are identical. Integers are confused with other

> *integers as well as with letters of the alphabet; they are sometimes read as fractions or as symbols"*

Western academics, in their confusion, will describe the cursive style as *"careless uncial"*. This form of writing cannot be anything but EGYPTIAN, and is nothing else.

2. Orientation—directional flow

Ancient Egyptian writing is normally from right to left. On some occasions, the direction is Boustrophedon (plough-wise) – that is to say, the lines proceed alternately from right to left, and from left to right.

Similarly, it is acknowledged by all that the direction of signs in writing varies greatly in the oldest "Greek" inscriptions, as it runs either from right to left or from left to right, continuing in boustrophedon fashion and alternately changing direction from line to line. Only gradually did the classical method of writing from left to right assert itself in the Greek system.

3. Two styles—uncials and cursive/ligatured

Just like the Ancient Egyptian writing system, the proclaimed "Greek" writings have/had two primary styles: the uncials and cursive, which was/is ligatured in special rules where some letters may be connected while others may not.

Front and center, Western academics bring attention to "Greek" as the Uncials writing system, since it also resembles present Greek writing. However, the fact remains that this Uncial style was one of two styles; the other being the cursive style of writing. Here again, as shown earlier, Ancient Egypt lead the theme of having two primary alphabetical writing styles: the sacred uncials, and the cursive style for civil and daily affairs.

E.G. Turner, in his book *Greek Manuscripts of the Ancient World,* page 1, writes:

> *"There are documents in which the letters are generally formed separately and not linked together .*
>
> *The term 'cursive' writing in a 'running' movement to a group of several letters which he will write in a single sequence".*

4. Cursive's connectivity/ligaturing rules

Roger S. Bagnall and Dirk D. Obbink, in their book *Columbia Papyri X,* speaking of what they insisted as a "Greek" text, on page 16:

> *"The hand is a rapid, angular cursive, bordering on the severe, with letters taller than they are wide.* <u>*Ligatures are common, but many letters stand as independent elements.*</u>*"*

This follows the unique Ancient Egyptian ligaturing rules of ligaturing different letters within a word. Certain characters may be joined to their neighbors, others to the preceding one only, and others to the succeeding one only. The written letters undergo a slight external change according to their position within a word. When they stand alone or occur at the end of a word, they ordinarily terminate in a bold stroke; when they appear in the middle of a word, they are ordinarily joined to the letter following by a small, upward curved stroke. With the exception of six letters, which can be joined only to the preceding ones, the initial and medial letters are much abbreviated, while the final form consists of the initial form with a triumphant flourish. The essential part of the characters, however, remains unchanged.

Here is an indirect admonition by a "bewildered" Western academic, E.G. Turner, in his book *Greek Papyri: An Introduction*, on page 61:

> *"The same kind of difficulty will occur as the student moves on from handwritings in <u>which the letters are capitals separately made to texts quickly written, where two or more letters or parts of letters are linked together and written in a long wavering line without the pen being lifted from the paper. In ligatures (the name given to strokes which combine in whole or part two or more letters) the basic shape of the letter may be distorted by what precedes and what follows.</u>"*

Unknown to Herbert C. Youtie [as well as ALL Western writers] is the very unique Egyptian ligaturing rules which invalidate such texts asbeing "Greek". Herbert C. Youtie, in his book *The Textual Criticism of Documentary Papyri, Prolegomena*, on page 47, expresses the same confusion that they all have:

> *"In fact, most of the errors utilized in my survey are not due directly to confusion of one letter with another but generally to misreading of groups of consecutive letters and even of entire words. They rest accordingly on the editor's failure to arrive at the writer's meaning".*

5. No space between words—no word separation

There is/was no separation between words in the Ancient Egyptian writing system. Words are never divided at the end of a line, the scribes preferring either to leave a blank space or to stretch out certain letters (hence called 'dilatable') in order to fill out the line. This is exactly the same in the proclaimed "Greek" texts!

E.G. Turner, in his book *Greek Manuscripts of the Ancient World*, on page 9:

> *"The scribe wrote without separating letters into words. Whatever the reason for it, it seems that the practice of writing without word division was adopted deliberately.*
>
> *. . . and it has become the reader's business to divide them correctly into words. This convention was eventually adopted also by the Romans, who in the imperial period discarded their intelligent system of dividing words from each other by spaces and points in favour of scriptio continua."*

E.G. Turner, in his book *Greek Manuscripts of the Ancient World*, in page 20:

> *"In Egypt, and especially in the Roman period, divisions between consonants are not avoided".*

Herbert C. Youtie, in his book *The Textual Criticism of Documentary Papyri, Prolegomena*, says, on page 3:

> *"The scribes do not divide their texts into words ..."*

Herbert C. Youtie, in his book *The Textual Criticism of Documentary Papyri, Prolegomena*, on page 50:

> "*the absence of word-division on the papyri.*"

6. Reading/Diacritic/Phonetic/Accent/Cantillation marks/signs

The very unique vocalization markings of Ancient Egyptian writings were found exactly in the proclaimed "Greek" texts.

Antonius N. Jannaris, in his book *An Historical Greek Grammar*, says on page 63:

> "*Associated with the letters proper are a number of complimentary symbols which serve to modulate or regulate the voice in expressing a word or sentence.*"

E.G. Turner, in his book *Greek Manuscripts of the Ancient World*, in page 13:

> "*Accents, too, will be found from time to time—acute and grave written in a downwards direction, the circumflex often made in two movements, and when set over a diphthong placed above the first vowel, or between the first and second.*"

E.G. Turner, in his book *Greek Manuscripts of the Ancient World*, in page 13:

> "*Accents are rarely written in prose literature, still more rarely in private letters. But they are likely to be used fairly frequently in texts of lyric verse, especially*

*in verse in difficult dialects. **In such cases their presence may help the reader to divide the words correctly**.*"

E.G.Turner, in his book *Greek Manuscripts of the Ancient World*, in page 20:

*"**In a verse text** (and very occasionally indeed in a prose text, cf. 58) a scribe **may mark the quantity of a long or short syllable**."*

21.8 SAMENESS OF EGYPTIAN PROTOTYPAL INTERCONNECTED LEXICON, GRAMMAR AND SYNTAX

The newly proclaimed "Greek Language" complies exactly with the much older Ancient Egyptian prototypal interconnected lexicon, grammar, and syntax such as the significance of verbs, verb roots, verb stems, verb classes and structures, the conjugation scheme for verbs, and Egyptian prototypal etymology/lexicon and word formation/derivation from a three-letter root (which signifies a certain general concept) into numerous patterns through the use of intermediate vowels and prefixes, infixes and suffixes, etc.

Point by point, from Chapter 15, grammatical highlights of the Ancient Egyptian grammar are an EXACT match in the later "Greek Grammar". A summary of major points:

1. Three Parts of Speech—"Greek", like Ancient Egyptian (and Semitic) grammar distinguishes three parts of speech: nouns, verbs, and particles.

2. The Verb Tree—Roots—Two Stems—Three

Branches/Classification—The linguistic structure of "Greek", like Ancient Egyptian [and later, Semitic languages], is centered on word roots or morphemes, which have a consonantal structure. Words are formed from roots by the addition of (unwritten) vowels, prefixes, infixes, or suffixes according to certain fixed patterns.

"Greek", like the Ancient Egyptian language, has two stems verbs to express an action or a state of being of a given subject—one for the instantaneous tenses and the other for the habitual and continuous tenses. Stem Verbs and derivations are two model stems.

"Greek", like Ancient Egyptian, verbs are commonly classified into 3 groups [active, passive and reflexive] distinguished by the character of their "stem" or "theme".

3. Verb Conjugation [Tenses, Moods, Voices]—Two Conjugations—"Greek", like the Ancient Egyptian language, is a synthetic language with a moderate to high degree of inflection, which shows up mostly in verb conjugation. There are two conjugations for all verbs:

- one for the instantaneous and the completed or perfect tenses and
- the other for the habitual and continuous tenses.

Verbs undergo conjugation [inflection] according to the following categories:

i. **Tenses**—Past, present and future with a total

variations of 8 categories/paradigms.

ii. **Moods**—3 indicative, subjunctive and imperative.

iii. **Voices**—3 active, passive and reflexive.

4. Word Formation/Lexicon—Nouns [adjectives, adverbs, pronouns]—"Greek", like Ancient Egyptian, words are formed from roots by the addition of (unwritten) vowels, prefixes, infixes, or suffixes according to certain fixed patterns.

5. Adverbs—"Greek", like Ancient Egyptian indeclinable words which define a verb and show place, time, method, quantity etc. are called adverbs. Adverbs can define adjectives and even other adverbs.

6. Pronouns—"Greek", like Ancient Egyptian, has the same personal pronouns as well as the enclitic forms of the pronoun.

7. Types & Structures of Syllables—"Greek", like Ancient Egyptian, has two basic types of syllables: short and long, with the same structure options.

8. Syntax/Word Order/Sentence Types—"Greek", like Ancient Egyptian, has the same exact sentence types to express various emphases between VSO, as detailed in Chapter 15.

–>>As common sense dictates : if it walks, talks, and looks like a duck, it is a duck. The proclaimed "Greek" scripts are nothing more than a Western academic heist of Ancient Egyptian scripts.

Chapter 22 : The European Languages

In the previous chapter, we discussed diffusion patterns of the ancient Egyptian vocalic/spoken and alphabetical writing forms into Europe, starting with Greece. In this chapter, we will cover the Italian [Etruscan and "Latin"] and the "Romance" languages.

22.1 ETRUSCAN: THE FOREMOST ANCIENT ITALIAN LANGUAGE

Among the early inhabitants of Italy, the most significant were the Etruscans. They left behind many inscriptions, mostly on graves. It is thought that they arrived on the eastern coast of Umbria several centuries before Rome was built, which was around 800 BCE. Their religious rites and architecture show an obvious affinity with Ancient Egypt. The Etruscans were newcomers who traveled westward during the early 1st millennium BCE. This coincides with the Assyrian assault on Egypt and its allies in Asia.

While the Etruscans built temples at Tarquinia and Caere (present-day Cerveteri), the few local nomadic tribes gravitated to Rome, then little more than a shepherding village.

Etruscans and Ancient Egyptians share many similarities

in culture, religion, building styles and techniques, language, farming techniques, etc. The newcomers were rich and introduced gold tableware and jewelry, bronze urns, and terra-cotta statuary. The true roots of the Etruscans are beyond the scope of this book. Yet, their arrival to Italy coincides with the Assyrian assaults on Egypt. The culture of the Etruscans is like nobody else's but Egypt. The "mysterious" Etruscans brought the first truly impressive architecture to mainland Italy. Little remains of their architecture, but historical writings by the Romans record powerful Etruscan walls, bridges, and aqueducts. As the nomadic tribes of Rome overpowered the civilized Etruscans, they borrowed heavily from themes already established by Etruscan architects. All their architectural styles are found earlier, in Ancient Egypt.

The Etruscans had an extensive trade with Egypt, and we repeatedly find small alabaster (as well as colored glass) bottles in their tombs, which have all the character of the Egyptian. Not only does the stone of the former proclaim, by its quality, the quarries from which it was taken, but the form and style of workmanship leave no doubt of the bottles themselves as being the productions of Egyptian artists.

The Etruscan alphabet was widely used by non-Etruscans as well as Etruscans in those influenced by Etruscan culture. Other inscriptions from pre-Roman Italy were mere graphic variations/errors of the Etruscan alphabet.

There are some 13,000 Etruscan inscriptions, the largest number by far in comparison to anything else in Italy until ca. 200 BCE.

This table provides a visual examination, showing that the depicted "alphabets" in the Mediterranean Basin were really never different alphabets, but a single alphabet: namely, Egyptian.

Phonetic Value	AE Alphabetic Script in varied directions	Moabite Script	East Greek				Classical Greek			West Greek	Etruscan	Archaic Latin	Classic Latin	
a	𐤀	✚	ΔΔ	ΔΑ	a	Α	α	Alpha	a	ΔΑ	A	ΔA	A	a
b	𐤁	𐤁	ΒΒ	Β	b	Β	β	Beta	b	ΒΒ	B	ΒΒ	B	b
g	⸝	⸜	ΛΛ	Γ	g	Γ	γ	Gamma	g	/((	)[∾]	)[∾]	C[∾]	g
d	◁Δ	◁	ΔD	Δ	d	Δ	δ	Delta	d	ΔD		Ͻ	D	d
h	⁊ ⁊	⁊	ΕΑ	ΑΕ	e	Ε	ε	Epsilon	ĕ	Ƒ	Ⴂ	Ⴂ	E	e
w	Υ	Υ			v					FC		⁊ M	F M	v
z	I	⊥	I	I	z	Ζ	ζ	Zeta	z,dz	I	ꟻ	I [M]	G [sd]	z
ḥ	H B	B	B	ΒΗ	h(ē)	H	η	Eta	ē	ΒΗ	B	B	H	h
ṭ	⊗	⊗	⊕	⊗⊕	th	θ	θ	Theta	th	⊕⊙	⊗			th
y	ᔐ	ᘔ	i	I	i	I	ι	Iota	i					i
k	ꓘ	ꓘ	Κ	ΚΚ	k	Κ	κ	Kappa	k	Κ	ꓘ	ꓘΚ	K	k
l	⟨L	⟨	LL	/Λ	l	Λ	λ	Lambda	l	L	J	J	L	l
m	ꟽ	ꟽ	ꟽ	M	m	M	μ	Mu	m	⌒	ꟽ	ꟽ	M	m
n	ꟻ	ꟻ	ꟻ	ꓕN	n	N	ν	Nu	n	ꟻ	ꟻ	ꟻ	N	n
s	‡	ᖴ		‡Ŧ	ks	Ξ	ξ	Xi	ks					x
˙ ˙	O	O	O	O	o	O	o	Omikron	ŏ	⊙		O	O	o
p	⁊	⁊	Γ	Γꓠ	p	Π	π	Pi	p	Γ	⁊	⁊Γ	P	p
ṣ	ꟼ	ꟼ			s						M			ś
q	φ	φ	Ϙ	Ϙ	q					Ϙ	O	Ϙ	Q	q
r	⦒	⦒	ΡR	ΡΓD	r	Ρ	ρ	Rho	r	ΡΡΡ	◁	◁	R	r
š	⟅ ⟆	⟆	𐤔⟆	𐤔⟆	s	Σ	σς	Sigma	s	𐤔⟆	⟆	𐤔	S	s
t	✕✚	✕	T	T	t	T	τ	Tau	t	T	⊤	⊤⊤	T	t
Phonetic Value	AE Demotic Script ("Phoenician") in varied directions	Moabite Script	V	V	u,û	Y	υ	Upsilon	ū	Υv	V	V	V	u
			ΦΦ	Ⓢ	ph	Φ	φ	Phi	ph	✕✚		✕	✕	ks
			✕✚	✕	kh	Χ	χ	Chi	kh	ΦΦ	Φ	O		ph
			ꟿΥ		ps	Ψ	ψ	Psi	ps	Υ⊥	⊥			kh
				Ω	ō	Ω	ω	Omega	ō		8			f
			East Greek			Classical Greek			West Greek	Etruscan	Archaic Latin	Classic Latin		

Etruscan writing usually runs from right to left. Archaic inscriptions, however, could also run from left to right, or they could be written boustrophedon.

The pre-existence of the Etruscan Alphabet in Ancient

Egypt is very obvious, as presented by Petrie in his book *Formation of Alphabets*. In addition, as detailed in Chapter 15, the "Etruscan Language" complies exactly with the much older Ancient Egyptian prototypal interconnected lexicon, grammar and syntax such as the significance of verbs, verb roots, verb stems, verb classes and structures, the conjugation scheme for verbs, and Egyptian prototypal etymology/lexicon and word formation/derivation from a three-letter root (which signifies a certain general concept) into numerous patterns through the use of intermediate vowels and prefixes, infixes and suffixes, etc.

22.2 THE RISE AND ABRUPT FALL OF THE ROMANS' LATIN!

The civilization of Italy by the Etruscans lasted a few centuries. From 510 BCE, the Romans continued to increase their power by conquering neighboring communities. The local tribes and their Campania allies began resisting the Etruscans around 510 BCE, and by 250 BCE the Etruscans were defeated.

It is the "sacred duty" of Western writers to elevate the status of the Romans in the history of the world. Western pride is dependent on the prominence of the Romans. Warmongers allotted a "new" language to this European "Roman Empire"; and they called it "Latin".

Western academics tried to make distinctions between the prominent Etruscan and this "new" Indo-European language, "Latin".

Yet, after all their attempts to split hairs and MAGNIFY minor graphic discrepancies in writing some alphabetical letter-forms, the fact remains that these were ALL distinction without a difference, as can be observed from the alphabetical tables and which the very same Western academics are showing in ALL their textbooks! The "differences" are a few letters turned 180 degrees, and that is all!

Despite the cavalier designation of a "new" language to the new empire as "Classical Latin", there was no difference between it, Etruscan, Greek and the Egyptian as being the real source of one and all. And just like the Ancient Egyptian writing system, "Classical Latin" had been two concurrent scripts: the book-hand and the business hand, the first aiming at being easy to read, the second at being easy to write.

As was the case in Ancient Egypt, there were various calligraphic types for various purposes of writings, such as Capitals and Minuscules. Capitals had two types, 'Square' and 'Rustic.' Another calligraphic variation is the 'Black Letter'.

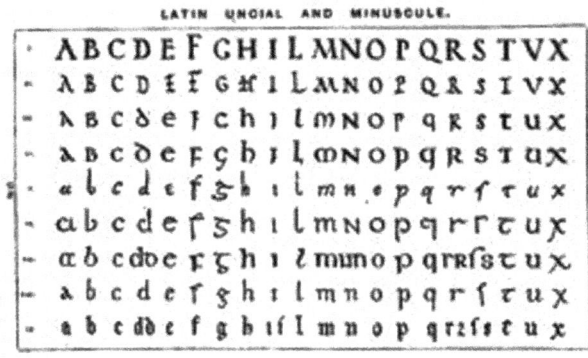

When evidence is provided for 'Roman' writings, we always find it—just like ALL others—to have its source in Egypt, because it is all Egyptian. A very few references (compared to the huge number in Egypt) are claimed to be found in Italy. Here, again, *the tail is wagging the dog.*

The "Latin Language" complies exactly with the much older Ancient Egyptian prototypal interconnected lexicon, grammar and syntax such as the significance of verbs, verb roots, verb stems, verb classes and structures, the conjugation scheme for verbs, and Egyptian prototypal etymology/lexicon and word formation/derivation from a three-letter root (which signifies a certain general concept) into numerous patterns through the use of intermediate vowels and prefixes, infixes and suffixes, etc.—all as detailed in Chapter 15 of this book.

Western academics laid claim to the vocalic tongues of Europe by declaring that vulgar Latin is traditionally divided into Western and Eastern halves. Eastern Vulgar Latin gave rise to the 'Eastern' Romance Languages (Italian and Romanian), and Western Vulgar Latin gave rise to the 'Western' Romance Languages (French, Spanish, Portuguese, and Catalan).

22.3 BROKEN EMPIRE—EASTERN ORTHODOX

In 312 CE, Christianity was made the official and only religion of the Roman Empire. A short time later, the Roman Empire split. Egypt became part of the Eastern (or Byzantine) Empire in 323 CE. The history of the political and doctrinal struggles within the Church during and after the 4th century has largely been written in terms of the disputes over the nature of God and Christ and the relationship between them.

Constantine became emperor in 306 BCE, and in 330 BCE he made Constantinople (also known as Byzantium) the new capital of the Roman Empire, moving the administrative functions away from Rome altogether.

The eastern and western sections of the Roman Empire split in 395 CE, leaving Italy without the support it once received from east of the Adriatic. When the Goths moved toward Rome in the early 5th century, citizens in the provinces welcomed the liberators.

Geoffrey Sampson notes that "script follows religion" in the case of Eastern European languages. Russians, Bulgarians, and Serbs use Cyrillic, while Poles, Czechs, and Croats use Roman, and the division coincides with that between the Eastern Orthodox and the Western Catholic churches. It has nothing to do with differences between languages, as the nations listed all speak fairly closely related Slavic languages.

If one looks at the letter-forms of the alphabets in Eastern Europe, it is easily observed that several of them look like *backward* "regular" Latin letters—and that tells us that they all came from the same source that was written, maybe, right to left. To make it "European", some maintained the same directions while others were turned 180 degrees to comply with its original orientation in Egypt.

22.4 WILD GOOSE CHASE OF A "LATIN" IN HISPANIA

Due to any lack of evidence, academics told us that very few people knew of this masterful language, and that this superior Latin died very abruptly as a result of the fall of the Roman empire!

In order to take cover for making up a "classical" Latin (since there was no evidence to support it in its presumably original home of Rome), academics led us on a wild goose chase in Iberia, where they claimed that it was deeply influenced by the Romans and that Iberians maintained Latin as their language. So, we'll check the facts in Hispania.

The role of the Romans has been totally exaggerated in the history of Iberia. A.T. Fear, in his book *Rome and Baetica: Urbanization in Southern Spain c. 50 BC-AD 150*, Oxford, 1996, sums up his findings [on page 269] regarding the fictional Romanization of Iberia:

> *"Therefore, the view that there was a conscious attempt to change native cultural practices by Rome appears to be incorrect".*

In addition to the statement above, more supporting evidence is found in the book *Egyptian Romany: the Essence of Hispania* by Moustafa Gadalla.

22.5 THE EGYPTIAN ALPHABETS OF HISPANIA

There was already a cultured language in use on the Iberian Peninsula prior to the arrival of the Romans. Classical writers from this era confirm the civilized pre-Roman Iberia, such as Strabo, in *Geography*, [3, 1, 6], who wrote:

> *"The Turdetanians are ranked as the wisest of the Iberians; and <u>they make use of an alphabet, and possess records of their ancient history, poems, and laws written in verse that are six thousand years old, as they assert.</u>"*

There was a thriving trade relationship between Ancient Egypt and the Iberian Peninsula, for several thousand years. Details can be reviewed in *Egyptian Romany: the Essence of Hispania* by Moustafa Gadalla. Our focus here will be strictly on the inscriptions found in Iberia.

Many unearthed artifacts, such as coins, lead tablets, ceramic pieces, tombstones and bronze objects, have turned up throughout most of the Iberian Peninsula. These artifacts have inscriptions that are described by many as "of an unknown alphabet", or as being "Iberian-Tartesian".

The number of the old inscriptions counted to date in Iberia is over 500, although many are in bad condition. They come from the regions of Andalusia, Extremadura, Castilla-La Mancha, Valencia, Murcia, Aragón, Cataluña, Navarra, etc. But they have also been found in some areas of France, Portugal, Italy, and North Africa. Engraved on lead, bronze, ceramic, and stone, Iberian texts are found in tombs, cemeteries, lintels of doorways to houses, ancient corrals, wells, etc. Because of the different (and difficult to write) surfaces used, there appears to be certain differences in "spelling". The disadvantages that they must have faced, such as transcribing them onto physical supports (lead, bronze, stone, etc.), become evident.

By comparing the Ancient Egyptian Alphabetical form of writing with Tartesian Iberian writings [shown below], the affinity between Ancient Egypt and Iberia become obvious. The first table below shows the Ancient Iberian-Tartesian writing and its comparison with the Ancient Egyptian writing, according to M. Gomez-Moreno.

[Source: *Prehistoric Iberia*, ed. By Antonio Arnaiz-Villena, (2000), page 167.] We have not changed the organization or order of the signs according to Gomez-Moreno. However, it is easy to see that these symbols/letters are exactly shown on previous tables of Ancient Egyptian alphabetical letter-forms.

Egyptian	Tartesian	Iberian
ᴠ Δ A	ΔΔA	ᴅᴘᴘᴘᴠ
＃ᴧ ᴋᴋ ＃	＃ᴋ ᴋ ᴋ	ᴋᴋᴋᴠ ＃
ʜ ᴋ	ᴋ ᴋ ᴧ ᴋᴘ	ᴋ ᴋ ᴧ
ʜʜ ᴋ ʏ	ʜʜ ʜʜ	ʜʜ ʜᴋ
ſ Λ	ᴧ	ᴋ ᴧ Λ
ᴧ ᴘ ᴋ	ᴧ ᴧ ᴧ	ᴧ ᴧ ᴧ ᴋ ᴧ
ᴏ ᴘ ●	● ᴘ ᴘ	ᴘ ᴘ ᴘ ᴏ ᴏ
ᴠʏʏʜᴛɪ	ᴋ ɪ ᴋ ᴋ ᴋ	ᴠʏʏᴛ ᴋᴋᴋ
ᴋ ᴋ ᴋ ᴧ	ᴋ ᴋ ᴋ	ᴋ ᴋ
ᴋᴋ ᴋ ᴋ	ᴋᴋ ᴋ ᴋ ᴋ ᴋ	ᴋ ᴋ ᴋ ᴋ
ᴍ ᴍᴧ	ᴍᴧ ᴍᴧ ᴍᴧ	ᴍ ᴧᴧ
ᴛ ᴛ ᴛ	ᴋ ᴛ ᴛ	ᴧ
ᴧ ſ	ᴧ ᴧ ᴧ	ſ ᴘ
ᴋ ᴋ ᴋ	ᴋ ᴋ	ᴋ
ᴋ ᴋ ●	ᴘ ●	● ● ● ● ᴋ
ᴋ ᴋ ᴋ ᴋ	ᴋ	ᴋ ᴋ ᴛ ᴋ ᴋ
ᴋ ᴋ ᴋ	ᴋ ᴋ ᴋ ᴋ	ᴋ ᴋ ᴋ
Δ ᴋ	ΔΔΔᴋᴠ	ΔΔΔΔ
●	●	● ●
ᴧ ᴧ Δ	Λ	ΔΔ ᴋ ᴧ
ᴋ ᴋ ᴋ ᴋ	ᴋᴧᴅᴘᴄᴋ	ᴋᴋᴄᴋᴋᴄᴄ
ᴋ ᴋ ᴋ	ᴋ ᴋ ᴋ ᴋ	ᴋᴋᴋᴋᴋᴋᴋ
ᴅ ●	ᴏᴏᴏᴏ	ᴏᴏᴏ

Some individual examples are included.

This alcoy tablet shows an inscription in the Ancient Egyptian demotic alphabet. It is one of several found in the ruins of the Iberian sanctuary of La Serreta.

This small lead tablet [shown below] is inscribed on both sides. It has a total of 117 letters or signs on the side on which the text begins, and 59 on the side on which it ends.

This lead tablet [shown below] was found in 1928 in the ruins of La Bastida de los Alcuses (Pais de Valencia, Spain), to the southeast of Jativa, a settlement destroyed circa the 4th century BCE. The writing runs from right to left, and is separated by horizontal lines. There are some-

EGYPTIAN UNIVERSAL WRITING MODES 309

times barriers of points, which separate different paragraphs. This is identical to the Ancient Egypt style and form of writing.

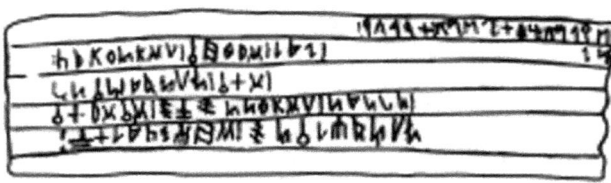

–>> **The conclusion is obvious: there was no difference between the Ancient Egyptian letter-forms and those inscriptions found in Hispania. Such alphabetical letter-forms pre-existed and were in abundant use in Ancient Egypt, as compared to a much smaller number in spotty locations throughout Hispania.**

A language, however, is much more than alphabetical letter-forms, and next we will review the Egyptian-Iberian linguistic 'oneness'.

22.6 THE EGYPTIAN-IBERIAN LINGUISTIC ONENESS

It is generally accepted that the Castilian (Spanish) language contains at least 4,000 "Arabic-sounding" words. Other Hispanic languages/dialects, such as in Murcia, have many more "Arabic-sounding" words. When the history of the "Arabic" language is studied, it becomes clear that "Arabic" is the Ancient Egyptian language, and that these thousands of apparently "Arabic-sounding" words found in Hispanic languages are of Egyptian and not Arabic or North African Berber origin.

These 4,000 "Arabic-sounding" words are the tip of the iceberg. Upon further examination of many words, taking into account the phenomenon of sound shifts and reversal of letters in words [as explained in an earlier chapter], as well as the impact of imposing the "Latin" alphabetical letter-forms to write existing spoken language/dialect after the Reconquest; there will be many more words that can find their origins in Egypt.

It is commonly acknowledged that the spoken language(s)/dialect(s) of the Iberian Peninsula, in the pre-Moorish era, sounded "like Arabic", but were not really "Arabic". Egyptian is the only language that sounds "like Arabic", which leads us to the conclusion (on a linguistic basis) that Ancient Egypt is the source of language(s) on the Iberian Peninsula.

The "common" language of the Iberian peoples is called by many different names—depending on the personal/religious/ethnic/cultural prejudices of the writer on the subject. Such a language can be called "Mozarabic", "vulgar Arabic", "colloquial Arabic", "Hispano-Arabic", etc. The use of these undefined and ambiguous terms indicates that the utilized language does not belong to any "officially accepted language". The reason is that the populace spoke the Egyptian language, which is older than all "politically/religiously recognized languages".

The present-day Iberian "official" and "co-official" languages have a high common measure of agreement between them. One may be characterized by a regular alternation of vowels and consonants, another appears as predominantly vocalic, and yet another as predominantly consonantal. Fundamentally, the same material is subjected to variants of differing rhythms.

...

To summarize, the source(s) of languages in the Iberian Peninsula, if tracked to "Latin" and/or "Arabic", will lead to Ancient Egypt as the sole source. As shown in Chapter 12, the pre-existence of Latin alphabet in Ancient Egypt is very obvious, as presented by Petrie in his book *Formation of Alphabets*. In addition, the "Iberian Peninsula's Language(s)" comply exactly with the much older Ancient Egyptian prototypal interconnected lexicon, grammar and syntax such as the significance of verbs, verb roots, verb stems, verb classes and structures, the conjugation scheme for verbs, and Egyptian prototypal etymology/lexicon and word formation/derivation from a three-letter root (which signifies a certain general concept) into numerous patterns through the use of intermediate vowels and prefixes, infixes and suffixes, etc.—as detailed in Chapter 15 of this book.

Apparent variations in the number of alphabetical letters in "the Iberian Peninsula's language(s)" as compared to the prototypal original 28 Ancient Egyptian alphabetical letters are caused by similar vocalic limitations, as detailed several times throughout this book, such as the phenomenon of sound shift, an inability/'laziness' to pronounce some groups of letters such as guttural and from-the-throat sounds which resulted in apparent 'soundless' like vowels; and how some phonemes [shades of the same sound of a letter] took lives of their own and became "independent" letters, etc.

22.7 WARMONGERS AND THE "ROMANCE" LANGUAGES!

During the later stages of the Moors' grip on Iberia, Castille became a dominant power in the north, and was the center from which the Reconquest of the peninsula was launched. The religious zealotry that followed the Reconquest included linguistic "purification". We are told that as the Reconquest succeeded in moving south, Romance languages "emerged"—how "poetic"!

The so-called "emergence of Romance languages" in Iberia was similar to what happened in Turkey about a century ago, when their leader, Mustafa Kemal Atatürk, after losing the Ottoman Empire in WWI, wanted to sever ties with the East by abandoning the "Arabic" alphabet for a "Latin" alphabet. His action did not change the Turkish language. He merely wrote the same spoken language in a different alphabet and a different direction (left to right), which, incidentally, complicated their writing system. The same thing could be said of the "emergence of the Romance languages": i.e., there was no change in the spoken languages, but merely a change in the specific form of writing.

The same situation applies to other places throughout the world: the invaders adopted the local language and in some cases changed letter forms so as to claim themselves the 'creator' of a new language, to be identified with them being the ultimate winners!!

PART VII : THE ANCIENT FUTURE OF THE UNIVERSAL LANGUAGE

Chapter 23 : Egyptian Alphabetical Vocalic Language [Past, Present & Future]

23.1 THE UNCHANGING EGYPTIANS

The Egyptians are remarkably traditionalist to a fault. Throughout the history of Egypt, the emphasis was on the adherence to traditions, and Egyptians were NEVER to deviate from such a principle. In the oldest surviving text of the world (5,000 years ago), the Egyptian scribe Ptah Hotep states:

> *"Don't modify/change anything from your father's (ancestor's) teachings/instructions—not even a single word. And let this principle be the cornerstone for teachings to future generations."*

The Egyptians never deviated from this principle. Early historians have attested to this fact, such as Herodotus, in *The Histories*, Book Two, [79]:

> *"The Egyptians keep to their native customs and never adopt any from abroad."*

Herodotus, in *The Histories*, Book Two, [91]:

> **"The Egyptians are unwilling to adopt Greek customs, or, to speak generally, those of any other country".**

It has been written and repeated that the Ancient Egyptians willingly changed their religious beliefs into Christianity, and a short time later, they willingly accepted Islam as a substitute for Christianity and adopted "Arabic" as their language (?!).

Because of the ironclad control of Islam over history writing since 642 CE, Moslem historians publicize that Egyptians forgot their identity and became a part of a big happy family called "Arabs". No one can dare oppose the line that Islam "saved" Egypt from the previous *Gaheliya* (ignorance era). As a result, we witness an intellectual state of terrorism that conceals realities by a cloud of dust—that the Ancient Egyptian vocalic language died and was replaced by this "new" language called "Arabic". The scheme to conceal the Ancient Egyptian alphabetical vocalic language as well as its primary role as the archetypal language of the world was shown earlier in Chapter 2 of this book and was elaborated about in later chapters of this book.

23.2 THE ENDURING EGYPTIAN ALPHABETICAL VOCALIC LANGUAGE

After concealing the (Ancient) Egyptian alphabetical writing system that makes everyone thinks of the Egyptian language as a collection of "primitive pictures" called hieroglyphics, their second blow was declaring that the

Ancient Egyptian language is DEAD and that it was replaced—out of thin air—by the "Arabic" language!

To say that Egyptians speak "Arabic" is totally false and illogical. It is the other way around: the "Arabs" long ago "adopted" and continue to speak EGYPTIAN.

When it comes to the Arabic Semitic letter-forms, they are all copies of the Ancient Egyptian letter-forms, as shown earlier in this book and as testified to by Western academia itself, such as by Isaac Taylor in his book *The History of the Alphabet*, volume I, page 145, who wrote:

> *"The internal evidence points to the same conclusion. The forms of the Semitic letters were not derived from the monumental hieroglyphics, but from the [Ancient Egyptian] cursive Hieratic".*

When it comes to the vocalic system of "Arabic" vis-à-vis Ancient Egyptian vocalic system, it is also worth repeating that the British Egyptologist Alan Gardiner, in his book *Egyptian Grammar*, page 3, stated:

> <u>*"The entire vocalic system of Old Egyptian may indeed be proved to have reached a stage resembling that of Hebrew or modern Arabic"*</u>

When it comes to the rest of the linguistic pillars of etymology, grammar, syntax, etc., later languages such as "Arabic" are nothing more than an EXACT copy of the Ancient Egyptian alphabetical language. Affinities and characteristics of the Ancient Egyptian language as described by Egyptologist Alan Gardiner in his book *Egyptian Grammar*, on page 2:

> *"<u>The Egyptian language is related</u>, not only to the Semitic tongues (Hebrew, <u>Arabic</u>, Aramaic, Babylonian, etc.), but also to the East African languages (Galla, Somali, etc.) and the Berber idioms of North Africa. Its connection with the latter groups, together known as the Hamitic family, is a very thorny subject, but the relationship to the Semitic tongues can be fairly accurately defined. <u>In general structure the similarity is very great</u>; Egyptian shares the principal peculiarity of Semitic in that its word-stems consist of combinations of consonants, as a rule three in number, which are theoretically at least unchangeable. Grammatical inflection and minor variations of meaning are contrived mainly by ringing the changes on the internal vowels, though affixed endings also are used for the same purpose.*

23.3 VOCABULARIES NOW AND THEN

Common vocabularies in any language change in different regions of such a language as well as in different eras. To provide a present-day example, let us take the word 'retarded' in Italy, which means (for their common use) 'late' or 'delayed'; as posted in train stations and airports for transportation vehicles. The very same word 'retarded', in English-speaking regions, is used to describe the 'mental incapacity of humans'. Similarly, within English-speaking countries, each region has different 'common' words in use. Also, 'common' words change over time—50 years ago, 100 years ago—etc.

Vocabularies in Ancient Egyptian texts likewise may have gone out of use or have had different meanings.

We find that many of the Ancient Egyptian vocabularies have been maintained in the 'conservative parts of the society' such as the [Egyptian] Sufis and among Baladi Egyptians, who use vocabularies not commonly used [or used differently] by those living in urban areas.

23.4 ARABIC CORRUPTION OF ORIGINAL EGYPTIAN LETTER-FORMS AND RESHUFFLED LETTERS ORDER/SEQUENCE

The only differences between the Ancient Egyptian alphabetical writing system and that of the present "Arabic" system lie in two [insignificant] areas:

> 1. Arabic reshuffled the order of the ABGD letters in the 10th Century CE to A,B,T, Th, G, H. Kh, etc.

> 2. Several Ancient Egyptian alphabetical letter-forms that had inclined [not vertical or horizontal] were all made vertical in the 10th century CE . Such changes led to having duplicates and triplicates of similar-looking letter-forms that represented two/three alphabetical letter sounds. To deal with such a problem, the "Arabs" added single, double, or triple dots to their "revised" letter-forms in order to compensate for their graphical carelessness of the original Egyptian letter-forms.

It should be noted that in the original Ancient Egyptian system, the last six letters in the Egyptian alphabet had a sonic-twin letter in the top 22 letters. These last six letter-forms have the same letter-form of each's primary letter plus an added dot or a bar to distinguish each from its prime sonic-twin. Western academics have always confused such distinctions of these last six letters of the 28-letter alphabet.

Here is an early "Arabic" text without dots from 8th century:

Here is another early "Arabic" script from 9th century CE, with no dots, which is ligatured even if some letters are not connected due to ink limitations; which looks exactly as Ancient Egyptian letter-forms:

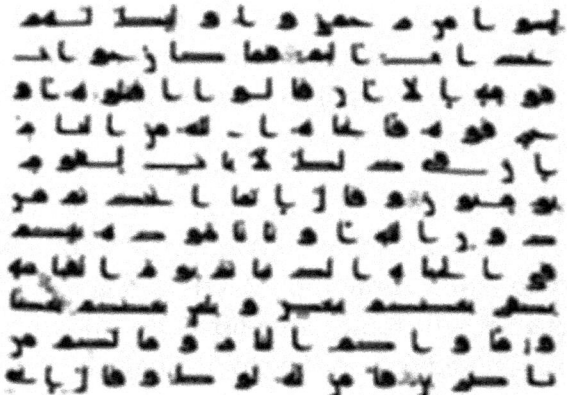

Here is an Arabic text after 10th Century [19th Century] with dots:

23.5 SAMENESS OF ALPHABETICAL WRITING SYSTEM

A summary of the highlights of the most common characteristics of Egyptian [Semitic] alphabetical writing are:

1. Ancient Egypt had 28 letters in their alphabets—just like later "Arabic"—with the same sound values.

2. Letters each can have up to four forms, as exactly in later "Arabic":

> o Detached – the letter as it appears by itself, no letters joining to it either before or after.
> o Initial – the letter as it appears when not preceded by a joining letter.
> o Medial – the letter as it appears when there are joining letters both before and after the letter.
> o Terminal – the letter as it appears when it is preceded, but not followed by joining letters.

3. Writing is normally from right to left—just like later "Arabic".

4. Old "Arabic" texts followed two Ancient Egyptian primary writing styles: the uncials and cursive, which was/is ligatured in special rules where some letters may be connected while others may not.

5. The rules for ligaturing different letters within a word in later "Arabic" are exactly the same as in the Ancient Egyptian alphabetical system. Certain characters may be joined to their neighbors, others to the preceding one only, and others to the succeeding one only. The written letters undergo a slight external change according to their position within a word. When they stand alone or occur at the end of a word, they ordinarily terminate in a bold stroke; when they appear in the middle of a word, they are ordinarily joined to the letter following by a small, upward curved stroke. With the exception of six letters, which can be joined only to the preceding ones, the initial and medial letters are much abbreviated, while the final form consists of the initial form with a triumphant flourish. The essential part of the characters, however, remains unchanged.

6. In both Ancient Egyptian writing system and later "Arabic", there is/was no separation between words.

7. Associated with the letters proper, in both Ancient Egyptian writing system and later "Arabic", are a number of complimentary symbols which serve to modulate or regulate the voice in expressing a word

or sentence being indicated by signs placed above or below the consonant or long vowel that they follow.

23.6 REINSTATEMENT OF ORIGINAL LETTER-FORMS AND ITS ABGD SEQUENCE

1. Follow the A.B.G.D. etc. sequence—which is already being used by Sufis and in all subjects of study such as mathematics, etc.—and abandon the illogical and difficult "Arabic" (introduced in the 10th century CE) of A,B,T,…

2. Restore the distinction of the last six letters of the Egyptian alphabet. These last six letter-forms have the same letter-form of each's primary letter plus an added dot or a bar to distinguish each from its prime sonic-twin.

3. Restore all letter-forms to those prior to the 10th century CE – the A,B,T,… changes.

Chapter 24 : Renaissance & Seeking the Universal Language The Ancient Future

24.1 ENGLISH LANGUAGE FLAWED DOMINANCE

At the present time, the English language is the most frequently used language of communication in the world, although not because it is a 'good' language. English is the language of the powerful during this time in history, and therefore it is the most important international language of communication.

Problems with phonetics, pronunciation and orthography are prominent in the English language. Richard A. Firmage, in his book *The Alphabet ABECEDARIUM*, on page 178, admits to the chaotic vocalization of the English language:

> *"For hundreds of years, right up to the present, linguistic reformers have lamented the inconsistency between the spelling of words and their pronunciation. No rules seem to apply here: letters are pronounced now one way, now another ... and yet another. Also, similar*

sounds are spelled with maddeningly different letters in seemingly arbitrary disregard."

Richard A. Firmage, in his book *The Alphabet ABECEDARIUM*, on page 289 admits:

"For centuries, the freedom and <u>lack of uniformity in English spelling</u> helped keep spelling-pronunciation differences to a minimum. But spelling became more fixed and the gap widened with the invention of printing. Noah Jacobs wrote that "English spelling is a monumental witness to the misguided erudition of pedants and printers... and could be abolished entirely in favor of shorthand without impairing communication. <u>We are in reality spelling imaginary sounds. The appearance of a word is irrelevant: different meanings can be attached to the same word</u> (sound, mean, bill); a word can be given a different meaning when differently pronounced (sewer, wound, lead); <u>and the same significance may adhere to words which do not look alike</u>" (such as transliterations of foreign words).

English speech is not phonetic – i.e. it is not spoken as it is spelled.

According to the Oxford English Dictionary, there are at least 13 separate sounds represented by the letter A alone.

Richard A. Firmage, in his book *The Alphabet ABECEDARIUM: Some Notes on Letters*, on page 227 wrote:

"English employs one of the greatest number of vowel sounds among World languages. The Oxford English Dictionary lists almost fifty vowel sounds that the five

letters represent, as well as other sounds that result from vowel combinations. Although some of these sounds are duplicates—both A and E can represent the same sound, for example— it is little wonder that English spellings and pronunciations can vary so greatly. This situation of different letters sharing sounds can prompt intricate linguistic and philosophic speculation. Jacques Derrida wrote of "Differance"—the substitution of an "a" for the normal "e" can be "written or read, but it is not heard. It cannot be heard. It is put forward by a silent mark, by a tacit monument." It is a purely graphic distinction—the written sign clothing the sound, as it were. So what then is the difference between "differance" and "difference"?"

Hans Jensen, in his book *Sign, Symbol and Script*, page 233, admits:

"<u>The English writing system</u> is notorious for its lack of correspondence to the phonetics of the language, and there have been numerous attempts to revise English spelling to make it more phonetically accurate.

To be sure, English spelling has its quirks, such as <u>multiple ways of writing the same sound</u> ([i] as in tea, tee, machine, people, amoeba), <u>multiple sounds for the same letter</u> ([o] as in woman, women, come, comb, port), and <u>silent letters</u> (debt, island, light, pneumatic), to name a few."

No one can ever pronounce a word in the English language without phonetics. In addition to the five basic vowels, there are other compound vowels such as 'oo', 'ou', 'ei', 'ie', 'au', 'eu', 'ee', 'ea' and 'y'. Moreover, the sounds of the basic five and other compound vowels are not consistent. There are also different sounds to the consonant letters of the alphabet, and to add to the confusion, some of them are often silent. The consonant letter 's' sounds as an 's' in many words, but it could sound as a 'z' in 'has', as an 'sh' in 'sure', or as 'zh' in 'confusion'. Then there are consonant sounds to some dual consonants, such as 'sh', 'th', 'ph', etc. The combination 'gh' in the middle of a word is never pronounced. And on and on.

There are other inconsistencies, such as :

– the verb 'read', in the present and past tenses, are written in the same way, but are pronounced differently
– the word 'race' has different meanings if it is a car 'race' or human 'race'.
– the words 'bear' and 'tear' have meanings as verbs and totally unrelated meanings as nouns.

The "26-letter English alphabet" is a degraded form of the 28 letters of ABGD. Also, **sometimes there are sounds in the English language that are not part of the "26 letters"**, such as the sound "**sh**", which is found in many English words like "shame", "sure"; "**th**" (as in "three"); and another sound for "**th**", as in the word "there". In short, the so-called 26 letters is an artificial number.

There is no such problem in the Egyptian language, as it is of a perfectly consistent tonal nature.

24.2 THE RENAISSANCE SEARCH FOR A UNIVERSAL LANGUAGE

Athanasius Kircher, known as the *'Renaissance Man'* and

The Last Man Who Knew Everything, emphasized two primary principles in his linguistic research and writings: that

1. All Languages of the world are reduced to One language.

2. This One Language has extended to All other languages.

Kircher, if not directly, has indirectly talked about the vocalic/alphabetical Egyptian language which is referred to as 'Coptic Language' in the sense that *Coptic* refers to/ means *Egyptian* and not just the Christian population of Egypt.

One of the most important topics during the [European] "Renaissance" was defining and adopting a *Universal Language*. These Renaissance scholars came up with the same exact details of the Ancient Egyptian alphabetical language. Their "invented" Universal Language walked like a duck [Egyptian], quacked/talked like a duck [Egyptian], etc. It is hard to believe that they were not copying from Ancient Egypt, but came out of thin air with the very same linguistic characteristics of the Ancient Egyptian alphabetical/vocalic language?!

Details of such Renaissance Universal Language studies can be found in *Imagining Language: An Anthology,* by Jed Rasula (Editor) and Steve McCaffery (Editor), Cambridge, MA, USA, 1998.

We choose here to highlight one of the most important points in the above-mentioned reference on page 348, where a Renaissance scholar wrote about their "proposed" Universal Language:

> <u>*The root of each word establishes its character*</u>, *for it is of the same nature, temper, constitution or genius. The root is an independent entity. The character is a dependent entity; a manifestation of its root. It is of like nature or of peculiar constitution attributable to its root. The properties of a character must agree with its word root, as a property of that word root and as offspring expressing it by its noticeable likeness to it."*

Was it a shear coincidence that ALL these Renaissance scholars and other later western academies were unaware that they are describing in minute details the Ancient Egyptian Alphabetical/Vocalic Language?!

ALL their work was nothing more than trying to 'reinvent the wheel' (so to speak) that was already 'invented' by the Ancient Egyptians and which continues to live since the Arab occupation of Egypt in 640 CE under the name of the conquerors "Arabic " language!

As they say: **"Denial [De-Nile] is a river in Egypt"!**

1

GLOSSARY

Animism – The concept that all things in the universe are animated (energized) by life forces. This concurs, scientifically, with kinetic theory, where each minute particle of any matter is in constant motion; i.e. energized with life forces.

aspirated – marked by release of a puff of air. Example: English p is aspirated in pie, unaspirated in spy.

attributes – the Divine qualities and meanings that are the real causative factors of the manifested creations.

Baladi – local, a term used to describe the present native silent majority in Egypt, which adheres to the Ancient Egyptian traditions, under a thin layer of Islam.

BCE – Before Common Era. Also noted in other references as BC.

Bilingual text – A text written in two languages with identical content.

Book of Coming Forth By Light (Per-em-hru) – consists of over 100 chapters of varying lengths which are closely related to the Unas Transformational/Funerary (so-called Pyramid) Texts at Saqqara. This book is only found, in its complete form, on papyrus scrolls that were wrapped in the mummy swathings of the deceased and buried with him.

CE – Common Era. Also noted in other references as AD.

cosmology – The study of the origin, creation, structure, and orderly operation of the universe as a whole, and of its related parts.

Cursive Writing – see **Writing, Cursive**

Duat/Tuat – (Ancient Egypt) the Underworld, where the soul goes through transformation leading to resurrection.

Etymology – 1) study of word origins: the study of the origins of words or parts of words and how they have arrived at their current form and meaning. 2) the history of a word: the origin of a word or part of a word, or a statement of this, and how it has arrived at its current form and meaning.

Homophony – A characteristic of several written signs expressing the same sound in the language. For example, the written 'too, two, to' are all pronounced 'tu', the opposite of Polyphony.

Image – actual or mental picture: a picture or likeness of somebody or something, produced either physically, by a sculptor, painter, or photographer, or formed in the mind.

mysticism – consists of ideas and practices that lead to union with the Divine. 'Union' is described more accurately as togetherness, joining, arriving, conjunction, and the realization of God's uniqueness.

neter/netert – a divine principle/function/attribute of the One Great God. (Incorrectly translated as god/goddess.)

Ostracon – A term used by archaeologists to refer to shards of pottery or flakes of limestone bearing texts and drawings.

papyrus – could mean either: 1) A plant that is used to make a writing surface. 2) Paper, as a writing medium. 3) The text written on it, such as "Leiden Papyrus".

Phonetic Complement/Indicator – A sign expressing a phonetic but non-semantic element above/below/attached to the basic letter.

"Pyramid" Texts – a collection of transformational (funerary) literature that was found in the tombs of the 5th and 6th Dynasties (2465-2150 BCE).

Re – represents the primeval, cosmic, creative force. His hidden name is Amen, which means 'secret'. All neteru (gods, goddesses) who took part in the creation process are aspects of Re. Therefore, Re is often linked with other neteru, such as Atam-Re, Re-Harakhte, etc.

Sign – something conveying an idea: an action or gesture used to convey an idea, information, a wish, or a command.

Sign, Phonetic – Any sign of full writing which expresses linguistic elements by means of visible marks, such as an Alphabetic, Syllabic and Word Sign, and, in some systems, a Prosodic and Phrase Sign. Phonetic Signs may be subdivided into two classes: (1) Phonetic semantic signs, such as word and phrase signs, (2) phonetic non-semantic signs, such as alphabetic, syllabic, and prosodic signs.

Sign, Prosodic – A sign or mark to denote a prosodic feature, such as quantity, accent, tone, and pause.

stanza – a group of lines of verse forming one of the divisions of a poem or song. It typically has a regular pattern in the number of lines and the arrangement of meter and rhyme.

stele (plural: stelae) – stone or wooden slab or column inscribed with commemorative texts.

Symbol – The same as a Sign, but not forming part of a system, such as the symbol of the 'cross' for Christianity, or 'anchor' for hope.

Thoth – represents the Divine aspects of wisdom and intellect. It was Thoth who uttered the words that created the world, as commanded by Re. He is represented as the messenger of the neteru (gods/goddesses) of writing, language, and knowledge.

Writing – A system of communication by means of conventional visible marks.

Writing, Alphabet or Alphabetic – A writing in which a sign normally stands for one or more single sounds of the language. Thus, in English, the alphabetic sign b stands for the sound b, while the sign c stands for the sounds k or s.

Writing, Cursive – A quick and superficial form of writing used for daily, practical purposes. Sometimes a cursive writing becomes monumental, developing at the same time a secondary cursive form.

Writing, Manual – Writing done by hand. Opposite of Mechanical Writing.

Writing, Mechanical – Writing done with a mechanical help, such as type or typewriter.

Writing, Monumental – A careful form of writing normally found on monuments and used for official display purposes. Opposite of Cursive Writing.

Writing, Pictorial – A form of writing using images.

2

SELECTED BIBLIOGRAPHY

Abdalla, Aly. *Graeco-Roman Funerary Stelae from Upper Egypt*. Liverpool, 1992.

Agrippa, Henry Cornelius. *Three Books of Occult Philosophy*. Montana, USA, 1992.

Ameen, Ahmed. *The Egyptian Customs, Traditions and Expressions*. Cairo, 1999 [Arabic text].

Assmann, J. *Agyptische Hymnen Und Gebete* (*Leiden Papyrus* p. 312-321). Zürich/Münich, 1975.

Barthes, Roland. Tr. By Annette Lavers and Colin Smith. *Elements of Semiology*. New York, 1968.

Betz, Hans Dieter, Ed. *The Greek Magical Papyri in Translation, Including the Demotic Spells*. Chicago, USA, 1986.

Baines, John and Jaromir Málek. *Atlas of Ancient Egypt*. New York, 1994.

Bowen, Richard LeBaron, Jr. *Archaeological Discoveries in South Arabia*. Baltimore, MD, USA, 1958.

Boylan, Patrick. *Thoth The Hermes of Egypt*. Oxford, 1922.

Breasted, James Henry. *Ancient Records of Egypt*, 3 Vols. Chicago, USA, 1927.

Budge, E.A. Wallis. *Amulets and Superstitions*. New York, 1978.

Budge, E.A. Wallis. *Cleopatra's Needles and Other Egyptian Obelisks*. London, 1926.

Budge, E.A. Wallis. *The Rosetta Stone*, 2 Vols. London, 1904.

Budge, E.A. Wallis. *The Decrees of Memphis and Canopis*, 3 Vols. London, 1904.

Budge, Sir E. A. Wallis. *Egyptian Language: Easy Lessons in Egyptian Hieroglyphics*. New York, 1983.

Budge, E.A. Wallis. *Egyptian Magic*. New York, 1971.

Budge, E.A. Wallis. *Egyptian Religion: Egyptian Ideas of the Future Life*. London, 1975.

Budge, E.A. Wallis. *From Fetish to God in Ancient Egypt*. London, 1934.

Budge, E.A. Wallis. *The Gods of the Egyptians*, 2 volumes. New York, 1969.

Cajori, Florian. *A History of Mathematical Notations*, Vol. I. Chicago, IL, USA, 1928.

Chejne, Anwar G. *The Arabic Language: Its Role in History*. Minneapolis, Minnesota, USA, 1969.

Clement Stromata Book V, chapter IV [www.piney.com/Clement-Stromata-Five.html]

Coward, Rosalind; and Ellis, John. *Language and Materialism*. London, 1977.

Daniels, Peter T & Bright, William. *The World's Writing Systems*. Oxford, 1996.

Daniloff, Raymond; Schuckers, Gordon; and Feth, Lawrence. *The Physiology of Speech and Hearing*. Englewood Cliffs, NJ, USA, 1980.

Davies, W.V. *Egyptian Hieroglyphs*. London, 1989.

DeFrancis, John. *Visible Speech, The Diverse Oneness of Writing Systems*. Honolulu, HI, USA, 1989.

DeKerckhove, Derrick; and Lumsden, Charles J., eds. *The Alphabet and the Brain*. New York, 1989.

Diodorus of Sicily. *Books I, II, & IV*, tr. By C.H. Oldfather. London, 1964.

Doblhofer, Ernst, Tr. By Marvyn Savill. New York, 1961.

Driver, G.R. *Semitic Writing: from Pictograph to Alphabet*. London, 1954.

Drucker, Johanna. *The Alphabetic Labyrinth*. New York, 1995.

Egyptian Book of the Dead (The Book of Going Forth by Day), The Papyrus of Ani. USA, 1991.

El-Aguizy, Ola. *A Palaeographical Study of Demotic Papyri in the Cairo Museum*. Cairo, 1998.

Ellis, Alexander John. *The Alphabet of Nature*. 1845.

Erman, Adolf. *Life in Ancient Egypt*. New York, 1971.

Erman, Adolph. *The Literature of the Ancient Egyptians*, tr. By Aylward M. Blackman. London, 1927.

Findlen, Paula, Ed. *Athanasius Kircher: The Last Man Who Knew Everything*. New York, 2004.

Firmage, Richard A. *The Alphabet ABECEDARIUM: Some Notes on Letters*. Boston, 1993.

Gadalla, Moustafa:
- *Ancient Egyptian Culture Revealed*, USA, 2007.
- *Egyptian Cosmology: The Animated Universe* – 2nd edition. USA, 2001.
- *Egyptian Divinities: The All Who Are THE ONE*. USA, 2001.
- *Egyptian Harmony: The Visual Music*. USA, 2000.
- *Egyptian Mystics: Seekers of the Way*. USA, 2003.
- *Egyptian Rhythm: The Heavenly Melodies*. USA, 2002.
- *Egyptian Romany: The Essence of Hispania*. USA, 2004.

Gaur, Albertine. *A History of Calligraphy*. New York, 1994.

Gardiner, Sir Alan. *Egyptian Grammar: Being an Introduction to the Study of Hieroglyphs*, 3rd ed. Oxford, 1994.

Gefin, Laszlo. *Ideogram: History of Poetic Method*. Austin, TX, USA, 1982.

Gelb, I.J. *A Study of Writing: The Foundation of Grammatology*. Chicago, IL, USA, 1952.

Gibson, John C.L. *Textbook of Syrian Semitic Inscriptions: Volume I: Hebrew and Moabite Inscriptions*. Oxford, 1971.

Gibson, John C.L. *Textbook of Syrian Semitic Inscriptions: Volume II: Aramaic Inscriptions including inscriptions in the dialect of Zenjirli*. Oxford, 1975.

Godwin, Joscelyn. *Robert Fludd: Hermatic Philosopher and Surveyor of Two Worlds*. London, 1990.

Godwin, Joscelyn. *Athanasius Kircher: A Renaissance Man and the Quest for Lost Knowledge*. London, 1979.

Goodspeed, Edgar J. *Chicago Literary Papyri*. Chicago, 1908.

Haikal, Fayza M.H. *Two Hieratic Funerary Papyri of Nesmin*. Bruxelles, Belgium, 1970.

Hare, Tom. *Remembering Osiris*. Stanford, CA, USA, 1999.

Hayes, William C. *Ostraka and Name Stones from the Tomb of Sen-Mut (No. 71) at Thebes*. New York, 1973.

Healey, John F. *The Early Alphabet*. London, 1990.

Helfman, Elizabeth S. *Signs and Symbols Around the World*. New York, 1967.

Herodotus. *The Histories*. Tr. By Aubrey DeSelincourt. London, 1996.

Horapollo. *The Hieroglyphics of Horapollo*. Tr. By George Boas, New York, 1950.

Husselman, Elinor M. *Papyri from Karanis*. London, 1971.

Ifrah, Georges. *From One to Zero: A Universal History of Numbers*. Tr. By Lowell Bair, New York, 1985.

Ifrah, Georges. *The Universal History of Numbers*. Tr. By E.F. Harding, New York, 2000.

Ifrah, Georges. *The Universal History of Computing*. Tr.by E.F. Harding, New York, 2001.

Iversen, Eric. *The Myth of Egypt and its Hieroglyphs*. Copenhagen, 1961.

Jannaris, Antonius N. *An Historical Greek Grammar, Chiefly of the Attic Dialect*. Germany, 1968.

Jensen, Hans. *Sign, Symbol and Script*. London, 1970.

Jensen, John T. *Principles of Generative Phonology*. Philadelphia, PA, USA, 2004.

Jones, Alexander, Ed. *Astronomical Papyri from Oxyrhynchus*, 2 vols. Philadelphia, PA, USA, 1999.

Kenyon, F.G. *Classical Texts from Papyri in the British Museum*. Milano, 1977.

Khaldûn, Ibn. *The Muqaddimah: An Introduction to History*, tr. From the Arabic by Franz Rosenthal, abridged and edited by N.J. Dawood. Princeton, 1969.

Maxwell-Stuart, P.G., Ed. *The Occult in Early Modern Europe*. New York, USA, 1999.

McDowell, A.G. *Village Life in Ancient Egypt: Laundry Lists and Love Songs*. Oxford, 1999.

Menninger. *Numbers Words and Number Symbols*, Tr. by Paul Broneer, Cambridge, MA, USA, 1969.

Nag Hammadi. *The Facsimile Edition of the Nag Hamaddi Codices*. Leiden, 1977.

Parkinson, R. B. *Voices From Ancient Egypt—An Anthology of middle Kingdom writings*, London, 1991.

Peacey, Howard. *The Meaning of the Alphabet*. Los Angeles, CA, USA, 1949.

Peet, Eric T. *Rhind Mathematical Papyrus*. London, 1923.

Petrie, W.M. Flinders. *The Formation of the Alphabet*. London, 1912.

Petrie, W.M. Flinders. *Illahum, Kahun and Gurab*. Encino, CA, USA, 1974.

Petrie, W.M. Flinders. *Abydos*. Oxford, U.K., 1978.

Piankoff, Alexandre. *The Litany of Re*. New York, 1964.

Piankoff, Alexandre. *The Pyramid of Unas Texts*. Princeton, NJ, USA, 1968.

Piankoff, Alexandre. *The Shrines of Tut-Ankh-Amon Texts*. New York, 1955.

Plato. *The Collected Dialogues of Plato including the Letters*. Edited by E. Hamilton & H. Cairns. New York, 1961.

Plotinus. *The Enneads*, in 6 volumes, Tr. By A.H. Armstrong. London, 1978.

Plotinus. *The Enneads*, Tr. By Stephen MacKenna. London, 1991.

Plutarch, *De Iside Et Osiride*. Tr. By J. Gwyn Griffiths. Wales, U.K., 1970.

Plutarch. *Plutarch's Moralia, Volume V*. Tr. by Frank Cole Babbitt. London, 1927.

Poehlmann, Egert; and West, Martin L. *Documents of Ancient Greek Music*. Oxford, 2001.

Pritchard, James B., Ed. *Ancient Near Eastern Texts*. Princeton, NJ, USA, 1955.

Pritchard, James B. (Ed.). *Solomon and Sheba*. London, 1974.

Rasula, Jed and McCaffery, Steve, Ed. *Imagining Language: An Anthology*, Cambridge, MA, USA, 1998.

Schuman, Verne Brinson, Ed. *Washington University Papyri*. 1980.

Sicilus, *Diodorus*. Vol 1. Tr. by C.H. Oldfather. London.

Silverman, David and Torode, Brian. *The Material Word: Some Theories of Language and its Limits*. London, 1980.

Taylor, Isaac. *The History of the Alphabet*, 2 vols. New York, 1899.

Turner, E.G. *Greek Manuscripts of the Ancient World*. Princeton, NJ, USA, 1971.

Turner, E.G. *Greek Papyri: An Introduction*. Oxford, 1980.

Wilkins, John. *Mercury or the Secret and Swift Messenger*. London, 1641.

Wilkinson, J. Gardner. *The Ancient Egyptians: Their Life and Customs*. London, 1988.

Several Internet sources.

Numerous references in Arabic language.

3

SOURCES AND NOTES

References to sources in the previous section, Selected Bibliography are only referred to for facts, events, and dates—not for their interpretations of such information.

It should be noted that if a reference is made to one of the author Moustafa Gadalla's books, that each of his books contains its own extensive bibliography.

Chapter 1: The Archetypal Primacy of The Egyptian Alphabet

1.1 The Divine "Inventor" of The Egyptian Alphabetical Letters – Plato, Diodorus, Plutarch, Gadalla [Ancient Egyptian Culture].

1.2 Remote Age of Egyptian Alphabet – Taylor Vol.1, Plato, Erman [Literature], Petrie [Formation], Gadalla [Ancient Egyptian Culture], Gardiner [Egyptian Grammar].

**1.3 The Distinctive Pre-Hyksos Egyptian Alphabetical Papyri – Erman [Life …], Taylor, Drucker, Parkinson, Gadalla [Egyptian Cosmology].

Chapter 2: The Concealment of The Supreme Egyptian Alphabet

2.1 Smoke Screening Thousands of Egyptian Alphabetical Writings – Gardiner [Egyptian Grammar], Budge [Rosetta Stone], practically all references.

2.2 Egyptian is dead, Long Live "Arabic" – Gardiner [Egyptian Grammar], practically all references.

2.3 The Mighty Western-Fabricated Egyptian Alphabet and "Sequence" – Gardiner [Egyptian Grammar], Baines, Budge [Rosetta Stone], practically all references.

2.4 The Double Talk and Double Take of Two [Egyptian Sourced] Alphabets –Taylor, practically all references.

Chapter 3: The Diversion of A Proto-Sinaitic "Phoenician Connection"

3.1 Mining History in Sinai – Gadalla [Pyramid, Culture, Romany].

3.2 'Proto-Sinaitic' Graffiti—A Manufactured Straw – Petrie, Driver, Drucker Gadalla [Romany], Culican, Weill, Daniels.

3.3 B'alat Who Saved The Day! – Gardiner, Petrie.

3.4 Understanding Names, Epithets and Titles of Egyptian Deities – Gadalla [Divinities, Romany].

3.5 Phoenicians' Homeland – Herodotus, Gadalla [Romany, ch.7], Baram, Kapitan, Weill.

3.6 'Phoenicia': The Egyptian Satellite – Gadalla [Romany, ch.7], – Baram, Culican, Weill.

Chapter 4: Genesis of Egyptian Alphabetic Letters/Writing

4.1 The Unfounded Obsession That Letters Were Derived from Pictures – Clement, Petrie, Diodorus, Plotinus, Plato, Plutarch, Gadalla [Harmony].

4.2 Differences Between Ideograms, Signs and Alphabetical Writing – Practically all references.

4.3 "Evolution" of Alphabet from "Signs" to "Real" alphabets – Drucker, Petrie.

Chapter 5: The Egyptian Sound Organization of Letters

5.1 The Universal Three Primary/Quantal Egyptian Vowels – Daniels, Healey, Sacks [Rise of Music], Ellis, Taylor, Vol.1, Pohlman, Polin, Turner, Chejne, Gadalla being a native Egyptian.

5.2 From Three to Five Vowels – Ellis.

5.3 The Seven Harmonic Tones/Vowels – Ellis, Firmage, Drucker, Jannaris, Gadalla [Rhythm].

5.4 The Infinite Vowels Derivatives – Ellis, Plato, Gadalla [Culture Revealed].

5.5 Consonants as Derivatives of Vowels – Ellis.

5.6 The 25 Articulated Alphabetical Letters – Ellis, Plato, Firmage, Diodorus, Plutarch, Gadalla [Egyptian Rhythm].

5.7 Balanced Phonology Range – Firmage, Petrie, Gardiner, Ellis, Taylor.

5.8 Special Phonetics of Each Letter – Daniloff, Firmage, Taylor, vol.1, Gadalla being an Egyptian native.

5.9 Sound Ligaturing of Letters in a word—mistaken as "syllable writing" – Daniloff, Firmage, Erman [Litr.], Taylor, vol.1, Gadalla being an Egyptian native.

Chapter 6: The Egyptian Alphabetic Writing Styles

6.1 The Devious Western Categorization of Egyptian Alphabetic Scripts – Davies, Hayes, practically all references.

6.2 False Distinctions of Cursive Writing – El-Aguizy, Petrie, practically all references.

6.3 The True Two Primary Egyptian Alphabetic Styles [Uncials and Cursive] – Clement, Drucker, Taylor.

6.4 Forms and Functions of Calligraphy – Taylor, Gaur, Gadalla being a native Egyptian.

Chapter 7: The Profession of Egyptian Scribes

7.1 The Writing Civilization – Gardiner, Davies, Gaur, Petrie [illahun], Hayes, Gadalla [Culture].

7.2 The Profession—Divine Scribe – Parkinson, Gadalla [Culture].

7.3 Writing Surfaces & Instruments – James, Erman, Baikie, Petrie [Formation], Davies, Turner [Manuscripts], Ogg, Hayes Gadalla [Culture].

7.4 Mobile Scribes – Gadalla [Culture, Pyramid, Historical, Exiled, Romany].
– **Egyptian Scribes and Mining Expeditions** – Gadalla [Culture, Pyramid, Historical, Romany].
– **Egyptian Scribes and Trade Expeditions in Africa** – Gadalla [Culture, Exiled].
– **Sea Expedition to Lebanon and Cyprus** – Gadalla [Culture, Romany].
– **Egyptian Scribes and the Foreign Security Guards** – Petrie, Gadalla [Culture].

Chapter 8: Multiple Writing Forms of a Single Document

8.1 Commonality Of Multiple Writing Forms – Budge [Rosetta].

8.2 Egyptian Magical Divination Forms – Budge [Rosetta & Magic & Amulet], Betz.

8.3 Egyptian Stelea – Wong, Budge [Rosetta], Abdalla, practically all references.

Chapter 9: Multiple Writing Forms of The Rosetta Stone

9.1 Place of its original Location – Budge [Rosetta, Vol.1], Jensen, practically all references.

9.2 Dating Falsehoods – Budge [Rosetta, Vol.1], practically all references.

9.3 Shameless Change of the Word 'Priestly ' To "Greek"! – Budge [Rosetta, Vol.1], practically all references.

9.4 Scandalous Cartouches "Decipherment" – Budge [Rosetta, Vol.1], Gardiner, Budge [Cleopatra], practically all references.

9.5 The Egyptian Three Functions and Forms of The Decree – Clement, Budge [Rosetta, Vol.1], Jensen, practically all references.

9.6 Shamelessly Substituting 'god/goddess for a Ptolemaic "King/Queen" – Budge [Rosetta, Vol.1], practically all references.

9.7 Self Serving Conjectural "Decipherment" – Budge [Rosetta, Vol.1], practically all references.

Chapter 10: The Beacon of the Ancient World

10.1 Egyptian Settlements Throughout The World – Diodorus, Herodotus, Gadalla [Culture, Exiled, Romany].

10.2 Ancient Egypt and The Seven Seas – Gadalla [Culture, Romany].

10.3 Ancient Egypt : The World Economic Engine – Diodorus, Gadalla [Culture, Romany].

10.4 The Dominant Egyptian Language – Erman [Lit.], Gardiner, Taylor, Petrie, Gadalla [Culture, Romany].

10.5 The Egyptian Mother Language of all Language Families – Taylor, Petrie, Gardiner, Gadalla [Culture, Romany].

Chapter 11: Common Characteristics of Ancient Egyptian Alphabetic Writing System

Petrie, Davies, Gardiner, Healey, Jensen, Daniels, Pohlmann, Assmann, Erman, Polin, Turner [manuscripts].
– **Necessities of Phonetic Notations** – Gardiner, Drucker, Polin.
– **Tonal Conformity Writing of Egyptian texts** – Burney, Vol. I, Turner, Stanford, Pohlmann, Gadalla [Culture Revealed], Gardiner, Drucker, Polin, Assmann, Erman.
– **Significance of Musicality in Ancient Egypt** – Sachs [Wellsprings], Gadalla [Egyptian Romany, Egyptian Mystics, Egyptian Rhythm].

Chapter 12: Letter-forms Divergence of World Alphabets From Its Egyptian Origin

12.1 Apparent Variations of Letter-forms in world alphabets – Petrie, Gadalla [Egyptian Romany].

12.2 Overview of archetypal 28 Egyptian letter-forms – Petrie, Assmann, Gadalla [Egyptian

Romany], El-Aguizy, Gadalla being a native Egyptian, internet resources.

Chapter 13: Sound Divergence of World Alphabets From Its Egyptian Origin

13.1 The Systematic Sound Variations – Taylor, Budge [Language], Driver, Gadalla [Egyptian Romany, Exiled Egyptians].

13.1 Causes and Effects of Sound Divergence – Taylor, Budge [Language], Driver, Gadalla [Egyptian Romany, Exiled Egyptians].

Chapter 14: Cavalier Designations of New Languages

14.1 Rewarding A New Language For Each Historical " Winner" – Taylor, Gadalla [Culture, Romany].

14.2 Fabricating "New" Languages From Egyptian scripts – Betz, Gardiner, Davies, Gadalla [Romany].

Chapter 15: The Primary Linguistic Characteristics of The Egyptian Language

15.1 The Four Distinctive Pillars of a Language – Gadalla [Romany].

15.2 The Egyptian Prototypal Interconnected Lexicon, Grammar and Syntax – Gardiner, Budge, Gadalla [Romany].

Chapter 16: Hebrew and Moses of Egypt

16.1 Moses and Writing – Taylor, Gardiner.

16.2 Moses and Moab – Gadalla [Christianity].

16.3 The Two Writing Forms [old & New!] – Gardiner, Petrie, Driver [Semitic], Budge, Druker, Daniels, Taylor.

16.4 Sameness of Egyptian Prototypal .... – Drucker, Taylor, Gardiner, Gadalla [Romany].

Chapter 17: The Ancient Egyptian Hegemony of Asiatic Neighbors

17.1 The Egyptian Settlement of Moab – Diodorus, Driver [Semitic], Daniels, Drucker, Taylor, Gardiner, Healey, Jensen [sss], Gelb, Chejne, Gadalla [Romany], Petrie.

17.2 False Designations of Various Alphabets in North Arabia – Taylor, Daniels, Healey, Petrie, Gelb, Jensen [sss], Driver [Semitic], Taylor, Gadalla [Romany, Culture].

17.3 False Designations of South Arabian Alphabets – Bowen, Petrie, Pritchard [Solomon & Sheba], Nyrob, Taylor, Daniels, Driver, Gadalla [Romany, Culture].

17.4 Arabic: The Stolen Egyptian Language – Diodorus, Taylor, Healey, Gelb, Daniels, Petrie, Gadalla [Romany, Culture].

17.5 Distinction Without A Difference—Summary – Petrie, Taylor, Driver, Daniels, Gardiner.

Chapter 18: The African Connections

18.1 The Traditional 'Ge-ez' Language – Taylor, Driver, Daniels, Gadalla [Exiled Egyptians].

18.2 Amharic—A Reshuffle of Ge-ez – Petrie, Taylor, Driver, Drucker, Daniels, Budge [Language].

18.3 The Direct Egyptian-Ethiopic Connections – Herodotus, Taylor, Driver, Gadalla [Culture Revealed, Egyptian Mystics, Historical Deception, Exiled Egyptians].

18.4 Eastern African Languages – Gardiner, Daniels, Gadalla [Exiled Egyptians].

Chapter 19: From Egypt To India and Beyond

19.1 From Egypt Via Yemen To The Indian Sub-Continent – Taylor, Petrie, Daniels, Gadalla [Culture].

19.2 The Two Primary Inscription Styles in Indian Sub-Continent – Taylor, Daniels.

19.3 The Apparent Large Number of Indian Letters – Taylor, Daniels, Drucker, Driver.

19.4 Punjab—Both Styles Together – Taylor, Daniels.

19.5 India & Far East – Taylor, Daniels, Gadalla [Culture].

Chapter 20: From Egypt to The Black Sea Basin

20.1 Affinities of Languages From Central Asia to The Black Sea – Taylor, Daniels.

20.2 Ancient Egyptian Settlements in The Black Sea Basin – Taylor, Daniels, Diodorus, Plutarch, Herodotus.

20.3 Pre-Existence of "Armenian/Georgian" Alphabets in Ancient Egypt – Taylor, Daniels, Petrie, Iverson.

20.4 Vocalic Limitation of Armenian/Georgian Tongue viz-a-vis Its Number of Alphabet – Taylor, Daniels, Driver.

20.5 Sameness of Ancient Egyptian Alphabetical Writing System in Later "Georgian & Armenian Languages" – Taylor, Daniels.

20.6 Linguistic Characteristics with Their Ancient Egyptian Roots – Taylor, Daniels.

Chapter 21: Greek: A Shameless Linguistic Heist

21.1 The Egyptian Settlers and Kings of Greece – Diodorus, Herodotus, Plutarch, Gadalla [Culture, Rhythm].

21.2 Greeks As Employed Security Guards in Egypt – Herodotus, Gadalla [Culture].

21.3 Greek Mercenaries and the Abu Simbel Inscriptions – Taylor, Driver, Gelb, Daniels.

21.4 Pre-Existence of The Proclaimed "Greek" Alphabetical Letter-forms in Ancient Egypt – Taylor, Petrie, Gelb, Drucker, Gadalla [Romany, Culture].

21.5 Robbing and Postdating Egyptian Scripts To Rename Them as "Greek" – Taylor, Turner [Greek Papyri, Manuscripts], Herodotus, Budge [Rosetta], Gardiner, Betz, Abdalla.

21.6 Vocalic Limitation Effects of Greek Tongue on the 28 Prototypal Alphabetical Letters – Taylor, Gadalla [Exiled Egyptians, Romany], Budge [Egyptian Language], Drucker, Driver.

21.7 Sameness of Ancient Egyptian Alphabetical Writing System in Later "Greek Language" – Taylor, Jannaris, Turner [both references], Healey, Youtie, Bagnall, Daniels, internet resources.

21.8 Sameness of Egyptian Prototypal Interconnected Lexicon, Grammar and Syntax – Taylor, Jannaris, Turner [both references], internet resources.

Chapter 22: The European Languages

22.1 Etruscan: The Foremost Ancient Italic Language – Taylor, Petrie, Gadalla [Romany, Culture, Christianity], Wilkinson, Baldi, Daniels.

22.2 The Rise and Abrupt Fall of the Romans' Latin! – Taylor, Gadalla [Romany], Daniels, Baldi, Lathrop.

22.3 Broken Empire—Eastern Orthodox – Taylor, Petrie, Gadalla [Romany].

22.4 Wild Goose Chase of A "Latin' In Hispania – Taylor, Petrie, Gadalla [Romany], Fear, Mierse.

22.5 The Egyptian Alphabets of Hispania – Petrie, Gadalla [Romany].

22.6 The Egyptian-Iberian Linguistic Oneness – Petrie, Gadalla [Romany].

22.7 Warmongers and The "Romance" Languages! – Taylor, Petrie, Gadalla [Romany].

Chapter 23: Egyptian Alphabetical Vocalic Language [Past, Present & Future]

23.1 The Unchanging Egyptians – Taylor, Petrie, Gadalla [Culture], Herodotus.

23.2 The Enduring Egyptian Alphabetical Vocalic Language – Taylor, Petrie, Gardiner.

23.3 Vocabularies Now and Then – Taylor, Petrie.

23.4 Arabic Corruption of Original Egyptian Letter-forms & Reshuffle Letters Order/Sequence – Taylor, Petrie.

23.5 Sameness of Alphabetical Writing System – Taylor, Petrie.

23.6 Reinstatement of Original Letter-forms and Its ABGD Sequence – Taylor, Petrie.

Chapter 24: Renaissance & Seeking the Universal Language—The Ancient Future

24.1 English Language Flawed Dominance – Firmage, Jensen, Taylor, Gadalla [Historical Deception].

24.2 Renaissance Search For A Universal Language – Findlen [Kircher], Rasula.

www.ingramcontent.com/pod-product-compliance
Lightning Source LLC
Chambersburg PA
CBHW071234160426
43196CB00009B/1063